HELLCATS OF THE SEA

CHARLES A. LOCKWOOD
Vice-Admiral, USN, Ret.
and
HANS CHRISTIAN ADAMSON
Colonel, USAF, Ret.

With a foreword by
Fleet Admiral Chester W. Nimitz, USN

D0186888

BANTAM BOOKS
TORONTO · NEW YORK · LONDON · SYDNEY · AUCKLAND

*This edition contains the complete text
of the original hard-cover edition.*
NOT ONE WORD HAS BEEN OMITTED.

HELLCATS OF THE SEA
A Bantam Book / April 1988

PRINTING HISTORY
Greenberg edition published in 1955

Illustrations by Greg Beecham.
Maps by Alan McKnight.

All rights reserved.
Copyright © 1955 by Greenberg: Publisher, a corporation.
Cover art copyright © 1988 by Chris Blossom.
Library of Congress Catalog Card Number: 55-10961
*No part of this may be reproduced or transmitted
in any form or by any means, electronic or mechanical,
including photocopying, recording, or by any information
storage and retrieval system, without permission in writing from
the publisher.*
For information address: Bantam Books.

ISBN 0-553-27059-1

Published simultaneously in the United States and Canada

---

*Bantam Books are published by Bantam Books, a division of
Bantam Doubleday Dell Publishing Group, Inc. Its trade-
mark, consisting of the words "Bantam Books" and the por-
trayal of a rooster, is Registered in U.S. Patent and Trademark
Office and in other countries. Marca Registrada. Bantam
Books, 666 Fifth Avenue, New York, New York 10103.*

PRINTED IN THE UNITED STATES OF AMERICA

O   0 9 8 7 6 5 4 3 2 1

THE TIME WILL COME

In my office was a large wall-sized operation's chart. On it, the distribution of submarines on combat patrols was reported by means of small magnetic markers. Each of these had the silhouette of a submarine on which the name of the sub it represented was printed.

Up where it should be in the Sea of Japan was the solitary marker that designated the *Wahoo*. I could not help but feel deep regret as I realized that inevitably this ship would be transferred to the port of other gallant but missing submarines. Up to that time, starting with the *Sealion*, twenty-one had been lost. Before V-J Day, the total was to increase to fifty-two submarines that were never to return to their home ports.

From that pathetic flotilla of missing ships, I cannot select a single one whose loss was greater or more deeply felt than the loss of any other. It just so happens that the *Wahoo*, by virtue of the circumstances that surrounded its two last patrols, symbolizes all that is fine, courageous, and self-sacrificing among submariners who paid the greatest price that man can pay for the defense of his country.

I knew them all. And I loved them all.

Long before the *Wahoo* was admitted to be missing—in fact soon after the *Time* article was published—I had made up my mind that by now the Japs would have lost so much "face" and be so alerted that the game of entering the Sea of Japan on the hitherto safe surface of La Perouse Strait would no longer be worth the candle. But, I resolved, there would come another day—a day of visitation— an hour of revenge. In time we would collect for the *Wahoo* and Commander Dudley Walker Morton and his men, with heavy interest. And in time we did.

THE BANTAM WAR BOOK SERIES

This series of books is about a world on fire.

The carefully chosen volumes in the Bantam War Book Series cover the full dramatic sweep of World War II. Many are eyewitness accounts by the men who fought in a global conflict as the world's future hung in the balance. Fighter pilots, tank commanders and infantry captains, among many others, recount exploits of individual courage. They present vivid portraits of brave men, true stories of gallantry, moving sagas of survival and stark tragedies of untimely death.

In 1933 Nazi Germany marched to become an empire that was to last a thousand years. In only twelve years that empire was destroyed, and ever since, the country has been bisected by her conquerors. Italy relinquished her colonial lands, as did Japan. These were the losers. The winners also lost the empires they had so painfully seized over the centuries. And one, Russia, lost over twenty million dead.

Those wartime 1940s were a simple, even a hopeful time. Hats came in only two colors, white and black, and after an initial battering the Allied nations started on a long laborious march toward victory. It was a time when sane men believed the world would evolve into a decent place, but, as with all futures, there was no one then who could really forecast the world that we know now.

There are many ways to think about war. It has always been hard to understand the motivations and braveries of Axis soldiers fighting to enslave and dominate their neighbors. Yet it is impossible to know the hammer without the anvil, and to comprehend ourselves we must know the people we once fought against.

Through these books we can discover what it was like to take part in the war that was a final experience for nearly fifty million human beings. In so doing we may discover the strength to make a world as good as the one contained in those dramas and aspirations once believed by heroic men. We must understand our past as an honor to those dead who can no longer choose. They exchanged their lives in a hope for this future that we now inhabit. Though the fight took place many years ago, each of us remains as a living part of it.

DEDICATION FOR THE NAVY

O Eternal Lord God, who alone spreadest out the heavens, and rulest the raging of the sea; Take into thy almighty and most gracious protection our country's Navy, and all who serve therein. Preserve them from the dangers of the sea, and from the violence of the enemy; that they may be a safeguard unto the United States of America, and a security for such as pass on the seas upon their lawful occasions.

From the *Book of Common Prayer*

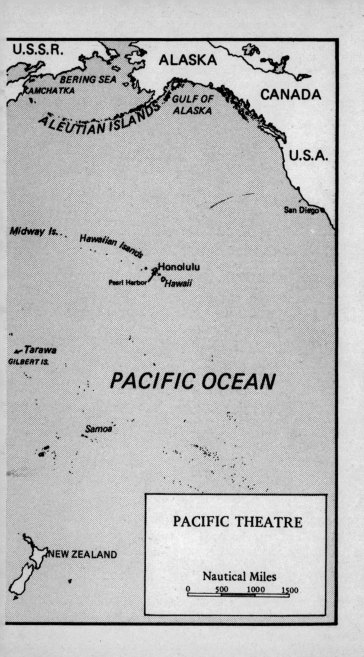

CONTENTS

FOREWORD

Although the public—and that part of our Navy that does its fighting on or above the surface—has a general idea of the great contribution made by our submarines toward defeating Japan in World War II, few outside the Submarine Service have the slightest knowledge of the men—and their problems—who served so gallantly in that dangerous service. That such work was dangerous is attested by the loss of fifty-two of our submarines during the struggle. Of these, all except a few were due to enemy action which, in most cases, claimed the lives of all on board.

During the war there was an almost complete blackout of information relating to submarines. And for the very obvious reason that such information, if publicized, could be valuable to the enemy and—what is more important—very dangerous to our submarines operating unsupported in enemy waters. The accounts, official and otherwise, of submarine operations that have appeared to date are accurate enough. But they leave something to be desired in reader interest as well as in the intimate details of our submariners—their hopes, fears, and thoughts in moments of intense danger. That kind of story could come only from men who were on the spot sharing those experiences.

Now, and here in this book—from the recollections and records of our wartime Commander Submarines Pacific, Vice Admiral Charles A. Lockwood—comes an intimate and thrilling account of one of the most difficult and dangerous submarine operations of the war. It was also one of the best planned and prepared blows against the Japanese Empire. The goal, of course, was to cut her off completely from the Asiatic mainland whence came her absolutely essential raw materials and food. War College planners, long before the war, had concluded that so long as Japan could draw sustenance from Korea and China she could not be defeated.

Operation Barney, so completely described in this story, was designed to wrest, at least temporarily, control of the surface of the Sea of Japan from our enemy and thereby demonstrate that, having done it once, we could repeat the performance as necessary.

Our experience with Japan's will to fight to the last man in the defense of the Empire convinced us that nothing less than complete isolation of her principal islands from the mainland could bring the leaders of Japan to a realization that the jig was up and that further fighting was useless. When the Marianas fell to our forces, the Japanese Navy knew the war was lost. Soon thereafter, the Japanese Government— through its Ambassador in Moscow—began secret efforts to secure Russian help to end the war—a fact well known to our high command.

In brief, Operation Barney was a break-through into the well-defended Sea of Japan, hitherto considered so safe and impregnable that Japanese shipping and navigational aids followed peacetime procedure. Here nine American submarines spent fifteen days of destruction and general hell raising before eight of them escaped to the Pacific Ocean and safety, leaving behind on the bottom one American submarine, the *Bonefish,* and her crew and some twenty-eight assorted Japanese ships, including one large Japanese submarine, for a total tonnage of 70,000 tons. That this bag seems so small compared to earlier results in the Western Pacific is due primarily to the earlier successes of our submarines in the open seas when so many Japanese merchant ships and quite a few important combat units were sent to Davy Jones' Locker. This operation took place from June 9-24, 1945, and was successfully completed at least six weeks before the first atom bomb was dropped on Hiroshima.

The success of Operation Barney can be attributed primarily to the unlimited faith Admiral Lockwood had in his submariners, and in his never-ending drive and zeal for the production of some device which would permit his submarine navigators to locate underwater minefields in time to pass by or through them safely.

With the skill and devoted co-operation of some of our scientists, an "Electronic Key" (labeled FMS) was finally produced. It would permit submarines to pass under the heavy minefields which guarded the few and narrow doors to the Sea of Japan—or Hirohito Lake—or Maru Nostrum—as that landlocked body of water was variously known from skipper to cook among submariners. Without Lockwood's stubborn drive and determination that project might easily have bogged down in bureaucratic snarls and inertia. Even after the FMS was successfully produced, Lockwood had to overcome the natural conservatism of his "show me" skippers—and that in itself absorbed much of his energy and endurance.

However, it was a foregone conclusion that Lockwood would succeed just as he did when confronted with the soul-depressing frustration of defective torpedo war head exploders in the first half of the war. I suppose it is possible to estimate how many enemy ships got a bit longer life as a result of our defective torpedoes, but I doubt if anyone can plumb the depths of depression reached by some of our skippers when our torpedoes failed to explode after hitting the target. Again it was Lockwood who sparked the remedy and who finally got scientists and home talent to lick that problem.

It would be difficult to overrate the importance to our surface fleets of the assistance given by our FMS-equipped submarines in locating and plotting the minefields in the East China Sea and in the mineable waters around Okinawa and the approaches to Japan. Had it become necessary to assault the main islands of Japan with landing forces—our ships would have profited greatly from a good plot of enemy minefields.

Lockwood's greatest disappointment came when his Boss— CINCPAC—declined to let him lead his submarines into the China Sea—as he had previously refused to let Lockwood go on combat patrols with his submarines in the far reaches of the Western Pacific. No one was more keenly aware of his disappointment than CINCPAC—who himself had to remain in rear areas at the end of a communication system throughout the war. No doubt COMSUBPAC well knows that CINCPAC displayed the same solicitude for Lockwood's safety that Lockwood himself had for the safety of experienced submariners when he learned that some of them were using recreation and rehabilitation periods on Guam to go along as passengers on B-29 bombing missions over Tokyo.

Not all of this story is devoted to Operation Barney

which Lockwood fills with intimate details at all points. He also tells about thrilling episodes of other submarine operations during the war—notably those of the *Wahoo*, the *Harder*, and the *Seahorse*. And in the telling he lets his skippers speak for themselves. But wait—read the book for yourself and be well rewarded for the time spent. I predict that once started, the story will not be laid aside until finished.

And now a word to my brother officers in Navy blue who sit in high places in Washington—and who occasionally sit as Selection Boards for promotion to higher rank, or who select naval officers for high command and difficult jobs. Do not overlook that crop of fine officers of experience and courage who fought our submarines in the war with Japan.

C. W. NIMITZ
Fleet Admiral, U.S. Navy

Berkeley, California
28 January 1955

DAMN THE TORPEDOES...SIR!

The shrill call of the telephone broke into my slumbers.

Perhaps I had been dreaming of a happier pre-war world where people sometimes slept a whole night through. But in those desperate days of 1943 I was so conditioned to hearing phone bells—and bad news—in the middle of the night that instant alertness and a tightening of the nerves had become automatic.

A bullet hole in my bedroom door was a grim reminder of December 7, 1941, and of an entire nation which had not been sufficiently awake.... What now, I wondered.

With practiced, ambidextrous motions, I switched on the bedside light and had the phone receiver collared almost before the first strident ring had ended. The luminous traveling clock on the bureau marked 0200. The date, I knew, was August 18.

Answering my none too blithe "Comsubpac," came the familiar, steady voice of Dick Voge—meaning Commander Richard G. Voge, Operations Officer to "Comsubpac," meaning me, Rear Admiral Charles A. Lockwood, U.S. Navy, Commander of Submarines in the Pacific with headquarters at Pearl Harbor.

"This is Dick, Admiral"—the background noise of teletypes told me he was in the Communications Room. Something must be urgent.

"Yes, Dick, what's brewing now?"

"Mush seems to be in hot water in His Nibs's private lake," said Dick, as he paused briefly and added: "Get me—sir?" This, in recognition of the mumjo-jumbo talk we had to use in telephone discussions at Pearl Harbor covering subjects regarded as secret. There could be listeners-in.

1

"Yes," I confirmed, "I get you. Shoot! What about Mush?"

My earlier placidity with respect to the call—my sleep was perforated by them every night—vanished with the mention of Mush and His Nibs's private lake. I knew then that the call had to do with Commander Dudley W. Morton, of the submarine *Wahoo*. Morton was engaged in a secret and highly dangerous mission in the Sea of Japan, known to us as Emperor Hirohito's private lake or bathtub. Mush was not only one of my star submarine marksmen but also the sort of younger man who wins his way into the hearts of his seniors.

"What kind of hot water?" I asked.

"His pickles are sour," answered Voge. "Again and again, he tries—but no soap. No clues. Mush wants to take a trip to Gooneyville to check his barrel of pickles. Wants travel orders right now."

Translated, this meant that Commander Morton was having trouble with his torpedoes—a trouble that had plagued most of our submariners but which we hoped to lick at an early date by replacing the old Mark 14 steam torpedo and its magnetic exploder with the then new Mark 18 electric torpedo with a brand new type of contact exploder. To say that Mush's radio message from the Sea of Japan was depressing is to put it mildly. It is bad enough when a skipper and his crew tempt fate by taking their submarine into highly dangerous waters, but it is a thousandfold worse when their weapons fail to function. Morton's reference to Gooneyville meant that he wanted to return to Midway Island to check his non-explosive pickles.

"Okay," I replied. "Tell Mush to make it on all four mains to home base."

For a minute or two after I had replaced the telephone and extinguished the light, I permitted myself to ponder the torpedo problem and then passed back into a slumberland where all torpedoes ran hot, straight, and normal; where new electric Mark 18's rolled off the production line to put an end forever to the temperamental "no soap pickles" which had made life hell for Mush and other frustrated submarine sailors.

At that time, the late summer of 1943, war in the Pacific had taken a substantial bite into its second year, and it should have convinced Hirohito and his advisers that Americans were not the soft pushovers he had expected. Our great sweeps by sea, land, and air were still to come. But the crucial battle of Midway had been won and so many of the Imperial Staff's slips were showing that even the Nips should have realized that their dreams of early destruction of the U.S. forces and Japanese expansion into the rich Asiatic "co-prosperity sphere" could be *only* dreams—strictly from the opium pipe.

They might have been even more convinced that immediate overtures for peace were in order, had not the inferior performance of our submarine torpedoes during the first eighteen months of the war unhappily added months to the length of the war and the expenditure of thousands of lives and millions of dollars.

Many other urgent matters demanded my attention at this phase of World War II, but none was more urgent than the maddening, frustrating torpedo failures of which Dudley Morton's experience was but one example.

Month after desperate month our submarines, manned by hundreds of keen young Americans, had crossed thousands of miles of ocean to attack an alert and relentless enemy with phantom weapons: torpedoes that ran deeper than intended and passed harmlessly under their targets; torpedoes that circled off their course and exposed their parent submarines to instant destruction; torpedoes that exploded long before they reached their objectives; and—worst of all— torpedoes that hit the enemy ships but, instead of exploding, kissed off like harmless balls in a billiard game.

The Mark 14 steam torpedo was an excellent target practice weapon before the war, but the addition of a heavy war head—750 pounds of TNT—and the installation of an unreliable magnetic exploder, already discarded by both the Germans and the British, had been its undoing. We in the field had battled valiantly to correct its defects. Admiral Nimitz had authorized me to inactivate the magnetic feature of the exploder, whereupon dud-hits rose to curse our efforts.

Our most recent experiments—firing live torpedoes against undersea cliffs in Hawaii in order to put the finger on the cause of our failures—had produced answers which indicated our firing pin as the criminal. Our Sub Base machine shops at Pearl Harbor were turning out scores of new pins even as Mush Morton's message came in. The *Tinosa*'s colossal bad luck on July 24—making eleven dud hits in a row—had triggered the experiments which were to solve forever our problem, and had restored the Mark 14 torpedo to its place of high honor among submarine weapons.

To the crew of a submarine—voluntary prisoners in their own submersible coffin—the sweetest music in the world is the percussion effects of some 750 pounds of torpex or TNT going boom into an enemy craft. As I had told Rear Admiral W. H. P. Blandy, Chief of the Bureau of Ordnance in Washington that spring: "The best morale builder in my trade is the sound of hearing your own torpedo explode against the hull of an enemy. On the other hand, there is no agony deeper than the silence that follows the firing of a well-aimed torpedo; when seconds, then minutes, turn into insufferable lifetimes as submariners count and count—and nothing happens."

This verbal tilt had followed a talk in Washington when I told a group of submarine officers serving in Navy Department Bureaus: "If the Bureau of Ordnance can't provide us with torpedoes that will hit or explode or with a deck-gun larger than a peashooter, then, for God's sake, get the Bureau of Ships to design a boathook with which we can rip the plates off the target's side!"

And, incidentally, that was no over-statement. In men like Mush Morton, and his kind, we had submariners who would attack a battleship with hand grenades if called upon to engage in that type of combat.

Dudley Morton was born in Kentucky in 1908, but appointed from Miami, Florida, to the Naval Academy's class of 1930. He was high-voltage, live-wire all the way through despite his deceptively slow and easy deep Southern drawl. At Annapolis, his classmates refrained from nicknaming him Dud because there was nothing whatever about Midshipman Morton to justify the appellation. Instead of that, they called him Mush by virtue of the soft and slow flow of his words. But all the mush in Morton's make-up was confined to his vocal cords. He had a veritable lust for combat and he was the deadliest kind of fighter—the cold kind. I had a chance to get a good look at Mush from the dock at Brisbane, Australia, before I met him face to face for the first time.

Medium-tall and on the slim side, he looked much younger than his years—in fact, almost boyish. His khaki shirt, open at the neck and with rolled-up sleeves, revealed brawn developed during his Academy days when Mush exercised his love of combat by going out for the manly arts of boxing and wrestling, plus a hefty dab at football. He had what a sculptor might call a square-blocked kind of face, a firm mouth, pugnacious chin, a pair of deadly-level dark eyes deeply set under heavy black brows and close-cropped dark hair. His eyes had the penetrating quality of a fine lens rather than a strong light, for there was nothing challenging or hostile in Mush's ordinary bearing. He was good-natured, with a broad vein of humor and a marvelous gift for the delegation of authority to the right people. The latter made him a superior submarine commander and lifted him to the rank of full Commander at the age of thirty-five.

However, I believe that it is high time for me to take the reader into my complete confidence. *Hellcats of the Sea* is not a story *about* Commander Mush Morton but a story *because* of him. It was this outstanding fighter's unsatisfied thirst for combat in the Sea of Japan that pulled triggers of invention. New departures in submarine operations which, over a course of about two years, compelled me, members of my staff, electronic specialists, and numerous submarine commanders to develop the FM Sonar and the technique of its use. FMS would permit Uncle Sam's submarines—disdainful of lethal mine fields and unafraid of radar and other invisible patrols—to penetrate the carefully distributed high-explosive Hellpots planted row on row by the Japs in Tsushima Strait.

This well-guarded waterway lies between Korea and Kyushu, southernmost of the so-called Home Islands of the Japanese Empire. Through this strait, aided by the mine finders of FMS, we could enter the Sea of Japan.

But before that goal could be reached, many things had to be done. Among others, brand new trails of scientific and inventive accomplishments had to be blazed. A way had to be found to locate and penetrate the rows of high-explosive Hellpots. Through constant application, the Naval Research Laboratory at San Diego finally developed an FM Sonar apparatus which, through a light-blob and a bell-tone, reported the presence of mines.

Among submariners who used it, this device was called Hellsbells. The nine subs which eventually entered the Sea of Japan by under-running mine fields with the aid of FM Sonar were called Hellcats. In June, 1945, they completed, and with flying colors, the job which Mush Morton, the *Wahoo*, and her gallant crew had so nobly started—at the cost of their lives—in August, 1943.

Having thus highlighted this up-to-now unwritten detailed "inside" history of a precedent-making mass penetration by submarines—beneath major mine fields into the Sea of Japan—let us backtrack to the time of its beginning. And, for all practical purposes, the day was Aug. 29, 1943, when the *Wahoo*, without her vaunted broom lashed to the top of the attack periscope to denote her usual clean sweep, entered Pearl Harbor.

U.S.S. Wahoo

2

THE FISH THAT FAILED

As always, when one of my submarines returned from war patrol, I was on hand to greet the ship and her crew as she tied up at Pearl Harbor's Submarine Base. We always strove to make these returns dramatic and colorful occasions. Usually, the weatherman played on our team. This August morning, as the *Wahoo* tied up at Pier #4, the sun was bright and the sky flecked by big white clouds. The cracker-jack band which Comdr. Eddie Peabody, USNR, had arranged for us opened the ball with the "Star Spangled Banner." Following that came the traditional "Hail, Hail, the Gang's All Here" and some dance hits of the day.

One of these, I recall, was the then popular "All I Want for Christmas Is My Two Front Teeth," and I could not help thinking that Mush Morton needed something with a bigger bite in it than that.

Anticipating the *Wahoo*'s arrival, a mail truck stood on the pier with several stacks of mail—always first on the agenda. And, a close second in popularity, big tins that contained freshly made ice cream and huge containers of orange and other fruit juices.

If a submarine could be said to have a hang-dog air, that kind of an atmosphere seemed to hang over the *Wahoo* as the gang-plank was shoved aboard. Instead of joshing and laughing, her crew members seemed depressed, outright unhappy. Of course, the ship and her crew would not get an additional star for their combat insignia in recognition of their just completed sixth patrol. There had been no damage to the enemy—thanks to pickles or fish, as torpedoes were also called, that failed to explode. All submariners set great store by those combat stars; hence the *Wahoo*'s crew, officers and men alike, felt pretty down in the mouth over this unproductive patrol.

7

On my arrival, Mush hopped down from the bridge and met me at the gangway. Returning my salute to the colors, he replied to my accustomed "Permission to come aboard, sir?" with a grave "Certainly, sir," and led the way down the forward torpedo room hatch to the wardroom below. Enroute, I noticed that the torpedo room was spotlessly clean, its bunks neatly stowed; the empty torpedo racks were mute reminders of torpedoes fired with all the thrill of the chase to produce only dismal failures.

In the wardroom we sat down with Morton's officers and my staff for a cup of coffee and a quick look through the *Wahoo*'s patrol report. In that setting I always sensed the import of a submarine's combat report. This sensation was increased by the feel of the ship and the nearness of her crew. It was better, far better, than meetings held in my own land-based office.

On this occasion Mush looked older than his years. Tired. Haggard. His despair over his patrol's poor record—not a single sinking, not a bit of damage to the enemy scored by a submarine which, up to now, had been a star performer. Obviously the situation had him down. Even Morton's junior officers, many of them growing boyish-looking full beards, looked mighty glum. I made up my mind to get all the facts in detail a little later on and then decide what to do about them. Just then I wanted to give Mush a chance to talk his head off if that was what he wanted to do. He did.

"Damn them—Admiral," came Mush's first salvo—"damn the torpedoes, sir!" He laughed in brief embarrassment. I joined in. Then he continued, "Either they do not explode or they run too deep or they explode too soon. They kill you—that's what they do. Kill you acting that way. The Sea of Japan is loaded with targets. It is full of ships that don't know there's a war on. And look at us. Look at the *Wahoo*. What did we do? Not one sinking! Nothing to show for our run. I'll bet every soul aboard feels as if the ship is naked without our usual 'clean-sweep' broom at the top of the periscope. Please, please load me up with torpedoes that will explode when they should! And give me a quick turn-around. That area is a honey."

Ah—there spoke a man after my own heart. No yessing. No beating around the bush. No stilted "By your leave, sir!" There spoke the real spirit of the submarine service in which

I had been raised. From me—yes, from me—Mush could have anything he wanted.

"Well," I said in a fatherly tone that was not difficult to muster, "tell me all about it. Just the highlights now. Later you can give me the complete details. The better informed I am, the more I can help you and other submariners in those waters."

Mush nodded, pulled briefly on his cigarette, and began, "We had figured our speed so as to get to La Perouse Strait at evening twilight. That would enable us to make our passage through it at night and on the surface. We would not have to dive until we were well into the Sea of Japan, probably near the Island of Rebun Shima."

As Mush spoke, I drew a mental picture of La Perouse Strait and its environs—a bleak and lonely stretch of water than runs between the needlelike terminal capes of the Island of Hokkaido to the south and Karafuto to the north. Facing each other across the chill currents of the Strait, at a distance of twenty-three miles, are two peninsulas, each with its lonesome mountain-framed lighthouse, Nishi Notoro Misaki on the north, and Soya Misaki on the south. About two-thirds of the way across the strait, going northward, stands a third lighthouse on a small reeflike rock called Nijo Gan. On the Sea of Japan side of the Strait, about forty miles west of the entrance, lie two islands, the northernmost of which is Rebun Shima.

Because the Strait was narrow and probably mined—but with a lane for Russian shipping, which was then neutral—and probably well patrolled, I requested Mush to describe his transit.

"Oh, there were a couple of tight moments," he answered with a grin. "We were challenged from shore and got the once-over from some kind of torpedo boat. We wanted to sink it but decided that it was not worth a torpedo. As we went through on top, we had our navigation lights burning and we kept them burning after we had been challenged. In fact, we ignored their challenge and changed neither course nor speed. Just went about our business as if we belonged there—and we got away with it.

"The torpedo boat came within a mile of us. They could have had tracking information on us because we had been using our SD radar during the day. Yep, perhaps our hearts bounced a bit between our tonsils, but if those Japs had acted up, I had my gun crew standing by with ammunition below deck—ready to let them have it at the slightest sign of trouble. But there were no signs."

Morton then went on to tell of the unsuccessful attacks, the pickles that failed to produce dead Marus. This part of the story began about midnight on August 14-15. At 2217 the *Wahoo* came upon three enemy freighters heading south— two medium, one small. Mush decided to attack the trailing ship because he felt that it could be sunk without giving warning to the next vessel which was some 6000 yards ahead. Five minutes past midnight, Morton dove for battle stations.

Now, it so happens, battle-stations aboard the *Wahoo* with Morton in command was completely unorthodox and unlike the attack routines on other submarines. Instead of manning the attack periscope himself—and thus directing the approach to the target and the firing of the torpedoes with his own eye at the periscope—Mush Morton had his Executive Officer handle the periscope and sing out the picture of the situation. Based on this information, and keeping an eye on the plotting board, where the approach was being charted, Morton would direct the attack and give the firing order when he believed it was time to do so.

Luckily, Lt. Commander Dick O'Kane,* his Executive Officer, was an excellent periscope operator. Together, they formed an unbeatable team. That morning at Pier 4 in Pearl Harbor—and purely to make conversation that would drag Morton away from his troubles, I asked him why he deputized his Exec to be his "eye-witness" at the periscope.

"Well," said Mush in soft Southern drawl, "I watch the plot and the TDC. That gives me the range, the bearing, and the length of torpedo run—everything I need. I can shoot when the range is right. If I run the attack from the bridge or the conning tower and forget that the targets look bigger than they are—especially at night—I'm liable to get trigger-happy or scared and fire too soon. With my system, Dick can get scared to death but I don't fire 'till I'm ready and until it is time to shoot."

---

*For another vivid account of submarine warfare read CLEAR THE BRIDGE by Richard H. O'Kane, Rear Admiral, U.S.N. (Ret.) Another volume in the Bantam War Book Series.

According to this peculiar routine, Mush would stand in the scanty space that separates the periscopes from the plotting table where he could keep an eye on each. With his back to the helmsman stood the ship's talker whose job it was—by way of a public address system that was piped to every compartment—to keep all personnel informed on what was going on during attacks or events of interest to all hands. Incidentally, and looking back, I often wondered during World War II how we—in the bowels of our tiny submarines during World War I—escaped blowing up through sheer curiosity when things were happening and the information percolated from bow to stern by the much slower mouth-to-ear process.

But anyway, during submerged approach runs and torpedo attacks, Skipper Morton swayed back and forth as O'Kane, his trusty and observant Exec, put an orb to the eye-piece on the attack periscope and his plotters produced the attack data.

"We dove at five minutes past midnight," recalled Mush, "and, after half an hour of getting into position, we fired our first torpedo at a distance of 950 yards. The fish had a depth setting of ten feet and the target a speed of seven knots. For all I know, she is still making knots. A miss? Anyway, no explosion!

"Almost an hour later, to the very minute, we sighted another ship. It was a large one and it was heading straight for us. I broke off the chase on the other vessel—a bird in the hand, you know—approached on the surface, dove, and attacked at 2220 yards. His speed was eleven and a half knots. We set the pickle at six feet with a run of 1150 yards. Duck soup." Mush grimaced briefly and ran a sun-tanned hand through his rumpled hair. "A sour pickle," he continued. "It struck at the point of aim, but the torpedo was a dud and it didn't explode. We surfaced and tracked the target for another attack. About 0415 we dove for a submerged approach. There was not much time to waste. Evidently no one aboard the freighter had noticed or heard our torpedo's run or hit. She maintained her course and speed. The moon was out, but just setting. Dawn hadn't quite arrived. So I went in on a sharp track to get him while there was still enough moonlight to see by.

"This time, to wrap it up quick, I fired two torpedoes. Both were set at six-foot depths; the run was about seven hundred yards—just a good niblick shot for a boat like the *Wahoo*. So help me, Hannah, both—"

"Torpedoes missed," I broke in, just to ease the situation. Poor Mush, he was having a hard time. "Were both of them duds?"

"No, one of them exploded at the end of the run—at 0423, five minutes after it was fired," he answered. "But, of course, now the jig was up. The Japs knew we were shooting at them. So I swung ship and headed directly for the target. I figured that by the end of the swing I'd be in a good position for a good up-the-kilt shot. It took me just sixty seconds. The distance was sixteen hundred yards. We kept count on our stop watches—what with the torpedo doing some forty-six knots, it should hit in about one minute. We waited for the explosion. We got one all right. But the darn thing broached and exploded before it reached the target."

Mush fumbled in his pockets for a match, found a half-gone packet of them, stuck a cigarette between his lips, lit it, and drew a few quick puffs.

"Well, that broke up the game!" he exclaimed. "It was daylight now. We couldn't clear the scene of action and the target was yelling bloody murder. For four solid hours we had been attacking. We had fired torpedoes in four attacks and had nothing in the bag to show for it." A brief but eloquent pause. "Damn the torpedoes!"

There was a long silence. We sat stiffly, almost like a habitat group in a museum.

"Did anyone get on your trail?" I finally inquired.

"Yep," grinned Mush wryly. "Naturally we dove and set course for deep water. About 0930 we heard echo-ranging. A Jap was probing for us. He turned out to be one of those small Otori Class Torpedo Boats. I evaded him. Later, I heard another echo-ranging ship, but I did not see him."

That night, Morton decided to move down on the Hokkaido-Korea route. The weather was fine and the moon was full. During the early morning of August 17, he fired a fish at a small freighter but missed. In the course of the day, which he spent submerged, the young skipper gave a lot of thought to the poor showing made by his torpedoes. He decided to use low-power shots in the hope that his missiles would have better depth control at low power. This meant that the torpedo's speed was reduced from forty-six to thirty knots.

Shortly before the start of August 18, he singled a large and heavily laden freighter from among several ships within range of his periscope. A run of 850 yards—a sure shot in anybody's bag—but no explosion. Another dud.

At 0300, while still seething from this latest addition to his pyramid of failures, Morton picked up a medium-sized freighter. Another miss and no explosion.

At 0314, a second torpedo was sped toward the same target. Through the periscope, O'Kane saw the missile broach and explode at the end of a twenty-second run.

At 0407, Mush Morton had cleared the coast for deeper waters and submerged to take stock. It was not an encouraging inventory.

In the brief span of four days the *Wahoo* had sighted an even dozen Japanese vessels of which nine were given chase and made the targets of ten torpedoes that either failed to explode, exploded too soon, or banged harmlessly on the enemy's hull. That night, as soon after sunset as he could surface, he sent me the coded radio requesting permission to return to Pearl Harbor which Dick Voge read to me over the phone much later that night.

How different these rows of blanks from the Morton-*Wahoo* score in March that year when, in ten days, the vessel sank every one of the nine targets it attacked and inflicted a total loss of nearly 20,000 tons.

I guess Morton realized what I was thinking as these recollections flashed through my mind that August 29 morning. He shook his head and tried to smile, but there was a sad down-tilt to his lips.

Yes—damn the torpedoes.

"Well," I exclaimed in much too loud a voice. And stopped. I was a bit choked up myself. "Tell me what you want—and I'll help you get it."

"In that case, Admiral," replied Morton, "I'd like to stock up with a new load of good torpedoes, fuel-up—and be on my way back as soon as possible. Tomorrow if I can."

This was speed indeed. Too much speed.

"Now wait a second," I told him. "Let me explain what the torpedo situation is, as of this moment. We have just finished a series of experiments with the old Mark 14 torpedo. The principal trouble was not in the torpedo itself, but in the magnetic exploder—the Mark 6 and its firing pin. I am absolutely sure that we have its troubles licked. We have inactivated the magnetic feature and the Base machine shop is turning out new, very light aluminum firing pins now. You can have the first batch when they are ready. A matter of a week or so. Or you can have the new Mark 18 electric. They are just in from the States and guaranteed to perform. They only make twenty-nine knots, but they leave no air bubble trails.

"Think it over, Morton. You can have either 14's or 18's—or both. Tell you what! Get your crew ashore for a week's rest at the Royal Hawaiian and when the *Wahoo* is loaded and ready, we will send you back to the Sea of Japan under the same kind of orders."

In my mind I had resolved that the *Wahoo* was not going to be ready in too much of a hurry. After a drubbing like that, I knew that Mush and his boys needed a real cooling off, and they were going to get it.

"Think it over," I repeated. "Meet me at noon at the office and we will have some lunch. Meanwhile read your mail and get squared away."

Morton thanked me and added, "I can tell you right now about the torpedoes. We'll take the new 18 electric. I like the idea of no give-away air bubbles on the surface."

His face broke into a wide grin. At that moment he reminded me more than anything else of my own two boys, Andy and Ted, when they had been told that they could go swimming instead of staying indoors tending to their homework. The gloom that had stood fog-thick in the wardroom when I came aboard had been driven off by the sunshine of eager anticipation. And so I headed back to the never-ending paper work on my desk, while Dick Voge whipped up plans for the *Wahoo*'s next patrol.

This last portion of the story about Mush Morton and the *Wahoo*—the last cruise of a gallant man and a gallant ship—is one that I would rather not write or, for that matter, even think about. Not entirely because it has a sad ending but because its ending unavoidably contains such a large amount of uncertainty. In war, Death itself is not too difficult to face nor is this Grim Commander necessarily an enemy. Under certain circumstances he can bring reliefs that virtually come under the heading of friendship. But where uncertainty, with respect to the when and where and how, of a man's passing goes hand in hand with Death, it is a different story, because then life ceases without the orthodox and orderly ending we have learned to accept, if not always to take for granted.

The *Wahoo* left Pearl Harbor on September 9 with orders that called for entry into the Sea of Japan through La Perouse Strait on September 20. She was to patrol the area below the 43° parallel while the *Sawfish* was to operate above it. Further, she was to leave her area after sunset on October 21 and report by radio as she transited the Kurile chain on October 23 when she made her way home.

In time, the scuttlebutt rumor was that the *Wahoo* had been sunk by mistake by a Russian patrol boat and that there were numerous survivors. We frequently hoped that it might be true but kept the matter quiet lest sorrowing wives and families be given false hopes. It is remarkable how many similar rumors regarding possible submarine survivors cropped up during the war. Any number of fathers, mothers, and wives wrote me personal letters saying they had heard "from a person in Washington who should know" that the—was sunk near a group of islands in shallow water and that it was expected there would be survivors. There are many variations of this story. Sometimes the water referred to was actually hundreds of fathoms deep, where escape from a sunken submarine would have been impossible. Sometimes it was the terrifically cold water of the Kurile Islands where a swimmer had no chance of survival. To raise such false hopes is thoughtless cruelty. Actually only about 5 per cent of the crews of lost submarines lived to tell the tale.

But that last message never came. After she entered La Perouse Strait for her second raid into the Sea of Japan, the *Wahoo* was never seen again. Nothing was heard from her—except this: In its October 18, 1943, issue, *Time* magazine carried a brief story about sea-warfare in Japan. It was headlined "Knock at the Door!" In part, the story read: "In the rough Tsushima Strait, where 2-decker train carrying ferries ply between Japan and Korea, an allied submarine up-periscoped, unleashed a torpedo. The missile stabbed the flank of a Japanese steamer. Said the Tokyo radio: 'The steamer went down in seconds, with loss of 544 persons.'

"Fifty miles across at their narrowest, Tsushima Strait is Japan's historic door to the Asiatic mainland. Over it, centuries ago, Regent Hideyoshi's armada sailed to battle the Koreans and sent home 38,000 enemy ears pickled in wine.

Upon it, in 1905, crusty Admiral Togo smashed the Russian fleet.

"Presumably the submarine knocking on the door last week was American. It had achieved one of World War II's most daring submarine penetrations of enemy waters, a feat ranking with German Gunther Priem's entry at Scapa Flow, the Japanese Invasion of Pearl Harbor, the U.S. raid in Tokyo Bay."

And, one might ask, why not include the British submarines which ran the Dardanelles in World War I?

The *Time* story did not say so, because in those days it was not always possible to name names, but today one can remove any doubt as to the identity of that submarine. It was—and could only have been—the *Wahoo*.

And, so far as anyone knows, that was the obituary of Mush Morton and his men.

My own notebook entry was different: "No news of 'Mush.' This is the worst blow we've had and I'm heartbroken. God punish the Japs! They shall pay for this. In fact, he's extracted pretty good payment in advance."

When we read the issue of *Time,* submariners in the Pacific who knew where Morton was made ready to celebrate his return. But the return of the *Wahoo* went from due to over-due; from that, to "Overdue and presumed lost." Then— but only after many weeks and months of waiting and when all hope of her return had vanished—was the *Wahoo* listed as lost with all hands. But she took a lot of Japs with her.

In my office was a large wall-sized operation's chart. On it, the distribution of submarines on combat patrols was reported by means of small magnetic markers. Each of these had the silhouette of a submarine on which the name of the sub it represented was printed.

Up where it should be in the Sea of Japan was the solitary marker that designated the *Wahoo*. I could not help but feel deep regret as I realized that inevitably this ship would be transferred to the port of other gallant but missing submarines. Up to that time, starting with the *Sealion*, twenty-one had been lost. Before V-J Day, the total was to increase to fifty-two submarines that were never to return to their home ports.

From that pathetic flotilla of missing ships, I cannot select a single one whose loss was greater or more deeply felt than the loss of any other. It just so happens that the *Wahoo*, by virtue of the circumstances that surrounded its two last patrols, symbolizes all that is fine, courageous, and self-sacrificing among submariners who paid the greatest price that man can pay for the defense of his country.

I knew them all. And I loved them all.

Long before the *Wahoo* was admitted to be missing—in fact soon after the *Time* article was published—I had made up my mind that by now the Japs would have lost so much "face" and be so alerted that the game of entering the Sea of Japan on the hitherto safe surface of La Perouse Strait would no longer be worth the candle. But, I resolved, there would come another day—a day of visitation—an hour of revenge. In time we would collect for the *Wahoo* and Commander Dudley Walker Morton and his men, with heavy interest. And in time we did.

To accomplish this, we would first of all have to devise means to penetrate the Sea of Japan on the surface or submerged as the occasion might direct. We would have to invent and build equipment that would permit our submarines to locate accurately the mines planted by the enemy in large fields in the three straits that form the doors to the Sea of Japan. Next time we would not knock on the doors. We would either pick the locks or dynamite the doors—whatever the situation demanded. And in my mind was the germ of an idea how this difficult job might be done.

Back in the early part of 1943 I still appeared in my role of a juggler who performed ambidextrous feats, keeping all sorts of things in perpetual motion—torpedoes, anti-submarine devices, pro-submarine devices, guns and other weapons, and so on ad infinitum. So many things that had to be changed, improved, invented, and discarded. So many new things unknown to the enemy. Because in war—as has been said by warriors throughout the ages—it is always the factor of the unknown that instills fear in the enemy and leads the way to victory.

My journey to one of the important unknowns in submarine warfare began in the late winter of 1942-43 when I had to go on a clean-up trip that took me all the way from Hawaii to the Aleutians; from Alaska to California. It was during a pause for breath at San Diego that the seeds for Operation Barney and the Hellcats—the basic formula for evolving the Magic Key—were sown in my mind.

3

MAGIC KEY FOR MINED LOCKS

The refit situation in San Diego was deeply discouraging. Hence, what had been intended for a breathing spell turned into a hatful of headaches regarding refitting problems. In the midst of them came dispatch orders to extend my visit and report to Chief of Naval Operations in Washington on the torpedo situation. This I knew would bring on a dog fight with the Bureau of Ordnance. Therefore, I was only too happy to accept a momentary diversion in the form of a visit to the Hush-Hush Laboratories of top-secrets in research and invention known simply as the San Diego Naval Research Laboratory. Established in a series of unimpressive buildings on old Point Loma, opposite North Island in the entrance to San Diego harbor, this incubator of ideas for defensive and offensive warfare on and under the surface of the sea was headed by Dr. George P. Harnwell, Director of the University of California's Division of War Research.

The visit was arranged by Captain Gordon Campbell—Hump, to his friends—Commander of the Submarine Squadron based at San Diego. He assured me that I would find a visit interesting as well as profitable.

"You'll see gadgets and things," promised Captain Campbell, "that'll make you think of a trip with Alice through Wonderland!"

By means of a quick telephone call, it was arranged that Dr. Harnwell would send a boat to North Island early the next morning to save the time it would take to drive by car around the bay to Point Loma. As a result, the day was still young when I met Dr. Harnwell in his office. If I had expected to meet a typical scientist, I was due for a major disappointment. Tall, broad-shouldered, straight, clear-cut, this noted scientist had none of the tweediness, thick-lensed glasses, and pipe-chewing habits popularly associated with

18

deep-stuff research. On the contrary, in his mid-forties, Dr. Harnwell had the suave smoothness of a Big Ten football coach in the habit of producing winning teams. As a matter of fact, as a scientist the Doctor was, indeed, providing Uncle Sam's combat teams with devices that did take many winning tricks. The same air of competence and success emanated from his immediate associates—Dr. F. N. D. Kurie, Dr. R. O. Burns, and Prof. Malcolm Henderson. In time, the latter was to become my strong right arm in bringing Operation Barney into being. But neither of us knew that on this raw and blustry April morning of 1943. In fact, I had not even given thought to the daring adventure which we were to name Operation Barney.

For several hours the four scientists dropped whatever work they had been doing and generously devoted their time and attention to showing me their Wonderland of Ideas. As we progressed, they courteously and patiently demonstrated or explained new weapons and protective techniques which, had we possessed them at our submarine bases in the Pacific, would have saved hundreds of lives and might have doubled our sinking scores. I felt that our present deck guns and torpedoes were almost as obsolete as bows and arrows and that "push button warfare" was just around the corner. Alas, it was to be many months before we would see this new equipment in action at sea, and many submarines went to Davy Jones' Locker for lack of the protection they would have afforded.

As a finale to our morning's peep into the future, Dr. Harnwell took me down San Diego entrance channel in a small motor boat to demonstrate a new device called the FM (Frequency Modulated) Sonar. To my unpracticed eye, it appeared to be a sort of underwater radar which projected on a PPI (Position Plan Indicator) screen—much like the screen on a television set—a lighted area which indicated the distance and direction of the sides of the channel our launch was traversing. Passing motor boats also showed as blobs on the screen and their steel hulls gave back a clearly audible, bell-like tone, a tone which I was destined to hear many hundreds of times in the far reaches of the Pacific in the years to come, a chime which our submariners learned to call Hellsbells because of the sinister, death-dealing enemies from which they echoed.

Dr. Harnwell explained that the FM Sonar had been

developed for mine sweepers in the Mediterranean but had proved unsuitable. In the disturbed, turbulent waters in which surface ships cruise, its efficiency in detecting mines was practically nil. However, he believed that a submarine operating in the quiet waters beneath the surface could use FMS to follow the channel into an enemy harbor.

If this were a work of fiction, this is the point where I would follow up the Alice in Wonderland theme by claiming that I—as we looked at the screen and listened to the chiming bells—was swept by a curious feeling of anticipation, that a low and disembodied voice whispered that here was the secret weapon which would knock the Mikado galley west of the Sea of Japan. However, truth compels me to say that at the moment I could see little future for the use of FM Sonar. This was mainly because our submarine targets at that stage of the war were on the high seas. The harbors of the Japanese Empire and its occupied territory were too shallow—far too shallow—to permit the entrance, undetected, of a submerged submarine. Once detected, without freedom to maneuver or go deep, such an intruder would have had no chance of escape. I wanted no part of such suicide missions. Submarines and submariners were too scarce and too valuable to be recklessly hazarded.

On the other hand, I was much impressed by FM Sonar's ability to see and hear nearby surface vessels. It was evident to me that such a device could be of great defensive value if used by a submarine, under depth charge attack, to locate and torpedo its attackers.

Curiously enough, I failed—and I have often wondered why I failed—to associate FM Sonar with its potential role of a mine detector when used by a submerged submarine in charting or penetrating mine fields. The reason for that could be that this pilot set had failed so abjectly in that direction when employed by mine sweepers. At any rate, on that particular morning, as my Hawaiian sun-tan faded into a wind-bitten blue, I made a mental note about the instrument and its potential use, subject to further improvements, as defensive equipment.

The immediate fruits of our morning cruise were arrangements between Dr. Harnwell and myself whereby I would initiate, and he would support, a request to the Navy Department to have an FM Sonar set installed on the first available submarine. That is, as soon as the first available

Sonar set was ready. In those fairly early days of electronic war production, these devices had been tailor-made in the Naval Laboratory by skillful hands and one by one.

Having, up to that time, spent all of my mature years in the Navy, I thought that I had some fairly accurate ideas with respect to the time it takes to stop and to change the flow and direction of red tape. But until then I never realized how much power and patience are required to cope with that frustrating current in wartime, especially when the inertia of almost unchangeable priorities is added to the problem.

However, not too much was lost by this expenditure of time and energy on my part because sets were not to become available for any use—even by the mine sweepers (which did not really want them)—until a contract had been let to and production begun by Western Electric in the early part of 1944. In fact, the delay gave me time to survey the problems posed by enemy mine warfare and to evaluate our available countermeasures. These studies convinced me that FM Sonar had the capabilities and potentialities we required and made me more determined than ever to get a set installed in a submarine. Hence, many months before the end of the full year that was to pass before I saw the first FMS set installed in a submarine, I had come to the realization that the mine doors into the Sea of Japan had to be unlocked by submarines and that FM Sonar was the magic key that could perform the marvel of unlocking them.

In the light of what afterward transpired, it was curious indeed that the fruits of my visit to Dr. Harnwell's Wonderland required such a long period of ripening, but as one Lewis Carroll character said so wisely to another: "Things get curioser and curioser!"

The combat activities of 1943-44 produced an endless chain of hectic days in the headquarters of Comsubpac in a converted bomb-proof shelter at the Submarine Base in Pearl Harbor. On the return from my tour, I found my desk piled high with stacks of papers that reminded me of the sky-line of Manhattan Island. First thing I had to do was report on my findings along the route of inspection from Alaska to San Francisco, from San Diego to Washington, to Admiral Nimitz.

Chester Nimitz is one of the easiest and, at the same time, one of the most difficult men in the entire Navy to talk to. It was easy going and smooth sailing, with a helping breeze, when you knew your subject and had all the answers at your finger tips. But it was up-wind all the way for those who tumbled and had to fish around for replies to his softly voiced, slowly spoken questions. And when it came to asking penetrating questions, he could make the average prosecuting attorney look like a schoolboy.

Bearing this in mind, I felt that I might be skating on thin ice when I brought up the subject of FM Sonar. I took special care in the presentation of my case, so that the Admiral would not jump to the conclusion that I had gone over to the Gadgeteers or joined the Buck Rogers Boys. Apparently I kept my presentation on a believable plane. Perhaps the fact that I did not claim too much for FM Sonar but placed the project on the basis of one experimental set for one trial submarine carried the day in my favor. At any rate, the Big Boss told me to go ahead and explore the matter and approved of my asking the Bureau of Ships to put the first available set aboard the first available submarine.

Perhaps one reason that influenced the Boss's favorable attitude was that my visit to Washington for the purpose of reducing the number of defective torpedoes issued to submarines had produced results. This to such an extent that Rear Admiral W. H. P. Blandy, Chief of the Bureau of Ordnance, had agreed to take immediate steps toward the improvement of our torpedoes. Briefly, "Spike," a lifelong friend, promised to take immediate action if I would assist by assigning a torpedo expert to his organization. This I did, with the happy outcome that the more important bugs that caused torpedo failures were eliminated within a few months. These improvements, unhappily, were not in time to give Mush Morton a batch of non-duds on his first venture into the Sea of Japan. However, they did come just in time to equip him with the new electric torpedo on his second invasion that was destined to have such a tragic ending. Most of us believed that our increasing losses of submarines in enemy waters could be ascribed only to mines. Several factors caused us to place the blame for those losses on mine fields. First and foremost, the Japs—whenever they sank one of our ships—had made a practice of shouting it to the high heavens. Now we began to lose ships in waters between Japan and Formosa, in the East China Sea, and in other waters including the Yellow Sea. But no shouting. This absence of Japan's crowing over our losses pointed to mines. Next, toward mid-1944, our Intelligence uncovered Japanese Notices to Mariners warning them to keep clear of certain areas in the Yellow Sea and elsewhere. Although the notices did not mention mines, they obviously pointed to the existence of mines in those proscribed areas.

Another feature that supported this conclusion was the steadily increasing number of floating or run-away mines discovered on the edges of Japanese waters.

On top of that, we also had fairly accurate knowledge of mine fields in the straits that lead into the Japanese Sea.

Into these troubled speculations over our increased losses was injected the news that the *Spadefish*, a brand new Mare Island-built submarine, Comdr. Gordon (Coach) Underwood, had received an FM Sonar installation and was even then undergoing trials at San Diego.

I heard the news with enthusiastic interest.

Was it possible that this new electronic gadget which had failed the minesweepers could be developed into a mine detector aboard submarines? My thoughts flashed back to the tests I had witnessed at San Diego in April, 1943. Determination to investigate further was born right then and there.

When the *Spadefish* poked her nose into the Submarine Base, Pearl Harbor, on June 23, 1944, I was on hand with a lot of questions for her commanding officer and his technicians.

I learned that, under the vigilant eye and skilled touch of Professor Malcolm Henderson, Skipper Underwood and the electronic specialists in the *Spadefish*'s crew had learned the technique of operating the rather temperamental sonar set of those pioneering days. Incidentally "Coach" Underwood was an ideal submariner, well-equipped mentally and constitutionally for sticking the nose of his sub into uncharted realms.

On arrival at San Diego from the Mare Island Yard, the *Spadefish* had been put through lengthy trial runs on the sonar device. Some of these runs, as I learned from Underwood, were made under dummy mines laid in simulation of a mine field; and some success had been achieved in detecting and locating mines. That was all I needed to hear. We made plans for further tests as soon as her torpedo firing training could be completed.

Naturally the FM Sonar device installed on the *Spadefish* created broad interest and wide speculation in submarine circles in Pearl Harbor. From the very start, I was to find that the personnel of submarines equipped with FM Sonar were not too enthusiastic about it.

As, month by month, the theater of war in the Pacific

U.S.S. Spadefish

moved closer to the Japanese home-islands, submarines were withdrawn from the now almost deserted Nipponese sea-lanes. Where once there had been such beautiful pickings, the traffic was now so thin that targets had to be "beaten out of the bushes" close to the coasts. But that did not mean rest for submariners. Instead, came urgent demands for their services in making of photographic panoramas of beaches and islands marked for invasion. This work, close inshore, was extremely dangerous, not only because of possible mines but because of unmarked reefs and similar obstacles.

It was my earnest hope that the FM Sonar could be the counter to both of these menaces. If that could be accomplished, then we could go on to train FMS equipped submarines to actually chart mine fields and eventually to penetrate them.

Contrary to the expectation of laymen, mines are not planted in wide areas in a pre-selected body of water. There is no comparison between the planting of a cornfield and the sowing of a mine field, since the latter is not densely sown. A field basically consists of two or three rows of mines which span certain shipping lanes, straits, or channels. Usually, the rows are fairly widely spaced at distances of from four hun-

dred to one thousand yards between rows. Nor are the mines, in the respective rows, planted too closely together—the intervals are from seventy-five to one hundred yards—so that each mine is far enough from its neighbor to avoid the danger of one mine setting the whole string off through chain reaction. When a mine detonates, it sets off an extremely heavy blast. Mines constitute the one and only enemy that a submariner really fears—the one and only thing against which a submariner had no protection until FM Sonar came into timely existence.

The Japanese mine with which we had the widest acquaintance—because our ships came upon so many drifters from the mine orchards—was their Type-93, a moored contact mine similar enough to our Mark-6 mine to be kissin' kin—namely a spherical, chemical horn-type that explodes when an acid in a horn is released through the breaking of the horn. These mines could be set at depths down to 246 feet, or even deeper; usually they were seldom planted below one hundred feet and then, as a rule, in tiers ranging from ten feet to forty feet to seventy feet. Since the draft of a submarine running on the surface is eighteen feet in standard trim, the top row of shallowly planted mines would offer a menace to submarines surfacing through a mine field. As a rule, the Japs set their mines no deeper than seventy feet. In very deep water, mine-dip caused by currents reduce a mine field's efficiency against surface ships. However, anti-submarine mine fields have been laid in waters as deep as eight hundred feet.

According to international agreements, mines are supposed to be armed only when the pull and weight of the cable provides tension on the mooring spindle. A drifting mine, free from that tension, is supposed to have its fangs drawn. Still, our boys never trusted this arrangement. They either gave them a wide berth or exploded them with gunfire.

As far as the presence of Japanese mine fields was concerned, it now seems—in the light of what we learned through submarine exploration of these dangerous areas—that Type-93 moored contact mines were planted in great numbers by the Japs fairly early in the war for the purpose of sealing off huge sea areas from our prowling submarines. Meanwhile, within their protective barriers, Jap merchant and other maritime traffic proceeded in perfect safety. Thus—taking time by the forelock—we found out about the high-explosive fences that blocked our entrance into the China Sea and north to Japan from Formosa. Another field blocked Formosa Straits and still others blocked the narrow waterways into the Sea of Japan.

As for mine fields and submarines, the normal thing for a submarine commander to do when he encounters a mine field is to give orders designed to take him and his ship some other place as rapidly as possible. As observed elsewhere in this volume, we suffered losses in those mine fields. It is, in fact, quite possible that as many as eight of our submarines were destroyed by mines, and we are quite certain that no less than three were victims of mines.

Though we took every precaution, we were lucky not to lose more submarines to enemy mines than we did. This is especially true considering the number of submarines that operated in areas later suspected of being mined. In the large open sea mine fields the Hellpots were planted so as to present what one might call a 10 percent threat to all of our vessels that entered those waters. In other words, the mines were distributed so that about one submarine in ten might be expected to sink. Naturally, this ten to one ratio was reduced by time—cables broke and mines either became supposedly harmless drifters or sank as a result of leaks or accumulated fouling. . . . But let us return to Pearl Harbor and the main track of our story.

Just as my braintrust and torpedo experts had devoted countless hours to perfecting and removing the bugs from our principal weapon, the torpedo and its exploder, so now our energies were arrayed against the problem of perfecting this passive weapon—the FMS—on which we pinned our hopes of conquering enemy mines in general and those in the Sea of Japan in particular.

In the first case we spent thousands of man-hours—and dollars—firing live torpedoes against the sheer underwater cliffs of Kahoolawe Island until we discovered the reason for duds; then we spent more hundreds of hours and dollars dropping dummy warheads from a crane-head until, eventually, we worked out the cure.

In the present problem, the expenditure of funds was small. But the man-hours devoted to the FM Sonar by me and by my battery of electronic experts far exceeded those expended on the torpedo.

From the day in June, 1944, when *Spadefish* brought the first set of FM Sonar to Pearl Harbor, until the crashing of Tsushima Strait mine barrier a year later, I was to greet almost innumerable sunrises from the bridge of a submarine bound to exercise areas where dummy mine fields had been laid.

To facilitate and speed the work, the Mine Force laid a field for us in the fairly deep and safe waters northeast of Barbers Point—off Brown's Camp. It was there we took the *Spadefish*, as soon as she was ready for patrol, to test her FM Sonar.

4

HELLSBELLS VERSUS HELLPOTS

On the morning of July 13, 1944, when I went aboard the *Spadefish* to undergo my maiden trip with sonar under a mine field—a dummy field, to be sure, but nevertheless a target that called upon the electronic detector to do its best—I was beset by cross-currents of thoughts and emotions.

I was so anxious to put the FMS to the acid test that I felt a twinge of impatience. Turning to Underwood, I asked, "Say, Skipper, do you think we could speed her up a bit? At this rate it'll take most of the morning to get there."

With a thinly suppressed grin, for the use of high speed was officially discouraged, Coach leaned toward the open conning tower hatch and ordered, "All ahead full!" Instantly the purr of the diesels changed into a subdued roar as their rpms were stepped up and the bone in the *Spadefish*'s teeth grew wider and longer and whiter.

As we sped westward along Ewa Beach, a couple of miles off shore, I cast a speculative eye on the part of the FMS set which was visible on the submarine's deck. What I saw was a gray-black and lifeless looking rubber sphere mounted on a short and slim steel shaft that rose from the deck of the submarine slightly abaft the bow-planes. This shaft extended down through the hull into the forward torpe-do room where gears, operated by electric motors, turned the shaft right or left as the sonar operator in the conning tower might direct. The rubber sphere, called a transducer, projected an electronic beam in any desired direction and collected an echo if the beam hit a solid object.

The sphere was about eighteen inches in diameter and yielded but slightly to the touch. Contrary to procedure used on minesweepers, the device had been installed on deck. As I studied it, it occurred to me that—from a submariner's standpoint—it might be preferable to place the sonar set in the keel of the sub rather than on the deck. If mounted in the keel, the set might not only give a better signal but might even prove usable on the surface. So mounted, it would not be affected by the noise of water gurgling through the deck gratings and the superstructure. Even on this millpond day, enough water rushed noisily over the *Spadefish*'s deck to give anyone who ventured forward from the bridge a good drenching.

Time and distance slipped by as I weighed the subject, and I had virtually made up my mind to suggest to Dr. Harnwell that he shift to keel-installation when a pair of danger buoys that marked the dummy mine field slipped from long range into close view. It was time to submerge, to cast the dice.

A dummy mine is merely a mine without the stuff that makes it explode. In this instance the mine field consisted of twenty Hellpots planted in two rows with some 150 feet between mines and about three hundred yards between the rows, which ran at right angles to the coast. The mines were planted at a uniform depth of thirty feet in order that ships could pass over them without danger of hitting them. We were about twelve hundred yards south of the buoys that marked the nearest row when Coach ordered: "Clear the bridge!" The bridge watch scrambled down the hatch and I eagerly headed toward that spot on the starboard side in the conning tower where the FMS receiving set was installed. Meanwhile the raucous echo of the diving alarm sounded throughout the boat.

To the observer, the sonar set of that day looked like a television set of today. Instead of the standard square screen, however, it had a circular scanning plate with a diameter of about sixteen inches. From its center extended a series of concentric circles with Range Markings that rose from one hundred to several thousand yards. Extending from the center of the screen to all the points of the compass, like spokes in a wheel, were the Bearing Lines which indicated the position of a mine as related to the position of the sub.

Running from the center of the screen and covering the compass area selected by the sonar operator (usually forward and from left to right over a zone of about 90 degrees) was a luminous sweep, almost hair-line thin. When the travel of the transducer beam was uninterrupted in the water, the luminous sweep ran straight to the edge of the screen. But when the beam of the transducer hit a mine or some other solid object—from a ship to a reef, from a school of fish to the wake of a vessel or even a mass of colder water—the luminous sweep formed a light blob on the sonar screen at that precise point. The operator was then able to note and report the distance of the mine, or other objects, from the ship and likewise its relative direction from the submarine's course.

At the same time, sound would emanate from a loudspeaker directly over the top of the sonar set. The fullness of the sound depended upon the quality of the blob. The loudspeaker would give tone to irregular and scratchy noises if the blob was a poorly defined light image. On the other hand, if the beam registered the small but almost pearshaped blob that was a sonar portrait of a Hellpot, the loudspeaker would produce the full, clear sound of a tiny bell. A skilled operator might fail to guess the source of flickering light blobs and their cacophony of sounds. But even the greenest hand would know the meaning of pear-shaped blobs and tolling chimes—the bells that heralded the presence of Hellpots and no doubts about it.

That morning aboard the *Spadefish*, we had barely reached periscope depth at sixty-two feet—the usual cruising depth of submerged submarines—when the conning tower watchers were electrified by the clear round tones of a tolling bell. At the same instant the sonar operator sang out, "Contact! Bearing—030!"

Briefly translated, this meant that a blob on the sonar screen indicated the presence of a mine slightly to the right of the *Spadefish's* course.

Any words that I might grope for to describe the tidal wave of triumph that swept through me at that moment would fall far short of describing what the sight of that blob and the sound of that bell meant to me. I had gambled much—even the blue chips of my professional standing—on the ability of FMS to pick the lock and open the doors that kept our submarines out of heavily mined waters.

Light and sound from the Hellpots! Hellsbells aringing! No longer would it be possible for these evil killers to lie in silent, invisible hiding in deep, dark waters waiting for my subs.

Hellsbells! I heard them then and I can hear them even now—a full decade after that momentous dive in the *Spadefish*—truly heavenly music. Memory records blobs glowing on the sonar screen like big juicy lightning bugs as our submarine, at a cautious three-knot pace, glided safely through the mine field. In the course of that July morning we made a dozen trial runs, tested and practiced the technique of operating the set, explored its promises, probed for its faults and limitations. I soon realized that the efficiency of a sonar set could not rise above the ability of the men who operated it. In other words, with the improvement and construction of FM Sonar sets, there was a corresponding need for the training of submarine captains and operators in their use. Confidence and a light touch on the volume dial were twin-essentials. Ham-handed operators who, through sheer nervousness, goaded their sets by turning on all the juice lest they should miss a mine, blocked their own goals.

Up to that morning, I sensed, Underwood's faith in the sonar device had been on the low side. Of course the set was far from perfect. But even miracles fall short of absolute perfection. That FM Sonar set was at least within range of perfection if we gave the device the time and study and patience it deserved. Up to that morning I had shared the almost universal viewpoint among submariners with respect to mines, namely that they constituted an unescapable occupational hazard, a sort of fatalistic attitude that if Kismet willed that your sub should hit a mine—well, that was it and nothing could be done about it. But from that time on, my viewpoint changed. Now I knew that Fate no longer decreed that mines had a Devil-given right to prey upon the splendid ships and fine young men I sent out on combat patrols. FM Sonar had changed all that. My unanticipated visit to Point Loma in April, 1943, had changed all that. I now felt it my personal responsibility to obtain as many Sonar sets as I could get as rapidly as I could get them and to spur the improvement of the sets as quickly as possible.

And, last but far from least, I resolved to take a personal interest in the training of skippers and operators in the use of Sonar sets during all operational trials before submarines were sent out on patrol, so as to instill some of my own abiding confidence into the men whose lives were to depend on FM Sonar. Confidence breeds success and perfection is the fruit of preparation. Equally applicable to the situation was the old story: "Give a dog a bad name and you might as well shoot him." I did not want this "dog" to get a bad name. In time, this decision was to eat heavily into my office working hours and rest heavily on my shoulders. But I hated paper work anyhow, and I have never regretted a single second of the hundreds of dawn hours I spent aboard submarines cruising through practice fields at Pearl Harbor, Saipan, and Guam. That, as it turned out, was as close as I was to get to the Hellpots.

I was now convinced that we had the passive weapon, the instrument which would pull the teeth of enemy mine fields. This was the key which would unlock the mine-studded doors that shut us out of the Sea of Japan. With this weapon in our hands and confidence in our hearts, we would complete the job which *Wahoo, Permit, Plunger, Lapon,* and *Sawfish* started in 1943—a job that demanded completion more urgently every day. The determination to collect in full

U.S.S. Permit

for the loss of Mush Morton and his lads never receded from the foreground of my thinking. It was not a driving, over-riding urge, but a resolve that was very much alive—one might call it a prefabricated but unlabeled piece of the jig-saw picture of operational planning that would fit into its proper position at the proper moment.

At about that time, I received information that one more FM Sonar was being built at the Naval Research Laboratory in San Diego and that it would be ready for delivery on August 15, not to the subs, alas, but to the minesweepers. The Hush-Hush Grapevine also had it that Western Electronic would have its first set ready in about sixty days and that from then on one set would be assembled each week—an ambitious program that was never realized.

This encouraging news was more than off-set by the information that all sets were destined for minesweepers. After all the correspondence, official and semi-official, that had been exchanged, the final pay-off was that the sets scheduled for manufacture were still earmarked for mine-sweepers that did not want them. First, because the performance of FM Sonar close to the surface was unreliable; next, because their unreliable performance actually increased the dangers of sweepers operating in mine fields.

My spirits, as reflected in my notes and in letters to my wife in the latter part of July, 1944, were at a low ebb. How my wife Phyllis managed to raise three children, drive for the Red Cross Motor Corps, listen to my troubles, and still come out of the war smiling was nothing short of miraculous—but she did.

As for the war, our losses had been heavy; thirty-four

submarines since the war began, nine of them in 1944. According to my figures, our loss in personnel was 216 officers and 1870 men. The gear for protective countermeasures, which I knew would check these submarine losses, was unbelievably slow in coming out to us. Reason: the invasion of the Marianas (then in progress) and the Amphibious Forces had top priority on electronics which we so sorely needed for several types of defensive equipment, not the least of which was FM Sonar.

I had no quarrel with plans for giving aid to the hard-pressed, hard-fighting lads in the landing craft. However, I was confident that if we were given a small share of the electronic gear they received, we could relieve them of a considerable load of worries. During the invasion of Saipan—when our forces ashore were having a bad time and Admiral Ozawa led his formidable Mobile Fleet of battleships, carriers, and heavy cruisers to attack our invasion fleet—the submarine *Albacore* and *Cavalla* contributed their bit to the success of the "Marianas Turkey Shoot" by sinking two of the enemy's five carriers on June 19, 1944.

Similarly, on June 1, 2, 3, and 4, the submarine *Pilotfish*, *Pintado*, *Shark*, and *Silversides*, in a wild battle north of the Marianas, practically wiped out a troop convoy bound for Saipan. Of the ten thousand enemy soldiers aboard those ships, six thousand were lost, and the four thousand who finally made it were deprived of their artillery, arms, and ammunition. Not a bad "assist" to General Holland Smith's Marines* and Army who hit the beaches on June 15.

After my first sonar trials, I naturally sought the earliest possible opportunity to make a personal report to Admiral Nimitz. I gave him a word-picture of our sonar cruises under the dummy mine field at Brown's Camp and voiced my hope that he would support my plans to ask the Navy Department to switch the delivery of FM Sonar sets, under construction and assigned to minesweepers in the Mediterranean, to Comsubpac. As the minutes slipped by and I warmed up to my subject, the Boss's questions grew shorter. My answers grew longer and more elaborate. Toward the end the interview was pretty much a monologue in which I gave full play

---

*For this famous Marine General's own story read, CORAL AND BRASS by General Holland "Howling Mad" Smith, another authentic volume in the Bantam War Book Series.

to the vitally important services I knew our subs could perform if they were equipped with FM Sonar. "Eventually, Admiral," I said, "with this new sonar, we'll crack the Sea of Japan without losing a ship or a man in the mine fields."

This was a clincher, for cracking the Japan Sea was a subject close to the heart of the Fleet Admiral. When our meeting came to an end, he granted me authority to try to obtain the sets then earmarked for minesweepers.

To be sure, my heart sang because I had been able to win his support. But! There was a big *but*. When I entered the Admiral's office on that occasion, I had been relatively empty-handed with respect to sonar equipment. I had only one FMS set, the apparatus in the *Spadefish* which the Boss had authorized me to obtain for trial purposes on a spring day way back in 1943. Almost fifteen months had passed since then. And now, as I left the Admiral's office on a mid-July forenoon in 1944, I had won his support in my efforts to get the sonar sets—a dozen or so—on the Western Electric's manufacturing schedule. This was a major go-ahead traffic light so far as I was concerned. But it was not mandatory in Washington where the Navy Department had the final say. Much battling was still to be done.

5

ADMIRALS KING AND NIMITZ APPROVE

There is no such thing as a submarine navy any more than there is a battleship navy. Big ships, small and medium ships, we all pull together for a common objective—victory. It was therefore natural that I should consider our submarines an integral and important part of Admiral Nimitz's "Pacific Pacifiers." They had won their spurs by letting daylight— and seawater—through hundreds of hulls of Japanese warships, transports, and cargo-carriers. Now the pattern of war was changing. It would soon demand the entrance of our submarines upon a stage that was heavily mined for the express purpose of keeping Americans out of Japanese homewaters. And I was determined to give our submariners every possible protection against Japanese anti-submarine measures.

Admiral Nimitz, the Big Boss of our naval forces in the Pacific, was now definitely in my corner. Reduced to its most important element, this spelled FM Sonar. With the Admiral's support, the project was bound to materialize. However, we needed pressure on the high level in the Navy Department which would eliminate the necessity for a dozen official letters. If I could bring the matter to the attention of Admiral King and enlist his favorable interest, the project's speed would gain considerable momentum.

But how to gain Admiral King's attention?

That was a large and, to me, baffling question. Then one morning out of the clear blue of a beautiful July Pearl Harbor day came the answer. There was to be a top-secret meeting of Uncle Sam's top-level strategists in Honolulu to discuss the then impending campaign to recapture the Philippines. Present Roosevelt was steaming Hawaii-ward from the States aboard the cruiser *Indianapolis*, which was later to carry the A-bomb to Tinian and meet her death from the torpedoes of a Japanese submarine. General MacArthur was flying up from New Guinea. Admiral King was winging his way to the Islands from Washington. Luckily for me, Admiral King arrived several days ahead of the hour when the *Indianapolis*, flying the Presidential flag from its mainmast, moored at 10-10 Dock in the solemn silence that had replaced all gun salutes in wartime. But long before that moment, I had been lucky enough to get my sonar case before Admiral King and to obtain from him the higher priority throttle-setting that was needed to expedite delivery into my hands.

This was how that happened: Following a kindly notification from Admiral Nimitz, I prepared to receive Admiral King at my office at one o'clock on the afternoon of July 25 and to show him our submarine line-up. The inspection, which lasted the better part of two hours, included climbing through a submarine which was fully loaded and ready for departure on a combat patrol. As always, Admiral King showed a keen interest in and thorough understanding of the equipment he inspected.

On his tour he was accompanied by his Chief of Plans, Rear Admiral Charles M. Cook, Jr., a submarine sailor from way back. Admiral Cook listened with attentive interest—

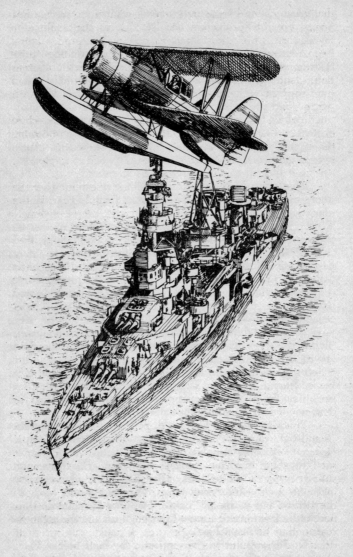

U.S.S. Indianapolis

that grew visibly warmer as I spoke—when I sprang my FM Sonar project. By now we had left the car that took us to Headquarters from the submarine base and entered Admiral Nimitz' office. This turned out to be a tailor-made opportunity. Admiral Nimitz followed my presentation with close attention, nodding approval at the right moments—if we had rehearsed the scene in advance, it could not have played with better effect.

When I had concluded my highly summarized speech of explanation, Admiral King—whose eyes had been following the argosies of clouds that sailed the sky—shifted his glance to mine and said, "All right. What do you need to implement this operation?"

"I need the eleven FM Sonar sets now building for the minesweepers in the Mediterranean and I need a share in the top-priorities for electronics in order to build more of them."

My right hand dove into my left breast pocket where—in hopeful anticipation of this request—I had placed a prepared statement of my most urgent needs. A quick grin spread over King's face as I handed two typed pages to him. He scanned their contents rapidly with the keen eye of the photographic reader, re-folded the sheets neatly into their proper folds, and handed them to "Savvy" Cook who placed them in his brief case as he gave me a reassuring look.

To my last moment I will recall the surge of pure, unadulterated joy that swept through me as I headed back to my office. I was indeed walking on the very clouds that Admiral King had been scanning not so many minutes ago. For all practical purposes Admiral King had promised to put pressure on production and to speed up the process of delivery of sonar equipment to our submarines.

Without realizing it, I began to hum *Anchors Aweigh*: "Stand Navy down the field. . . ." A mood, a positive feeling of victory swept over me. For all practical purposes, the sonar sets were in our hands and aboard submarines. Enough submarines with enough sets to realize my long cherished project to invade the Sea of Japan. To avenge Mush Morton, the *Wahoo* and its men. To make Imperial Hirohito and his henchman Tojo knuckle under. To make Japan and the Japanese realize that no longer was the Sea of Japan safe for their dreams of Empire or to transport rice for their bellies.

To be sure, my spirits did not remain at that high altitude of enthusiasm for long. There were still handicaps to overcome here at home. On the other hand, the submarine conference to be held at Hunters Point Navy Yard in a few days—on August 7—was no longer the potential high hurdle it had been before my meeting with Admiral King. He had given me a formidable "persuader" to use on Washington conferees who might prove recalcitrant or reluctant.

Yes, sir!

As the calendar pages turned from July to August, I completed my plans for the most important submarine meeting of the year with respect to the war in the Pacific.

My staff for that conference was a power-house of combat-tested experts. Included were: Captain Bud Yoemans, Strategic Plans; Commander Bill Irvin, Subpac Communications; Commander Bob Ferrall, Material Officer; Commander Harry Hull, Special Weapons; Commander Spike Hottel, Base Torpedo Officer; and last but not least, Flag Lieutenant Vince Bailey, ex-Harvard man just in from submarine patrols.

The caliber of the representatives from Bureaus and builders was equally heartening and I was especially glad to see Commander Rawson Bennett, II, from the Electronics Desk in The Bureau of Ships, whose whole-hearted support we needed—and won—to obtain a cut of the priority pie for which we anhungered, as the Bible says.

The Pacific War was getting into high gear and everyone wanted a share in it. I found that Commander Dan Daspit of early *Tinosa* fame—with four enemy ships to his credit—had been assigned to push as rapidly as possible production of the very hush-hush equipment to increase the offensive power of submarines, which we so urgently needed to check our losses. I knew that he would not fail us in our current difficulties. An additional submarine officer had been assigned to assist FM Sonar operations at San Diego U.C.D.W.R. Laboratory.

The conduct of war from a desk that does not submerge even to wastebasket depth is, as a rule, so full of frustrations, disappointments, and hopes that turn into nightmares that the smooth precision with which everything went at the Hunters Point séance made me suspect that this was too good to last, that something had to break with a bang and hit me with a wallop. The chore of running Submarines Pacific could never be that pleasant.

The next stop was San Diego and my next conferee, Dr. Harnwell. Subject: Acquiring FM Sonar sets from minesweepers that did not want them for the use of submariners who were lukewarm or outright hostile toward placing their lives and their ships at the tender mercies of Hellsbells.

Chances are, I thought, as we headed south from San Francisco, that something has gone haywire on the sonar subject. True, no further news on the matter had reached me at Hunters Point and—using past experiences as a yardstick—it simply did not measure up that no news could be good news. So I set course for Point Loma with my fingers crossed.

6

HELLSBELLS CHART MINE FIELDS

A smile, as brilliant as a Diamond Head rainbow, spread over the face of Dr. Harnwell and glints of happy excitement highlighted his eyes that August morning when he met me at the dock of the Point Loma Naval Laboratory. Again, to save time, I had crossed San Diego Bay by launch from North Island.

"Three cheers and congratulations," he shouted before the bobbing little motor boat was close enough to the dock to permit me to jump ashore.

"What?" I yelled. "What did you say?"

"You got 'em!" he replied.

"What've I got?"

"The sonar sets," he answered. "A message just arrived. Eleven sets that are being assembled by Western Electric have been released to you instead of to the minesweepers."

My heart dove and surfaced—sank and rose—or just went up, up, up in steadily ascending spirals. I had won the battle of Washington. But how? And through whom? Admiral King? Admiral Nimitz? Or Savvy Cook? Chances are that all of them had pulled their weight at the oars.

From San Diego I returned to Pearl Harbor. In mail awaiting me was a letter giving gratifying proof that the Hunters Point conference had vastly improved the position of the submarine war in the Pacific. The letter was from Captain

Frank Watkins, ex-*Flying Fish* and ex-commander of a submarine division, writing from the Submarine Desk in the Chief of Naval Operations Office. He wrote: "Since my return from the conference, I have noted a difference in the tone of all submariners' requests, directives, etc., which originate here. They speak with conviction and force, for they know what you and your boys want—and they will move mountains to get the thing rolling."

Unfortunately there were some mountains they could not move. The bottleneck in electronics was terrific and production was not yet in high gear.

In the early fall of 1944, two new FM Sonar sets—one made by the Point Loma Naval Research Laboratory Staff, the other manufactured in the Western Electric plant at Los Angeles—arrived at Mare Island for installation in submarines. The boats to receive these instruments were the *Tinosa* and the *Tunny*. We had reached the last week of November, 1944, when the *Tinosa*, an old and valued friend of seven successful combat patrols, pulled into Pearl Harbor from States-side. On this trip she had a new skipper who was to prove himself one of the best—Commander Richard C. Latham. The first factory-built FMS set was mounted in the *Tinosa*'s keel. All sets that followed were also keel-mounted. This change had been decided upon as a result of the tests with the *Spadefish*.

I was naturally eager to see this new gear in operation, so in the gray dawn of Thanksgiving morning—as soon as the torpedo nets at the entrance were opened to admit the night shift of patrolling destroyers—the *Tinosa* stood out the channel to the practice field of dummy mines planted near Brown's Camp on the west coast of Oahu. Again, as on my maiden trip aboard the *Spadefish*, the day was ideal. The water was so unruffled that on our first trial run, while still surfaced, our FM Sonar revealed clear "blobs" of mines at satisfactory ranges. This seemed too good to be true and, in fact, was, for it required very little roughening of the sea to spoil this rosy picture. However, our submerged results were excellent. Time and again we picked up mines that registered the distinct nearly pear-shaped screen blob and the ringing bell tone. The set functioned much better with the transducer mounted in the keel.

My cup of joy was brimming; the success of a long

cherished plan now seemed assured—but there was a long, hard road still to travel.

The first definite step along that road—namely to bring the ability of FM Sonar as mine detectors into play against actual high explosive Hellpots in enemy waters—was taken in the orders issued to Dick Latham and his *Tinosa* for the eighth War Patrol of that vessel. It was to take place in the Nansei Shoto—Formosa—East China Sea areas. This was Dick's first war patrol as skipper, and he left Pearl Harbor on a mission of fifty-eight days' duration on December 4 after a full week of intense FM Sonar training under my personal supervision. In addition to his regular orders, Latham was to explore along the edges of some sections we believed to be covered by mine fields. Because of this—because of the inviolate secrecy that surrounded FM Sonar and its use—the *Tinosa* was under sealed orders when she set her course westward. As usual, I was down at the base when she got underway. This was always a time of introspection for me, a time to check, mentally, a ship's orders and make sure we had done everything humanly possible to ensure the safe accomplishment of her mission. This time, just for extra good measure, I silently made a prayer to the God who rules the great waters for her safe return.

Meanwhile, much of the news that came to Pearl Harbor from the fighting fronts was good. From a submariner's standpoint, the fall of 1944 had been a highly successful season. Night after night, the decoding machines unfolded stories of victory: the *Archerfish* had sunk the huge carrier *Shinano*; *Sealion* had sunk the battleship *Kongo*; *Darter* and *Dace* had sunk two heavy cruisers; the bottom of Luzon Strait was carpeted with enemy merchantmen—yet none of these victories compensated for the loss of ten fleet submarines with about eight hundred American submariners, especially since many of these losses could have been prevented by the timely provision of adequate defensive equipment.

Yes! In the brief space of four months we had lost ten submarines. We suspected mining in four instances, and post-war reports show we were probably correct except for one—the *Tang*—which, while operating in the shallow waters off the China coast where she might have struck a mine, was actually sunk by one of her own torpedoes that made a circular run.

This was not so good—in fact, it was outright bad. Again I felt robbed and cheated because the protective devices, the electronic marvels we needed so badly to prevent the losses of men and ships we could not afford to lose at any cost, were so slow in arriving.

Again and again, in the small hours of the night, I asked myself and my Maker why it is that we Americans always have to learn about war the hard way—the ostrich way—by stocking our hopes for peace in the sands of unpreparedness. True, we emerge from wars with marvelous weapons and equipment, but we go into them with so much that is obsolete and lose so many thousands of lives and millions of dollars before once again we can surpass our opponents. Somewhere, in between, there should be a realistic medium course.

In July, Guam had been secured and, with the permission of Fleet Admiral Nimitz, I had moved submarine tenders into Tanapag Harbor, Saipan, and Apra Harbor, Guam, in order to refit and rearm submarines practically in the front lines. This saved the wear and tear, the time and fuel involved in the three-thousand-mile trip from the Empire to Pearl Harbor. The Seabees, with their bulldozers, had leveled off a site in a beautiful coconut grove selected by my Deputy, Rear Admiral John (Babe) Brown, on the windward side of Guam. There, working parties from the tenders *Sperry* and *Apollo,* berthed in Apra Harbor, had set up dozens of Quonset huts for the use of submarine officers and men recuperating between patrols.

We named it Camp Dealey after the heroic captain of the *Harder* who went down with his ship west of Luzon under depth charge attack by enemy destroyers. But Sam Dealey and his gallant crew did not go alone. As befitted their heroic deeds, they took with them sixteen enemy ships—six of them destroyers or destroyer escorts—to light their way across the darkness of the River Styx.

I decided to use the Christmas season (certainly nobody in the Pacific in 1944 could call it a "holiday") to make a trip to Saipan and Guam preparatory to moving down lock, stock, and barrel in January, 1945. Pearl Harbor was getting so far from the fighting front that people seemed to consider it a suburb of Washington, and I was expecting any day to receive a white feather for my desk inkpot.

Admiral Nimitz had commenced building his headquarters on the top of Cincpac (Commander-in-Chief Pacific) Hill almost before the firing stopped. Actually, the Marines hunted Jap diehards in the nearby jungles for months after he moved in, and we lost five submarine men near Camp Dealey in an ambush.

The chief purpose of my trip to Guam was to make sure that all preliminary arrangements for the moving of my Submarine Pacific Advanced Headquarters from Pearl Harbor to that recently hard-won island were being made. The harbor dredging was of vital interest to me, for I wanted not only anchorage for three submarine tenders and one 2500-ton floating dry dock, but also facilities for the venerable *Holland*, our first real submarine tender built in 1929, a vessel of 5000 tons and some 350 feet long. Modern tenders are of 8600-ton displacement and run up to 492 feet in length. These tenders might have been called Alladin's Treasure Arks, for such indeed they were. There is hardly an item, among the hundreds needed aboard a submarine, that cannot be obtained aboard a tender. "We've got everything, from beans to bullets," is the proud and truthful boast of tendermen. From their stores can be drawn anything in the food, apparel, and supply line, as well as torpedoes, diesel oil, and ammunition. In their capacious shops, all but major overhauls can be accomplished.

This move on my part, which took place in January, 1945, did not, of course, close the Comsubpac office in Pearl Harbor. Among those I left at the latter headquarters were the following: Rear Admiral J. H. Brown, Deputy Comsubpac; Commodore Merrill Comstock, Chief of Staff; Captain John Corbus, Operations Officer; Captain E. E. Yeomans, Strategic Planning Officer; Lt. Comdr. Lawson Ramage, Personnel Officer, and Commander Harry Hull, Special Weapons Officer.

On my return to Pearl Harbor—preliminary to preparing for my final move from Hawaii to Guam—I was greatly pleased, but not surprised, to receive good news from the *Tinosa*, now on patrol. As previously mentioned, in connection with her patrol toward the East China Sea, she had been given special and secret orders to search for Japanese mines around Okinawa. This now famous battleground was soon to be invaded. The *Tinosa* found and charted many mines; then, entering the East China Sea by passing north of Formosa, she located and charted another mine field. The *Tinosa* was thus the first FM Sonar-equipped boat to put the device to effective use against the real McCoy.

This submarine's success brought to a triumphant close a year in which American submarines, with two assists from British submarines, had sunk forty-nine men-of-war and 503 merchant ships. The war, for the submarine forces, was going well—so well, in fact, that soon there would be no more targets at sea. Only the Sea of Japan remained to be cracked.

7

ASPECTS OF SEA-WAR CHANGE

I returned from Guam to Pearl Harbor in time to see the New Year—1945—ushered in. Hopes in all our hearts were high; the far horizons looked wonderfully clear. Optimists believed we would wind up the war in this new year. The more cautious felt we could not invade the home islands until fall—and that was bound to be a long and bloody job.

Admiral Nimitz Headquarters looked like the base for an African safari about to penetrate the Congo jungles; cartons and boxes filled the offices; everyone was packing; Guam was the next stop.

The Admiral and I had several hasty conferences. I always reported to him frequently because the very nature of my responsibilities demanded that we work in close accord, but these early January, 1945, conferences dealt with new agenda. Both our headquarters, closely linked as they were, would require in Guam new operational and communication techniques. In addition, our conversations recognized and developed the fact that the war, now in its fourth year, was changing drastically so far as submarine operations were concerned. From a war of independent operations by submarines, it was becoming one of close coordination with our fleets and air forces.

At the beginning of the war, submarines in pitifully small numbers were scattered over the tremendous reaches of the

Pacific in a valiant attempt to whittle down the enemy's navy and merchant fleet, to prevent his ill-gotten spoils of conquest from reaching the Empire, and to wipe out convoys of troops and supplies sent to consolidate his forward positions. Those were desperate days, pre-radar days, defective torpedo days.

Then, as the numbers of our submarines increased, the size and stiffening protection of enemy convoys necessitated the formation of coordinated attack groups. These we named "wolf packs" after those of our resourceful but less successful enemies in the Atlantic. Our wolf packs showed the world how wolf-packing really should be done. They frequently left the Japanese escorts to steam dismally into port, leaving their convoys in the safe hands of Davy Jones.

And now, as of January, 1945, the advances of our surface, ground, and air forces had just about deprived the submariners of the areas that had been wonderfully rich in targets. Gone were the fat, loot-laden convoys that tried to blast their way back to the Empire. Vanished were the huge transports, piled high with munitions and packed to the rails with enemy troops, headed southward from the enemy's homeland.

Instead, what little ocean transport the enemy had left skulled along the coasts in a dispirited effort to sneak home from the co-Prosperity Sphere, Japan's crumbling Asiatic empire in the southlands—or to carry rice, beans, coal, and iron ore in small ships from Manchuria and Korea.

Naturally, with this change came new and less exciting jobs for our submarines—such as the Lifeguard League, designed to save downed aviators from death on the seas. No matter how inspiring this lifesaving job might be, long stretches of standing lifeguard duty could be monotonous as well as highly dangerous. Quite often, saving aviators meant working in shallow waters close inshore where dangers from mines and depth charges—and even shore batteries—were ever present. It was a sort of sitting-duck existence in which subs, if set upon by enemy planes or anti-submarine patrols, had but slim chances of survival. Another new job, locating and charting enemy mine fields off beaches marked for invasion, was no seagoing picnic. And at the bottom of the list of new *musts* loomed the break into the Sea of Japan which would call for deeds and daring that surpassed the running of the Dardanelles by British submarines in World War I. Tough

U.S.S. Holland

work, all of it. But we had the men with the guts and skill to do it, as well as ships that could not only deal out punishment but take it.

It seems to be part and parcel of the make-up of inanimate devices to develop streaks of mulish obstinacy. You move along at a good trot; everything is fine. Then suddenly—trouble and a dead stop. FM Sonar was no exception to that rule. On the heels of my elation over the *Tinosa's* accomplishment, I was not prepared for the letdown that followed the less than mediocre results we obtained from the next two FMS-equipped submarines to arrive at Pearl Harbor from Mare Island in January, 1945. They were the *Bowfin*, commanded by Commander Alec K. Tyree, and the *Tunny*, skippered by Commander George E. Pierce. Both dashed my spirits with FMS trials that left much to be desired.

So far as the *Bowfin* was concerned, the sonar situation

was so discouraging that we simply were not able to make her
set workable by the time she was scheduled to go on patrol.
Hence, much to our regret—for we needed more mine field
exploration—we had to keep her out of mined waters. If
nothing else, this decision made it amply clear that FMS was
no longer a secondary device but a primary factor in extending
the operational range of submarines. That, incidentally, was
the point on which so many submariners showed peculiar
blindness. They regarded it as a device that existed for the
purpose of *pushing* them into dangerous mine fields. Whereas, in fact, the FM Sonar had been acquired and developed
for submarines to *protect* them against mine fields in areas
which they would be called upon to enter in the normal
conduct of the war. To the day of the A-bomb, there were a
few submarine skippers who held to the former viewpoint.
But, I am happy to say, there were many more who were

itching to break into the Sea of Japan with the aid of FMS, where worth-while targets awaited their torpedoes.

We had the same trouble with the *Tunny* that we had had with the *Bowfin*. Circuits overheated; tubes gave inferior performances; and there were no electronic technicians on hand trained to handle this new, complicated, and temperamental gear.

The situation required action—and fast. Hastily summoned electronics experts met in my office. We drafted a top-secret wire to Dr. Harnwell in San Diego asking that he send his best FMS specialist to do some heavy trouble-shooting at Saipan. And Dr. Harnwell, bless him, replied immediately, saying that he would send his right-hand man, Professor Malcolm Henderson, with two of his best assistants to Saipan early in March, and that they could remain with Comsubpac as long as they were needed.

His reply was handed me from a panting jeep as my staff and I piled aboard a NATS plane Guam-bound. As the plane took off, I regarded with satisfaction the able and combat-tested officers who would constitute my immediate staff: Captain "Dick" Voge, Operations Officer; Commander "Bill" Irwin, Communications Officer; Lt. Comdr. "Ed" Hines, Flag Secretary; and Flag Lieutenant "Bob" Vaughan.

About a week before that date, the *Holland*, which was to be my flagship at Guam, had left Pearl Harbor for its new home base. Aboard were supply stores and members of my communications and office staffs. Skipper was Captain C. Q. Wright, with whom I had served in World War I submarines when we were both fairly fresh out of the Academy. The Headquarters at Pearl Harbor, I left under the overall command of Deputy Com. Sub. Pac., John Brown, and my Chief of Staff, Commodore Merrill Comstock. They would have to handle that particular job. And did, to the hilt.

Training for mine detection and mine field penetration was first put into high gear at Saipan and then shifted to Guam under ideally isothermal water conditions. Distances to the training areas were considerable and the danger of lurking enemy subs was ever present. Occasional echo-ranging contacts and periscope sightings indicated the presence of enemy subs. However, they never seemed to fire at such small game as submarines so we eventually forgot all about them. I recall, for example, that off Pearl Harbor it was several times necessary for destroyer target groups to order all U.S. submarines to surface and then thoroughly depth-charge a suspected enemy sub. After all, we had not invited them to participate in our training exercises! Post-war reports indicate that enemy submarines were often present off our bases but chiefly for observation purposes. What a waste of time, diesel oil, and sometimes lives!

The waters off Saipan and Guam were much too deep to permit planting anchored mines. We solved the problem by borrowing a minesweeper which, when requested, would lay a string of three or four dummy mines suspended forty-two feet below buoys. This was ideal, for the buoy served as a visual mark from which we could check, by periscope, the ranges obtained by our FM Sonar.

We selected the forty-two-foot depth because our reports indicated that Japanese mines were, as a rule, set at depths of approximately three, thirteen, and twenty-three meters. Forty-two feet represented an average setting and was convenient for training.

Following the discovery by the *Tinosa* of mine fields off Okinawa and north of Formosa, various questions arose as to the existence of mines in other nearby localities. Our invasion forces and our Fleet were moving northward toward the main islands. Iwo Jima was marked for the next invasion. Okinawa, across the way in the Nansei Shoto, was second on the list. What our surface ships would find in those localities in the way of mine fields was important; they must have freedom to maneuver for bombardments, and they must be free to attack and pursue any enemy force which might be sent against them. Iwo Jima we did not have to worry about, since the waters about it were too deep for mining. But Okinawa and the nearby East China Sea were shallow and suspected areas.

Intelligence reports told us that an enemy mine field extended from the south end of Kyushu—the southernmost of the main islands of the Empire—all the way down to Formosa. And we suspected that one, perhaps two, of our submarines had been lost in that area. For our own safety as well as that of the Fleet, we would be forced to investigate these suspected areas as soon as FM Sonar-equipped boats were available.

8

FMS COACHING IS BIG LEAGUE

The drone of the Beachcraft's engine changed from a steady rhythm into a percolating gurgle as its pilot retarded the throttle while he swung down to land on Saipan. Through the window on my left, I saw the maze of large and small runways from which Army and Navy aircraft of all kinds operated around the clock. Everywhere, the island's face was scarred by ruins and shell craters. Brand-new construction stood out against the eternal green of the tropical landscape. For a moment the harbor, thick with anchored ships and speeding small boats, swept beneath me. I caught a glimpse of the submarine tender *Fulton* and alongside it a nest of submarines. One of these had to be the *Tunny* which, according to the despatch received by me on Guam the previous day, had just arrived under command of Commander George E. Pierce. Additional newcomers to Saipan included Professor Malcolm Henderson and two other sonar experts, Lt. (jg) Robert Dye and Chief Technician Nigretti. Thus the scene was set and the members of the cast assembled for the *Tunny*'s FMS rehearsals. The day was March 2, 1945, and my plans for the next two days were to spend every available hour putting the *Tunny* and its set through their paces under dummy mines planted outside the harbor some five miles from the *Fulton*'s anchorage.

As the plane taxied up to the Operations building and cut the engines, Captain G. E. (Pete) Peterson, the senior submarine officer at Saipan, came forward to meet me. We climbed aboard his waiting jeep and threaded our way at top speed (for who ever saw a jeep drive with any regard for life or limb or heart condition?) through the jumbled mass of bulldozers, graders, bomb trucks, and jeeps that jammed the still unfinished highways. In due time, with our hearts back in their normal locations, after a short boat ride, we arrived aboard the *Fulton*.

There—tall, dark, thin, and in his early forties—was Professor Malcolm Henderson. His broad grin and enthusiastic air indicated that to him, even as to the youngsters in our subs, this being out in the front lines was adventure—adventure plus the added thrill of seeing his beloved FM Sonar prepared to test its cunning against the real thing, the Hellpots of Okinawa, Formosa, the Yellow Sea, and Tsushima Straits. The firm clasp of his hand inspired confidence that he could do a man-sized job in making that preparation thorough and adequate.

From that early March day when we met on the *Fulton* until the triumphant Hellcats swept back from the Sea of Japan on the Fourth of July, the worthy professor was to see very little of California and almost enough of submerged submarine operations to be entitled to wear a Dolphin pin, the highly revered emblem of the undersea service. Among the millions who gave so willin'ly the best they had, "Mal" Henderson was an outstanding 'iver of brilliant ideas and valuable time. He was a real education to us sailors who are seldom exposed to scientists.

On the morning of March 3, we were under way at the crack of dawn for the exercise area with its half a dozen suspended dummy mines. It looked like a fine day—and so it was until we submerged and began our runs under the targets. At periscope depth, alack and alas, the day became one of those there's-no-joy-in-Mudville affairs. When it came time to bat at mines, FMS—our mighty Casey—struck out. Not now and then, but time and again. Run upon run, made under conditions that were close to ideal, produced no score whatever. Blobs on the screen dissolved into shapeless light patterns. Instead of bells we heard mousy scratchings. At close range and at far range—at any range—the performance was "lousy." The presence of three or four *DE*'s, destroyer escorts, in the area pinging for enemy submarines did not add peace of mind to the situation. Frequently their pings registered on us and, but for our trusty escort who always hovered near, they would undoubtedly have given us a sample of their wares. . . . Certainly something was wrong with our horoscope that day.

Even Malcolm Henderson showed the strain. As for

DE (Destroyer Escort)

me—I was sweating—nothing strange about that with the
water temperature standing at 80 degrees. But this was the
cold and clammy kind that tells you you are in a tight corner.
How could I expose the lives of my men and the safety of
their ships to a device that only worked now and then—a
device so unreliable that it would black-out at the moment
when it was most critically needed?

I watched the *Tunny*'s sonar screen and listened for its
sound effects. I also watched the *Tunny*'s crew and had my
ears tuned for their comments. What I saw and heard was not
encouraging. The men were disturbed, unhappy, depressed;
tempers were short and talk was in monosyllables—a strange
atmosphere aboard the *Tunny* which had always been a happy
ship with a fine record of sinkings and of service. Poor
George Pierce! He was under high pressure being, as it
were, between the Devil and the deep blue sea, with me in
the undesirable role of Belzebub himself. George and all the
other submariners who, behind my back, called me Uncle

Charley, regarded me, I believe, as a staunch friend—a title and a friendship I would be loath to lose or abuse.

When we returned to the *Fulton* near sunset, I went alone to my cabin for a session of stock-taking and a bit of soul-searching. In the ship's safe I had placed the sealed orders I had written for the *Tunny* on Guam—orders that its Captain would open only after he was well out at sea from Saipan on his next mission. They directed the *Tunny* to barge head-on into the nest of Hellpots that fringed the East China Sea, to penetrate the mine barrier from east to west.

Quite an order! It was based upon firm faith in FMS to deliver mine information to eye and ear—accurate and instantaneous:

Could FM Sonar actually do that? If not, I had but one choice: tear up the order; forget mine field penetration. . . . Should I?

A knock sounded at my cabin door and at my "Come in," George Pierce entered. I called for a pot of coffee and we sat down to talk over the events of the day. . . . He wasn't even worried! Here I was, feeling as though ten years had suddenly been added to my age, but he looked fresh as a daisy! What a marvelous thing is the resilience and resourcefulness of youth.

"Admiral," he said, "if the damned gear won't work, we'll just run deep and go under the mine fields."

Yes, that might work but it wouldn't help us to chart mine fields for the protection of our own submarines and surface ships; nor to aid minesweepers who had to clear mined areas. Just getting through the mine barrier was not my entire problem. But George Pierce, who had lost his brother Commander J. R. Pierce to Japanese guns and depth charges which destroyed the *Argonaut,* and who was himself about to embark on a patrol from which he might not return—George had come to me to talk about a hat! He had just been made a Commander—which in happier times should have called for a bottle of champagne—and he had no brass hat!

"Could you do me a favor, sir? You have a pipe line back to San Diego; could you tap "Hump" Campbell (the Senior Submarine Officer there) to get me a brass hat, size 7⅛, and send it out so I'll have it when we get back from this patrol?"

It's amazing how little it takes to break tension and restore confidence.

"George," I replied, "I'll order a dozen if you want them and they'll be in Guam waiting for you."

When we joined Peterson and his officers at dinner in his cabin, I felt that, as the Spanish say, "tomorrow is another day," and that it would be a good one—at least it couldn't be worse.

Malcolm Henderson did not join us for dinner. He and his lads were grabbing a bite in the *Tunny* while they dug into the vitals of her FMS.

Just after midnight came a tap at my door and Henderson reported that they had located and repaired the trouble. He declared the set ready for another set of trials at dawn. These, he predicted, would prove the FMS set to be on the beam.

In the gray light of the false dawn we met aboard *Tunny* and stood out for the exercise area. This time things were different. The sonar set proved to be in perfect working order. Henderson and his boys had wrought miracles. With an average sea condition, say about four-foot waves, we consistently picked up mine blobs on the screen and echoes on the loud-speaker at highly satisfactory distances. Now and then my ranging thoughts touched upon the *Tunny*'s orders in the *Fulton*'s safe. More and more, it looked less and less as if I would have to tear them up. But I kept my fingers crossed.

The smooth-working process of the FMS also produced a much improved attitude toward it on the part of the men of the *Tunny*. The whole ship—from conning tower to battery room, from forward to after torpedo rooms—was alert to the work of that mine detector. As the day tapered off, it was interesting to watch the crew change from hostile to friendly—confidence had replaced doubt. Smiles took the place of long-drawn faces; lively comments replaced staccato whispers and bright eyes, those of dull stares. Yes, the *Tunny* had all the earmarks of being a happy ship again.

That night I removed the *Tunny*'s sealed orders from the safe, not to tear them up, but to give them to George Pierce. Henderson had told me that he had no fears whatever that the ship's FMS would fail again.

"It's okay," he assured me. "Nothing can happen to it unless the boys give it too much juice—dial it up to the point of producing hot channels. But after working with us for two days, I'm absolutely sure that the operators won't do that."

So, instead of tearing the orders to shreds, I handed

them to Pierce with the traditional submarine God-speed blessing of "Good hunting." At the same time I sent a radio to Admiral Nimitz on Guam, who knew of my plans for the *Tunny,* and reported her ready. In this despatch I also requested permission to go with her, explaining that the entire trip would take only from twelve to fourteen days.

At 0200 the communication watch officer woke me with the Admiral's reply: "Sorry that the answer must be negative."

Asking permission to go on this patrol was not just playing hookey on my part. This was new and controversial equipment whose effectiveness was questioned by many of my own officers and men. I had seen more of its operation than anyone in submarines and I wanted to see it in action against the real thing. . . . "Oh well," I thought to myself as I switched off the light, "it's the same in the Army."

9

TUNNY'S SONAR SHOWS VALUE

The next FMS-equipped boat scheduled to arrive was the veteran *Tinosa* which, in December and January, had carried out three separate mine searching missions and had successfully located fields off Okinawa and the north end of Formosa. I was most anxious to have her report at first hand. On learning of her arrival, closely followed by the *Spearfish,* I hopped aboard the trusty little Beachcraft which the Commander Marianas, Vice Admiral Johnny Hoover, permitted me to use. On I flew to Saipan, where the two FMS veterans were ready to have their sets tested before they left on patrols in mined areas.

We were out at crack of dawn with *Tinosa* next morning. Her Commanding Officer, Lt. Comdr. Dick Latham, was enthusiastic about his set and about its performance at Okinawa and north of Formosa. However, he was not enthusiastic about the life of an FM Sonar sailor.

It was not the danger involved in mine-detecting missions that wore him down but the lack of targets with which

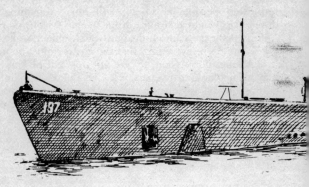

U.S.S. Spearfish

he had been cursed on his last patrol. The performance of a submarine, her skipper and crew, was naturally judged by the damage they had inflicted upon the enemy. In fact, the additional stars for the coveted combat pins were dealt out accordingly. (Was it Napoleon who was credited with saying, "Give me enough ribbon and I'll conquer all of Europe"?)

Of course, we took care of obvious unfairness in such matters, but blame for the lack of targets we had to lay at Admiral Bill Halsey's door—his carrier strikes against Luzon and Formosa had frightened everything larger than sampans off the sea lanes.

The first day out with *Tinosa* was not too productive. The sea was rough with a strong wind which drifted our mine-suspending buoys so badly that by mid-afternoon we had lost all but one and had to call the minesweeper to locate and pick them up before dark.

The next day was not much better. We made various runs from periscope depth down to two hundred feet but the *Tinosa*'s set was in need of adjustment and the bell tones were most reluctant to answer up. That night Professor Henderson came to the rescue with a lot of midnight oil and circuit testing that put the set in excellent order. At the same

time, the *Spadefish* was champing at the bit to get away on patrol.

So we left *Tinosa* in port and worked with Commander Bill Germershausen, the new skipper of *Spadefish*. This pioneer set, now improved by the latest alterations, performed beautifully. The *Spadefish*'s sonar technicians, Chief Radioman P. L. Majone and Ch. Radio Tech. N. Pike, were especially adept and her set was in excellent adjustment. We gave Captain Germershausen orders to sail the following Monday on a mission which included establishing the southern limits of the Tsushima Straits mine field. We needed to know just where we should lay down our starting line for the forthcoming breakthrough. Since the FMS sets were subject to over-heating, we wanted to conserve them until actually needed.

I also instructed Germershausen and Latham, as well as all skippers who followed them, to pick up—forcibly if necessary—prisoners from the Yellow Sea and near Tsushima Straits. Prisoners—especially men of the enemy armed forces—seldom came aboard voluntarily. Swimming teams had to be formed to go out and drag them in. Sometimes they avoided capture by drowning themselves. From prisoners thus obtained—one of them the captain of a small steamer—our Intelligence Officers at Cincpac H.Q. gleaned further valuable data as to possible mine field locations.

With the *Spadefish* off and away, we once more turned our attention to the *Tinosa*. By and large, the results among the dummy mines on that second day's training were very encouraging. I recall that at lunch—Latham and his officers, Henderson and myself, sitting around the wardroom table—we compared notes while we relaxed and took aboard the excellent chow for which the submarines were noted.

Suddenly the lanky figure of Latham's Communications Officer stood at my side. He held a file-board for my attention. Glancing quickly, I saw that it was a secret radio message which the Communications Officer had just run through his decoding machine. The radio was from Pierce aboard the *Tunny* and it read:

"Completed passage through the East China Sea mine field. Have charted rows of mines spaced about one thousand yards apart. Position about 170 miles north by west of Okinawa. Am now in the East China Sea and have charted 222 mines in the vicinity of Latitude 29-20 North, Longitude 127-10 East. FM Sonar gear running like sewing machine."

I scanned the message quickly. Then I read it slowly. Then I read it aloud. And each time I went through it, I was more and more impressed by the importance of its contents. Here was another FMS contribution. Here was proof positive not only of the presence of mine fields but of the ability of FMS-equipped submarines to penetrate these hellish barriers and to take inventory of them as desired. It goes without saying that I was itching to report personally this highly important information to Admiral Nimitz as soon as possible. But I thought he was still back in Washington and would not return to Guam for another day or so. Meanwhile I radioed *Tunny*, ordering her to return to Guam at once with a detailed report and congratulating George Pierce on his good work. Then Henderson and I renewed our task of putting the finishing touches on *Tinosa*'s FMS gear. We finally checked her out that afternoon, St. Patrick's Day—the seventeenth of Ireland, as my Dad called it—after her FMS had given us several fine demonstrations. Maybe those sets have Irish amperes running through their systems.

Returning to Guam the same day we finished with *Tinosa*, I found to my surprise that Admiral Nimitz was at

H.Q. and made a date with his Chief of Staff to report early next morning. The fact that the next day was the Sabbath meant nothing to the Big Boss. Except for perhaps a swim or an extra game of horseshoes, Sunday was like any other working day.

Looking very fit in spite of his long trip, the Admiral greeted me with an appreciative smile. Also, he gave my verbal report close attention.

"Well, Lockwood," said he, "it looks like your favorite gadget might really pay off. I'll send congratulations to the *Tunny*."

"Thank you, sir—and may I order her skipper, Commander Pierce, back to San Diego—on his return to Guam—on temporary duty to pep up production there and at Western Electric? His first-hand knowledge will be invaluable to the scientists and technicians. Also his story should be highly inspirational to the plant and laboratory personnel."

The Admiral assented and then I tossed what I hoped might be a touchdown pass: "Admiral," I said, "I've just completed FMS training runs on the *Spadefish*. She sails tomorrow. She's got an excellent set with fine technicians and one outstanding operator. We are sending her to locate the southern limits of that Tsushima mine field—and it is an important mission. I'd like permission to go with her."

The pass was incomplete. The Admiral said he could not take a chance on having me captured. . . . I knew "too damned much about our future plans."

"But, Admiral, if we come to grief on this mission— which I'm sure we won't—there'll be no prisoners."

But the pass remained batted down. I would have to figure out a better play next time.

However, Admiral Nimitz did agree to another scheme I had in mind. For some months, the Bureau of Ships and the Naval Research Laboratory, Anacostia, had been urging competitive tests between the FMS and three other mine detectors which that Laboratory and a group of Harvard scientists had built. Actually one might have thought—from the feeling evinced and the correspondence which had been batted back and forth—that it was Harvard vs. California in the Rose Bowl. I was not interested in the old-school-tie angle. But I was certainly in the market for the perfect mine detector— one that would be the answer to the submariner's prayer.

The time was opportune, since we had all of the mine

detectors under consideration mounted either in *Flying Fish* or *Redfin*, both of which were available on the West Coast and nearly ready to head west for Pearl Harbor and Guam. San Diego, obviously, was the logical place for the tests.

Upon receiving Cincpac's approval, I sent off secret dispatches assuring attendance of my outfit and asking participation by interested Bureaus and Offices, including Commander Submarines Atlantic, Rear Admiral C. W. (Gyn) Styer; I alerted my staff experts and scheduled trials for April 24-27 at San Diego.

The intervening month was spent in many diverse activities. By now, FMS-equipped submarines were rolling in like autos off a Detroit production line. The *Seahorse*, Commander H. H. Greer, was next to be put through her paces. To this sub went the distinction of being the first submarine whose FMS trials were run in Guam.

Since testing FM Sonar had now become big business, an undue amount of my time was spent in flying back and forth to Saipan. While this was refreshing, and the visits to Saipan kept me in touch with our organization in Tanapag Harbor, they were also time-consuming.

Therefore we shifted FMS training activities to Guam where my flagship, the veteran *Holland*, was moored in Apra Harbor. Coincidental with this change, another shift was made. "Barney" came to town in the person of Commander W. B. Sieglaff, former skipper of *Tautog* and later of the *Tench*, with numerous patrols and thirteen sunken enemy ships behind him. Having Barney ordered to my staff was a stroke of super-fortune. Immediately he struck me as the ideal man to help me with the FM Sonar program. Widely experienced, resourceful, quiet—with a delightful vein of humor—Barney, as he was affectionately known, radiated energy and determination in every line of his dark, square-jawed countenance.

And so, staring early in April, day after day, Barney and I greeted the sunrise from the bridge of submarines proceeding out through the entrance nets of Apra Harbor. Our destination was the training area we had laid out in 1600 fathoms of water ten miles west of rugged Orote Point which marked the entrance to Apra.

10

BARNEY BOSSES "BARNEY"

When I shoved off in April for the Sonar tests scheduled for San Diego, Sieglaff took over all the planning and training for the break-through operation which we named "Operation Barney" in his honor.

In laying it out, he had the help of our Operations Staff officers, Captain R. G. (Dick) Voge and Lt. Comdr. N. G. (Bub) Ward, and I never completely relinquished my spot on the training team. Ringing Hellsbells had gotten into my system like a narcotic and furnished a challenge that was too interesting, too exhilarating, and at times too maddening to be given up.

I have neglected to mention that tentative plans for entering the Sea of Japan were discussed in January, 1945, at a staff conference in my office at Pearl Harbor before our transfer to Guam and following the *Tinosa*'s success around Okinawa. But at that time, our ideas as to how to effect the break-through into the Emperor's private ocean were pretty nebulous. We were not even agreed as to which entrance, La Perouse or Tsushima, should be used. Tsugaru Strait—between Japan's two northernmost main islands, Honshu and Hokkaido— was never considered because it is narrow, tortuous, and capable of being heavily mined.

Now, as we renewed our invasion thinking, the number of boats to be sent in would, of course, depend upon the number of FMS sets available in submarines; however, we were all in accord that a considerable number should be present in the Sea at all times, so as to prevent the enemy from concentrating all his anti-submarine strength against one or two ships. That was about as far as we had progressed when the arrival of FMS-equipped submarines began to step up and a tentative date began to be discussed for launching the attack. It was at this point that Barney Sieglaff entered the picture and he and Dick Voge got down to work.

In describing Dick, my Operations Officer, I find myself repeating the phrase I especially like to use when it is appropriate: "typical submarine officer." He had been C.O. of the ill-fated *Sealion* on December 8, 1941, when the Jap bombers struck at Manila, Cavite, and various air fields. The *Sealion*, undergoing an extensive overhaul and unable to dive, was a sitting duck for the Japs, who wrecked her with two hits from twenty thousand feet and took the lives of four of Dick's crew.

Voge was of the studious, investigative type, always working on problems—night attack techniques, torpedo spread tactics, patrol plans. When he was not working on Force Operating Plans or a new rotating patrol area to extract more tonnage from the enemy, he was busy dashing off a poem or composing a cheering night message to the boats out in enemy waters. Rhyming and humorous twists of words or ideas came naturally to Dick and many of his masterpieces are still current in the Service. Our nightly information messages were always long—deliberately so—in order to permit slipping in some important news or urgent orders without alerting the enemy by a longer-than-usual message. When business was slack, Dick put in news regarding recently arrived heirs in the Submarine Force. Letters from mothers frequently came with such announcements and many a father out in the Pacific, worrying about the coming blessed event as well as the enemy, had his mind set at rest regarding at least one worry.

It was therefore into very capable and experienced hands that I entrusted the layout of Operation Barney.

On March 20, Barney, Professor Henderson, and I put the *Seahorse* and her FMS installation through their paces off Guam. The sea was fairly rough, so that our surface runs netted nothing; however, the water was an 81 degree isothermal down to 150 feet, which was as deep as we went. In addition to her Sonar installation, *Seahorse* (already made famous by the nineteen-ship record of the redoubtable Commander Slade Cutter), had a new skipper Commander H. H. Greer, who was an FMS enthusiast. There were no halfway measures in Harry Greer's plans. When we finished the day's work and were standing back to Apra, he came down to the wardroom where Professor Henderson and I were vilifying each other in a game of cutthroat cribbage and quietly said, "Admiral, we are all ready; our gear is perfect; may we have the orders to break into the Sea of Japan?"

"Sorry, Greer," I said, "I'm really sorry I can't let you punch the first hole. One sub in the Sea of Japan would have a mighty hard row to hoe with all the A/S opposition the Nips could bring to bear. I want to send all the boats we can muster in at the same time, hit the Japs like a tone of bricks, and pull out before they can properly organize their opposition."

Greer was keenly disappointed. He had plenty of confidence in his equipment but had encountered a lot of sonar skepticism from other skippers. He wanted to prove how right he was and be the first to crash the mine barrier.

And so it was arranged that *Seahorse* was to check the southern limits of the Tsushima mine barrier, which *Spadefish* was already attempting to define. Enroute, we directed her to check the mine field north of Formosa, reported by *Tinosa*.

Commander E. H. (Steiny) Steinmetz came next with the *Crevalle*, and on March 26-27 we gave her the standard "treatment." Her preliminary working-up had not been good and the personnel had plenty of doubts. The chief trouble, as we found out the first day, was in the tuning and adjustment of the set and the inexperience of the operators. Too, we all expected greater ranges than the set was capable of delivering— ranges that were actually more than we needed.

With two submarines already sniffing at the Tsushima barrier, we sent *Crevalle* off on a regular shooting patrol along the China coast with an additional mission of following after *Spadefish* and *Seahorse* in locating the Tsushima mines.

With the results obtained from these three ships, we constructed a fairly accurate plot of the southern limits of the mine field and laid down a tentative starting line for Operation Barney.

How accurate were the plots made by our submarines of these and other mine fields strung along the border of the East China Sea from Kyushu to Formosa, or just dropped in clumps in the shallow Yellow and East China Seas, we did not know until after the war when reports from the mine sweepers became available. One ex-Lieutenant, then a minesweeper sailor, now a stock broker, Harold D. Barnard, Jr., of San Jose, Calif., whom I met at a Rotary luncheon, told me: "We certainly had to hand it to the submariners who charted those fields. In clearing them out, all we had to do was to use their charts and we knew exactly where to put our sweeps in the water. The mine detection and navigation of those little boats must have been amazingly accurate."

11

BIG BOSS STURDY PILLAR

Sinking scores by submarines had not been impressive during March, 1945, because of the lack of targets. Hence the news of a kill by one of our subs always raised a cheer among the H.Q. staff. Not received with a cheer, however, was the news with which I was awakened in the morning watch of April 2, 1945. The Staff Duty Officer handed me a priority despatch reading: "Sank *Awa Maru* off China Coast north of Formosa Channel. Picked up one survivor."

The *Awa Maru* had been granted safe conduct from Japan to Saigon to carry some ten thousand Red Cross food packages to our prisoners of war there. She was marked with white crosses which, at night, were lighted. She was on her return trip when she was hit at 11:00 P.M. of April Fool's Day by four torpedoes from the *Queenfish*, Commander C. Elliott Loughlin, a fine officer with a fine ship and crew and seven enemy vessels to his credit.

Elliott Loughlin had fired, in a dense fog, at what he believed was a destroyer escort. *Awa Maru* was not sounding her fog whistle, as required by rules of the road at sea. This neglect undoubtedly was a major contribution to her destruction.

Of course, the Japanese radio and diplomats screamed for vengeance and the head of the captain of the *Queenfish*. To my mind it was a regrettable but honest mistake abetted by *Awa Maru*'s neglect. A ghastly mistake, it is true, but such things happen in wars. . . .

Next day, by despatch from the Navy Department, Admiral Nimitz was ordered to convene a general court martial for the trial of Commander Loughlin on charges of negligence in obeying orders. In the light of what we later found out

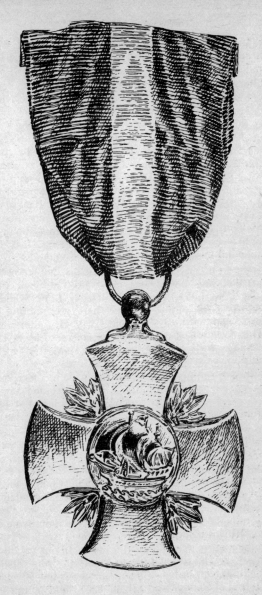

Navy Cross

about the illegal cargo activities of the *Awa Maru*, it is my humble opinion that Loughlin deserved a medal for ending her hypocritical career. The sentence received by Elliott Loughlin was: A reprimand by the Secretary of the Navy—a sentence which I am confident James V. Forrestal carried out with deep regret.

In the midst of our sorrow about the bad luck of the *Queenfish*, the *Bonefish*, Commander L. L. (Larry) Edge, came up for FM Sonar trials. Barney and I, with Lt. (jg) Dye and Ch. Tech. Nigrete, climbed aboard at 0600 as, accompanied by a minelayer, Captain Edge headed his ship for the practice area beyond Orote Point. The coming patrol was to be Larry's first experience with FMS and he, as an electronics expert, was looking forward to it with keen anticipation. Already we had news, via the scuttlebutt, that about July 1 he would receive orders to the Electronics Desk in the Bureau of Ships—orders Fate decreed he would never receive.

Larry, from the deep South, with his fine-featured face and dark coloring, plus his soft drawl and traditional charm of the men from below the Mason–Dixon Line, could have doubled for a romantic lead. But there was nothing of the dilettante, nothing theatrical about Larry. His quiet Southern voice denoted authority, competence, and assurance. He was all business at sea and his ship was spotlessly clean and excellently organized.

As usual, the first runs of the day gave mediocre results. But as the set warmed up and "Dinky" Dye and Ch. Tech. Nigretti—Malcolm Henderson was at the moment back in San Diego—plied their trade of trouble shooting, locating a broken wire and correcting troubles with the reversing switch and the loud speaker, ranges improved and bell tones cleared up.

Skipper Edge was right on the ball all the time, especially when it came to making repairs or adjustments, for on his prospective job back in Washington intimate knowledge would be invaluable. I sent a despatch that night to Professor Henderson making further suggestions on improvements to insure greater reliability.

I was indeed thankful for the results of our various mine field surveys. Reports of these came in from *Spadefish*, *Seahorse*, and *Crevalle*, still out on their special missions. With the insecure position which FMS held in the esteem and confidence of many of our skippers, the loss of one of these specially equipped boats would have been a crushing blow to morale. With so many people skeptical as to the capability and reliability of FMS, Barney, Malcolm Henderson, and I—and our few disciples—had a rough time injecting assurance into the unbelievers. Certainly, half-hearted use of the mine detector would never produce the necessary results. Undeniably, it was as temperamental as an opera singer, requiring constant tuning and attention to its delicate innards. Its temperament called for strong-willed, expert impresarios to handle the situation. We needed training, training, and more training to breed confidence; we needed successful experience to strengthen that confidence. As one of the Hellcat skippers wrote me during preparation of this book, in a very heart-warming letter:

"The No. 1 thing which sticks in my mind is that Operation Barney was and is a tribute to your personal leadership. I talked with most of the C.O.'s in Guam back in May, 1945. None of them was overflowing with confidence. Yet all of us believed in it because of your personal interest and your conviction that it could be done."

He was talking not of me alone, but of Barney Sieglaff and Malcolm Henderson and our small band of enthusiasts. We evidently lent assurance to them even as the quiet support of Admiral Nimitz lent strength and confidence to me. And I am thankful that we few *did* have the conviction and *did* keep our faith in spite of adversities, for our Hellcats, nine little ships, were destined to deliver to the enemy a mortal blow.

Before the next FMS-equipped submarine arrived for trials, the long expected Kamikaze charge of the Japanese Navy took place. We knew that their oil fuel stocks must be running terribly low. Seventy-six of their tankers running fuel up from their southern holdings had been sunk by our submarines. No oil or other fuel was getting into the Empire except from across the Sea of Japan. All possible "ersatz" substitutes were being utilized, including oil boiled from pine roots. With their dwindling stocks of fuel, the Japanese Combined Fleet would soon be immobilized in harbor, but we did not believe they would give up without a final suicidal battle to the death.

On the night of April 6, my notes recorded: "Much excitement today. Planes report remnants of Jap Fleet acting suspiciously. Am crowding as many of my boys as I can into

Yamato

exits from the Inland Sea. Maybe the Japs plan a banzai charge. Certainly if they stay where they are, sooner or later they will be bombed to smithereens by the B-29s."

At 12:30 A.M. on April 7 I recorded: "Now have three reports from subs in Bungo (southwest exit from Inland Sea) that two battleships and eight destroyers are heading south at 22 knots. If we miss them, I'll bet my bottom dollar Admiral Spruance (Commander Fifth Fleet) doesn't. It looks like the banzai charge we expected."

And that's about what happened. Our submarine *Threadfin*, Commander J. J. Foote, made the first report. He was in excellent position to attack the giant battleship *Yamato*—which *Skate* had hit with two torpedoes on Christmas Day of 1943—but according to standing patrol orders he was required to report first and attack afterwards. This strict adherence to orders cost him his chance to shoot at, and possibly to sink, the largest battleship in the world. His procedure was entirely correct. Our orders were designed to give important

information, such as this, to commands that should receive it instantly. Had *Threadfin* attacked before reporting and been lost in the attack, *Yamato* and her task force (the other reported battleship was actually the cruiser *Yahagi*) might have been able to reach their objective and wreak incalculable damage upon our supply fleet at Okinawa. Two other submarines gave chase but never were able to attack. In the meanwhile, however, Admiral Spruance and Vice Admiral Marc Mitscher, with his carriers, took up the chase and next morning both big ships, plus four of the destroyers, went to their deaths beneath a hail of aircraft bombs and torpedoes. Thus died the once mighty Imperial Japanese Navy.... And we must admit it died with its boots on.

On April 15 Barney and I rode with the *Bowfin* to the exercise area. Her skipper, A. K. (Alec) Tyree, bore a name already familiar to me. I had had the pleasure of pinning a Navy Cross on his brother, John A. Tyree, a seven-goal man, as polo players might say, after an adventure-packed patrol by the *Finback* in which he, with a single four-inch gun, engaged three armed merchant ships. Only one escaped. He took a grave risk that might have been adjudged unwarranted, but many a medal awarded in any war represents just the shade of difference which separates a commendation from a court martial. At the time of which I write, John had been transferred to a job as a White House aide. When I protested vigorously to the President's Naval Aide, he replied that I should consider it an honor to the Submarine Force.

"Yes," I said ungratefully, "I consider that the Japs should also be happy."

Alec Tyree got into the sinking game rather later but he was destined to uphold the family honor with a bag of five ships.

When we finished with *Bowfin* after another session on April 18, we packed her off to check the limits of a possible mined area at the eastern end of Tsugaru Strait. There we believed two submarines had been lost. Post-war reports indicate that three were so destroyed. *Bowfin* found mines and she also found two enemy ships, which she dispatched, and then dashed back to Guam for final training prior to Operation Barney.

12

RADAR TRICK FOILS *SEAHORSE*

During the very hours of the very day we had such a pleasant training cruise with *Bowfin*, one of her sister ships, far to the northwest of Guam, wrote a log of quite another kind. Seventeen of the twenty-four hours of April 18, 1945, were spent by the *Seahorse*—and the four-score human beings who depended upon her for survival—on the bleak and black pastures that form the bottom of the East China Sea. A dark, cold, and dismal place of ooze and silence that stretched in all directions hundreds of feet below the blue surface waters that reflected the heavenly images of sun and moon, stars and clouds.

In telling me about his experiences aboard the *Seahorse* on that occasion, Captain Greer said: "We got caught—and caught good! Except for a crew that did not know the meaning of defeat or fear and a submarine with a larger factor of safety than even its designers realized, we would not be here today. Sixteen hours of hell and Japanese depth charges. But what worried me most were my constant fears that I would not live to bring you the information about mines and mine fields which, with the aid of my sonar, I had collected, as per your orders. Unless I could surface and tell you by radio what the situation was regarding mines, I had failed. No man enjoys failure. The one hope we all held was to report the mines we had found.

"Our damage was extensive. Both of our periscopes were useless. The periscope windows were shattered and both had flooded. We were blind, deaf, and dumb unless or until we salvaged enough of our transmitter to get on the air. Both gyros were a shambles but, thank God, I had our armored tank compass compensated before we left."

Years have passed since the Hellcats dared execute Operation Barney in the Sea of Japan, and largely because of mine field explorations performed by submarines such as the *Seahorse*. But even now, in the book of Harry Greer, his moment of deepest disappointment in that entire decade was the hour when he realized—deep on the ocean's bottom—that the damage done to his submarine was so great that it could not possibly be put in shape in time to join the Hellcats on their hush-hush expedition.

Seahorse's catastrophe was as keen a disappointment to me as it was to Greer. Crashing the Sea of Japan would have been a fitting climax to her already illustrious career. The fact that Greer was so enthusiastic about my particular baby—the FMS—and had asked to be the first to penetrate the mine barriers into the Sea of Japan made his disaster doubly ironical.

As things turned out, it was nothing short of a double-barrelled miracle that Greer and his boys came back at all—with their lives as well as with the information that they had located and charted ninety-seven mines in one of the sectors they had been sent to investigate.

To start things off on a thoroughly sour note, a few days after she left Guam, the *Seahorse* met up with a B-24 Liberator that did its best to perforate her with machinegun

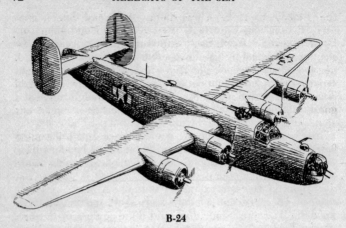

B-24

bullets and blow her to pieces with depth charges. The
incident happened at dawn one March day some six hundred
miles northeast of Luzon. The sun was still low in the sky as
the *Seahorse* plowed along on the surface at standard speed.
The ocean was empty. And so was the sky until a speck
appeared on the southwestern horizon. Submarines are always leary of unidentified aircraft. Therefore Greer was about
to pull the plug when one of his lookouts shouted that the
plane was an American bomber. At almost the same moment
the *Seahorse* flashed the recognition signal.

Being the officer of the deck at the moment, Greer kept
a close watch on the bomber. He saw it approach the submarine in a long, straight dive and had made up his mind that
the plane intended to do a frisky buzz on the sub, when he
was aware that high-humming bees were flashing past the
sub. To be sure, they *sounded* like bees, but they *acted* like
bullets. Which they were. Streams of them.

"Lay below!" Hank shouted to his lookouts. "Scram!
Quick! They're shooting at us."

Last man down, he reached for the toggle that secures
the coming tower hatch and yelled as he came, "Flood
negative! Take her down. Fast. Catch her at three hundred
feet."

At this moment, just as the sub started to slip below the
surface, Greer heard the heavy crrrump, crrrump of depth
charges exploding close to his vessel. Several more bomb

thuds followed. Then all was silent. After some fifteen minutes, Greer took a cautious periscope peep and then surfaced. But only after he was sure that the sky, as well as the sea, was completely free from friends as well as foes. A nearby sub, the *Blackfish*, had witnessed the shooting and reported the plane's number as 5786 or 5783. Why the patrol bomber made no attempt to attack the *Blackfish* is anybody's guess. Both were in a safety lane—and the bomber pilot was eighty miles out in his navigation.

A few days later, Greer began his probings for mine fields in the areas to which he had been assigned. As I have said, he belonged to that group of submariners who were out-and-out sonar enthusiasts. His confidence is reflected in the following comment:

"The *Seahorse* demonstrated that she could run through mine fields, around mine fields or, if necessary, zigzag through a line of mines like a football player running through a broken field.

"After we had counted ninety-seven mines and recorded the density and size of a field north of Formosa, we headed into the East China Sea but with no luck. By now, I was so sure of the FMS that, on one occasion, I actually risked the *Seahorse* in steering for a blob which, in the eyes of some observers, could have been a mine but which, according to the screen and the tone on my Hellsbells speaker, was not a mine but a bottom echo. This was a stupid thing to do, but I did prove that the contact *was* a bottom echo and *not* a mine.

"Next, on to Tsushima. Alas, our work there had to be on one side of the barrier. Remember that you threatened to execute me if I penetrated mine fields in the Sea of Japan before you had your pack ready to strike a real blow. I do not recall how many days we spent sniffing at that first line of mines, but it seemed like ages. In addition we were under observation. The Japs probably wondered why I did not go in or go away.

"The Straits of Tsushima live up to their reputation of being very strongly defended. There is every evidence the enemy is making maximum use of radar and radar detection in his defense. Our SJ, which used to give us such an enormous advantage, is being made almost a hindrance by his detectors and by his ten-centimeter radar-equipped escorts and planes who can 'home' on it.

"The enemy's radar anti-submarine measures were so

constantly active as to give us the feeling of being on the defensive instead of the offensive. We would not have felt quite so naked had we been able to determine the direction and source of our APR signals. Six or seven different signals could be heard at most any time in Area Nine, and at least two of these would be saturation pips.

"The performance of the FMS was, in my humble opinion, adequate. For a prototype, our FMS was all that could be expected. The fact that the *Seahorse* delivered the goods speaks eloquently."

How true! The *Seahorse* and its gallant crew certainly did deliver the goods and the goods speak eloquently not only of superior ability but also of inspiring courage. The endless hours of gruesome waiting, spent by the *Seahorse* on the ocean's bottom—from 0536 in the dawning to 2236 in the late hours of the night—present a showdown incident of the kind for which submariners are constantly prepared yet for which they have spine-tingling dread—namely death. Not swift explosive death, but death by slow degrees through asphyxiation of suffocation at the bottom of the sea.

The minute hand on the *Seahorse*'s conning tower clock stood at 14 minutes past 5 A.M. on April 18, when the lookouts on the ship's periscope shears sighted two Japanese patrol boats. Dawn was just breaking and the sea was overcast with a filmy haze. Evidently, the Japs had the sub in their sights. Thick columns of smoke poured from their stacks as they built up speed and headed toward the *Seahorse*. The latter also opened up her engines in the hope of showing the enemy a clean pair of heels. At first, pursuit ran its course in a silence that was broken aboard the *Seahorse* only by the resonant roar of its full-throated engines. Then the largest and nearest Jap vessel fired several rounds from its forward deck gun. The first shell fell some four thousand yards astern the submarine. The others splashed closer and closer—too close.

At 5:36, in conformance with orders, the *Seahorse* pulled a swiftly executed dive. When under, Greer made a 90-degree change in course. In anticipation of listening pursuit as well as depth charges, Harry rigged for silent running and for depth charge attack. At the same time, he kept a sharp down angle on the boat until it reached three hundred feet.

At 0543, he fired a couple of false target shells—new devices designed to misguide electronic ears and eyes. Then the *Seahorse* withdrew into the complete motionless silence of a hibernating snail. The false target shells are fired from small signal tubes in the after and forward torpedo rooms. These shells have the length of roman candles, with a diameter of three inches. Only, instead of releasing shooting stars or fiery balls, they let loose huge clouds of gas bubbles that form, so far as sonar beams are concerned, a solid body from which a sonic echo can be obtained. In releasing these shells, Captain Greer hoped to confuse the Japs so they would pick up one or the other of the gas clouds and bomb it to their heart's content while the sub played possum and eventually slipped away into more hospitable waters.

As the minutes ticked off, Harry Greer did some mental back-tracking to figure out how he got himself into this unpleasant position. He finally concluded that the trouble began before dawn when he was fooled into believing that a ten-centimeter radar beam which registered on his screen was of American origin. Japanese radar was not known to operate in that range. As we were to learn—when we put all the pieces of the Tsushima Strait jig-saw puzzle into their proper places—the lower gateway into the Sea of Japan was not only subject to a wide range of enemy air and sea activities, but was "patrolled" by an extensive array of Jap electronic devices that ran all the way from the Alpha of land-, air-, and sea-based radar to the Omega of sono-buoys, listening devices that were anchored in shallow waters.

During the dark stretch of pre-dawn morning—while the *Seahorse* was completing the job of topping off her batteries so that she could remain submerged all day if necessary—her conning tower watch made the near-fatal mistake of assuming that a nearby vessel with a 10-CM radar set was a friendly submarine, an error to which Captain Greer subscribed long enough to get into extremely hot and very deadly waters.

When dark of night was replaced by light of day, Greer was to learn that the neighboring ship was about as friendly as the airplanes that visited Pearl Harbor on the early morning of December 7, 1941. His radar contact turned out to be a brand new Nipponese frigate that was fast and, for its size, heavily armed. At first, Greer thought that he could make a surface escape from the frigate and its companion but when a Jap plane joined the chase, Greer decided to submerge. In fact, he had no other choice.

There are times when the rather clipped language of a Navy war patrol report—which is written under the stress and impact of combat—conveys the grim picture of what submariners think and do when their vessel is nailed to the ocean floor like a wall-to-wall carpet—not an opening, not a crack wide enough for escape, anywhere. A world so quiet that the men in it can hear only two terrible sounds—the spine-chilling crrrumps of depth charges . . . and the thumpings of their own hammering hearts . . . outside and inside sounds that seemed to be at the same level.

But let us read Harry Greer's combat report. And let us start at the very moment when the near-fatal radar misinterpretation is made:

0303—Interference on the SJ Radar at 060° and 315° T. Both very similar to SJ interference. Interpreted it to be the USS *Crevalle* with a wide-bearing width. Know now they were Japs. Made no attempt to exchange recognition signals as the tuning of our SJ falls off whenever it is keyed. Bearing remained steady until—

0512—Radar contact on two small targets at 8000 yards. Radar interference very strong and steadied on us.

0514—Dawn is breaking and sighted two patrol boats—very hazy. Opened out at full speed. Escorts appeared larger than PC's but not as large as destroyers. Range opened out slowly as smoke poured from the escorts.

0530—Larger and nearest patrol boat fired four rounds. Sounded like 3 or 4" guns. Splashes about 4000 yards astern.

0536—Submerged in a record-breaking dive, north of SHIRO SE. Changed course 90° and rigged for silent running and depth charge. Went to 300 feet.

0543—Fired two false target shells.

0615—"Pinging" of the patrol boats drawing astern.

0620—Screws changing course and bearing now steady at 180.

0625—First eight or nine depth charges in quick succession very accurately placed slightly above and on either side.

"We were Christians after that first charge," continued Greer's letter to me. One cussing machinist's mate trying to keep the warped engine room air induction closed was shut up by his helper saying, 'Don't you do any sinning around me just now!'

"We were knocked below 300 feet in nothing flat. Stopped the motors and settled to the bottom.

"No trouble staying on the bottom since the auxiliary tank had flooded itself through a valve backed open by the barrage. Salt water commenced pouring in through the SD mast packing gland and engine room induction, fuel oil through a ruptured emergency vent fitting in #5 F.B.T., hydraulic oil through ruptured line to SD mast, air through several fittings and even fresh water spouted from the ruptured engine cooling system.

"The Christmas tree showed three deck hatches open. Emergency lights went out in after half of ship and all in all, things looked pretty grim.

"Ship was a shambles of broken glass, smashed instruments, objects torn off the bulkheads, and quantities of cork and dirt and hydraulic oil over everything. It was undoubtedly the worst beating anyone on board had ever taken.

"Another such pattern could possibly have finished us. But the Japs, who had averaged well up to now, made their first mistake by losing contact after the attack. The two patrol boats could be heard 'pinging' and searching carefully but their screws began to get farther away."

Time dragged on with leaden shoes as Greer and his men waited with knife-sharp senses for what was to come. Death had cast a heavy shadow, short and black—like those of periscopes at noon—just to show that he was near. Would he come even nearer?

An hour after the first full-out blitz, they heard the pingings of searching electronic beams—fleshless and boneless fingers that probed and picked among the rocks and wrecks and reefs that litter King Neptune's junk yard, searching in the ever-constant hope that they might touch the metal hull of the submarine they wanted to destroy—electronic ears that listened with fiendish patience and superhuman skill for the slightest sound that was alien to that of the sea itself.

Comes an echo from steel. . . .
Comes a foreign sound. . . .

Follows then the merry-go-round of extinction! Camouflaged patrol boats steaming in steadily shrinking or expanding

circles... white froth in their boiling wakes... miniature vol-
canoes rising from the ocean as depth charges exploded
astern... one by one... a dozen... two score... the works!

Meanwhile, in the submarine, Greer and his men sat
tight. In silence. In darkness. Not a device, started or
operated by human hands, was in motion.

Talk was kept at a minimum—and then only in whispers.

Moving about was at an absolute minimum—and then
only in stocking feet.

Over-cautious?

Perhaps!

But one never knew what kind of deviltry the enemy
might be up to in the realm of new and secret listening or
locating devices.

Greer wisely decided to take no chances. Also, there was
no way of knowing at that moment how long the *Seahorse*
might be forced to stay under. Or how long it would be before
they could bring her to the surface in the event that vital
parts of her machinery or equipment had been seriously
damaged.

The more men stirred around, the more oxygen they
consumed. And, aboard a sub—pinned to the ocean ooze—
oxygen is as precious as life itself. In fact, it is life.

At 0815 a sudden shower of depth bombs—not heavy,
but close enough for each to be felt aboard the sub. "It made
us grope even deeper into the mud," Greer said.

This was evidently a going-away shower—or at least it
pretended to be one. All signs of enemy presence ceased. No
beat of ships screws. No pingings. No depth charges.

It could mean that the ocean above the *Seahorse* was
open and free. Again, it could mean that Jap patrol boats—
engines dead—were lying in wait to ambush the sub should
she try to move or show a periscope.

Earlier in the war *Sculpin* had fallen for that trick. As a
result, she was lost with a large part of her crew.

When noon came and there were still no signs of Japs,
Greer took a cautious inventory of his communications equipment. He found that his SD, the aircraft detector, and the
APR, an enemy radar warning device, were completely out.
He also learned that his surface radar was only partly effective. Torpedo tubes and door were inoperable. The after
section of the engine air induction was ruptured as were the
freon lines of the *Seahorse*'s air-conditioning system. All were

under the heading of dangerous damage, and the freon gas could be fatal.

Throughout the ship, men were assigned to cleaning up and making repairs, but under a blanket of silence so that give-away sounds of wrenches or hammers could not be heard through enemy hydro-phones. At the same time, the listening aids that did function were manned by the ship's best operators.

This latter precaution paid off. At half-past two o'clock in the afternoon the sonar man, pressing the head-phones to his ears, sang out that he could hear pinging and fast screws in the distance. No orders were needed to make every man freeze where he stood. The pinging came nearer, then drifted off; nearer, then drifted off. Greer could visualize the patrol boat steaming in a huge circle, the center of which was a mile or two south of the *Seahorse*. Now came the crrrump, crrrump of depth charges. Twenty of them. The drum beats of death.

Then silence. No crrrumping. No pinging. No sound by man or his machines.

Aboard the *Seahorse*, work was resumed with velvet gloves.

Then the merry-go-round of pings and crrrumps returned at seven minutes before six o'clock. This time the Jap dropped seventeen of his unwelcome ash cans, but the center of his circles was farther off. When he returned at 9 P.M. to have another go at pinging, Greer estimated that he was some twelve miles off the target. Only ninety minutes remained of April 18 when Greer decided that he might as well try to get off the bottom. "Stand by to surface!" No surfacing—no survival.

Could the gallant old *Seahorse* make it? Would the batteries and all the electrical gear do their jobs? Once up, would the diesel plant do its stuff, or were sea valves and exhaust valves hopelessly jammed? And lastly, had the Japs really gone over the hill?

Greer's watch said 2236 when he gave the order to surface. With the efficiency of robots, an efficiency that was far from automatic but was the result of months of training, the men who pushed buttons and pulled switches went through the take-her-up routine. And the *Seahorse*—getting slowly unstuck from the bottom mud—answered the command and rose nobly to the surface.

So far so good, thought Greer with a prayer of thanks as he felt a current of clean, cool air sweep through the open conning tower hatch and caught a glimpse of the clear star-lit sky above him. One by one, he started the diesels. A broad grin swept over his face as the last, the starboard after main engine, caught on and changed the muffled songs of its companions from a dulcet trio to rip-roaring quartette. But the grin was soon wiped out. Greer learned that his antenna had been wrecked, that his starboard reduction gear was much too noisy, that his periscopes were smashed beyond hope of repair at sea, and that his radio transmitters were out of commission. Until his communications were repaired, Greer had no way of sending his vital information about mine fields to submarine headquarters in Apra harbor.

Repairs were under way, on deck and below, when Greer got word that his operators had come upon the same 10-CM radar beam that had nearly resulted in his destruction that very morning. Leaving the job of supervising repairs to Lieut. R. V. Welch, his Executive Officer, and Lieut. J. F. Sporer—the latter with ten and the former with eight patrols under their belts—the Skipper centered his attention on the radar screen in the conning tower so that he would have first hand information on the source of the 10-CM emanations. Instead of setting his course straight for Guam, Greer decided to hug the west coast of Kyushu. In that manner he hoped to become lost against the landmass of the island. Despite this precaution the 10-CM beam continued to sweep the *Seahorse*. That was bad. Pretty soon its bearing on the submarine became almost constant. And that was worse. As the hours slid by and the *Seahorse* plowed its stealthy way along the coast at sixteen knots, its best possible speed, the enemy radar pattern grew indistinct and drew astern. By three o'clock in the morning it was gone. With this load off his mind, Greer started battery charging. About four hours later he submerged gingerly west of Danjo Gunto to, as the Log read, "lick our wounds."

During that day of April 19, there were only two unto-ward incidents. About four o'clock in the afternoon they heard one depth charge, but not at close range. Some two hours later another depth charge was registered at about the same range. By then, the *Seahorse* did not feel quite as helpless as it had that morning. Two torpedo tube outer doors in both torpedo rooms were in working order. The bow

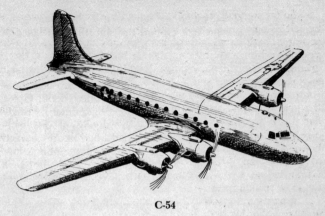

C-54

planes were in commission, but unreliable, and the air-conditioning functioned on an off-and-on basis. In submerging that night, Greer had some trouble getting his submarine under. She broached three times before finally reaching and steadying at periscope depth. The day and night of April 20 was divided between surface and near-bottom in about equal parts and was uneventful except for endless hours of hard and precise work. Their old pal Mr. 10-CM was no longer around, but there was enough Japanese activity all around the *Seahorse* to make her extremely cautious over making either a show or a sound of herself.

The spur that drove Harry Greer with the sharp prongs of a Spanish rowel was the galling realization that his vessel was dumb as well as blind. His periscopes were blacked out. His radio—the vessel's priceless voice—was still silent despite the hours of toil his able and enthusiastic technicians had poured into it. Finally, at 2300 on the evening of April 21, Greer's communications officer reported that the radio men had repaired the TBL transmitter and that a jury-rig antenna was ready.

"If, by chance, the Captain wants to send a signal to NKN—" joked the officer.

Greer handed his young communications officer a top-secret message which had been coded and ready for hours. Absolute silence held throughout the control room as the radioman—hunched over his tubes and switches—established contact with a far-off receiving station. But cheers rang and smiles showed as word got around the ship that the voice of the *Seahorse* had been restored and was once more on the air.

"Set a course for Guam on all four mains," said the Captain as he turned the deck over to his exec and went below for some well-earned and badly needed sleep. Greer had delivered his message. The *Seahorse* had done its work.

Later, in describing some of the details of this truly hair-raising incident, Greer said: "I had been depth-charged before, but nothing like this. The six-hundred-pounders close aboard were new to me. Each salvo would rock us like a hobbyhorse. What must have saved us was the depth charges going off *overhead*.

"I had thoughts of surfacing and gunfighting my way out. Thank God, I didn't try. Our ready ammunition lockers were flooded and my guns were unworkable. This hopeless gesture would have resulted in the loss of a submarine, crew, and the vital information I had to get to you.

"There is one interesting story on the first salvo. My torpedo and gunnery officer, Joe Sporer (one of the bravest men I have ever known), was watching the after torpedo room clock to see if his cutie hit (I don't think it did) when all of a sudden the clock came off the hatch trunk and headed for him. With calm, collected foresight he *caught* the clock, noted the time, and put it away safely. I have forgotten the time, but it is in the patrol report. This is sort of like a murder trial when attempts are made to fix the time accurately. Joe fixed the time of the first salvo accurately for us.

"The next sixteen hours were busy ones. The officers and men performed magnificently. Repairs were made if possible; there was no confusion, no outward manifestation of fear, and no lack of intelligent effort. American men, nurtured in a democratic way of life, have the ability to rise to unexpected heights under intense pressure. For example, our one disciplinary case, a youngster still in the process of growing up, had caused considerable trouble between patrols with his overenthusiastic consumption of malt beverages. As a result he had been to mast and was in general disrepute. But in the time of crisis, this boy was a pillar of strength. He succeeded in partially plugging our leaking gland (with clothing hammered in with chisel and maul) and later, when we got up on the surface, in gas-welding the gland until the leak was under control."

When at long last the pressure of the exploding ash cans had ceased, the *Seahorse* surfaced by blowing safety. "I could hear the seas breaking on deck from the conning tower but our one gauge still read seventy feet," continued Captain Greer. "Knowing that we were on the surface, I had the quartermaster stand by to open the hatch and I grabbed him around the ankles with both arms—because of the heavy air pressure inside the ship—and ordered him to open her up. It opened like a cork leaving a good bottle of champagne. We were both blown up to the bridge, but, thank God, not overboard into the sea."

The *Seahorse* reached Guam, in company with the *Sea Dog* and the *Torsk*—just as May got onto the calendar. Admiral Brown, who was in command during my absence at San Diego, and Commander Sieglaff, who headed Operation Barney, agreed with Skipper Greer that the *Seahorse* could not be got ready in time to join up with the Hellcats. Some other sub had to take its place, and there was the *Sea Dog* just arrived and ready, willing, and able under its highly competent skipper, Commander Earl T. Hydeman, to lead the pack into the Sea of Japan. That decision reached, it was a matter of high-priority hustle on the part of the submarine tenders at Guam, and of Lt. (jg) Robert H. "Dinky" Dye and Ch. Tech. Nigrette, to transfer the *Seahorse*'s FMS outfit to the *Sea Dog*. Mine-cable guards also had to be installed and the officers and sonar operators trained—quite an order on short notice.

Our last training run for *Bowfin* on April 18 was 0938 and at 1240 I climbed aboard a NATS C-54 plane bound for Pearl Harbor enroute to the mine detector tests scheduled for April 24-27 at San Diego.

Arriving at Submarine Base Pearl Harbor after a twenty-three-hour trip at 1930, April 18—having lost a day crossing the 180th meridian—I found that exercises the next day included special tests for *Skate*. She was scheduled to fire some of the very hush-hush defensive decoys which I had seen performing in a fresh-water reservoir back of San Diego in August, 1944. Too, she would fire some of our homing torpedoes and run tests of her FM Sonar.

This was a feast too tempting to miss and, in spite of a

U.S.S. Torsk

mountain of papers on the old familiar desk, I asked to be taken out for the show.

The USS *Whitman*, a destroyer escort, took me out next day before even the myna birds were awake. Then followed an exciting morning of trying to locate and attack the *Skate* while she attempted to throw us off the track with "pillenwerfers" and decoys. The DE sailors were good and located her more often than not. Then I shifted to the *Skate* and, by suggesting a few tricks, we baffled the DE and surfaced to find her chasing a decoy some five thousand yards from us.

The Captain of the *Skate*, Commander R. B. (Ozzie) Lynch, was one of our top-drawer skippers. Then in his first command, he had won his spurs in the veteran *Nautilus* and was devoted to his ship and her equipment. In addition, he was a camera enthusiast and had rigged his German-made camera to take pictures through the periscope—the forerunner of scores of such installations to be made.

To wind up the day, I shifted, via a torpedo chaser, to a Landing Craft Infantry boat to observe the performance of homing torpedoes fired at her by the *Skate*. Their uncanny ability to seek us out was amazing and on the second run, as a result evidently of the failure of a cut-off switch, the torpedo struck and wrecked the LCI's starboard propeller, leaving her to crawl home on one shaft.

Next day Ozzie led the *Skate* and me through a regular Virginia reel among the mines off Brown's Camp. His FM Sonar set was a joy to watch and I packed my bag for the flight to San Diego feeling like the heavy-end winner of a championship boxing bout. . . . The world was my oyster!

Flying back with me were Captain Bud Yeomans (Subpac. Strategic Plans Officer), Captain Bill Irvin (Subpac Communications Officer), Commander George Pierce (skipper of the *Tunny* which had recently penetrated the East China Sea barrier), and Commander Eddie Fahy (Subtrainpac Electronics Officer).

We arrived at San Diego on Sunday, April 22, to find *Flying Fish*, Commander R. D. (Bob) Risser, and *Redfin*, Commander C. K. Miller, ready to go. An impressive battery of electronics experts had gathered, including Harnwell, Henderson, and Kurie from Naval Research Laboratory at San Diego and Dr. Hayes and Mr. Richards from the NRL, Anacostia. Representatives of Bureau of Ships were also present, plus R. Admiral Styer (Comsublant) and his electronics staff.

The tests at sea, which began on April 24 and lasted for three days were conducted in two mine fields outside San Diego harbor. One field was in shallow water about thirty fathoms and the other in about fifty fathoms. The water was not isothermal as it usually was at Guam, but dropped from about 56° F at 50 feet depth to about 48° F at 150 feet. Such a temperature gradient works to the disadvantage of the mine detector, but these were about the conditions we could expect in Tsushima Strait.

Flying Fish had two FMS transducers, one on deck and one in the keel. Similarly located were the transducers for her SOD (Small Object Detector). The *Redfin* had two detectors MATD (Mine and Torpedo Detector) and OL (Object Locator) mounted the same manner as in the *Flying Fish*.

Incidentally, the name of the FM Sonar was changed about this time to QLA, which apparently were not initials for any words. To avoid confusion I will continue to call it the FMS. When I returned to Guam, I found that Barney Sieglaff already had coined a slogan for it: "Swing and Sway with QLA."

13

SHADOW OF RUSS BEAR LOOMS

One day while making FMS runs in *Flying Fish*, I was operating the gear. At extremely long range I picked up a blob with a faint bell tone which I joyfully classed as a mine, since no surface ships could be seen in that direction. The experts, however, did not agree with me and called it a patch of kelp.

The sound, they declared, was too scratchy to be a mine. Eventually we passed under this blob and, when we surfaced at the end of the run, there was the "patch of kelp" hanging on our port bow plane—a large thirty-three-inch dummy mine. I didn't let the experts forget that "patch of kelp" for some time.

During the tests, we observers shifted from ship to ship and made the runs under similar conditions and depths for each set of apparatus. Each partisan group rooted for its own invention. There was no denying that ranges obtained with MATD, SOD, and OL were consistently longer than those obtained by the FMS. However, the identification of the target by the FMS blob and bell tone was more positive than the mere spark shown by the other three. Furthermore, the FMS operated at frequencies above the normal enemy listening range, whereas the others operated in frequencies near those of the enemy's sonar, thus presenting a hazard of detection.

To my mind, for the Japanese war, FMS was the answer.

With this decision in hand, I flew on to Washington with Admiral Gyn Styer and most of the experts. There Gyn and I spent five days in conferences with practically the whole Navy Department, including the Secretary of the Navy, the War Priorities Board, the Bureau of Ships, the Bureau of Ordnance, and the Submarine Officers' Conference which, back in 1937-38, had accomplished the history-making feat of designing the Fleet type submarine which accomplished such wonders in World War II.

To Commander Rawson Bennett of the Electronics desk and his boss Ned Cochrane, Chief of Bureau of Ships, I presented the FMS case and was promised a continued and accelerated flow of these mine detectors. Also, Commander Bennett promised me twenty-four SV Radars to equip submarines for the job of radar pickets against enemy aircraft which were raising such hell with our small surface ship pickets off Okinawa. These sets had to arrive in time to equip twenty-four subs before the invasion of Kyushu—Operation Olympic—scheduled for November 1, 1945.

As in any good serial story or comic strip, we were about to move on to another chapter and other scenes.

When I arrived back aboard the *Holland* at Guam on May 18, I found my headquarters a regular beaver pond of activity. Captain Dutch Will, the senior Squadron Commander present, with Barney Sieglaff, had kept the FMS project boiling, and Captain Dick Voge not only had the plans for Operation Barney ready and checked by all our staff officers, but he had sent a top secret copy back to SORG (Submarine Operational Research Group) at Pearl Harbor asking their evaluation.

The nine submarines which were to take part in crashing the Sea of Japan were in Apra Harbor or arriving soon. Every dawn saw Barney and me rubbing the sleep out of our eyes as we climbed aboard subs bound for final tests beyond Orote Point. Often we went out in different ships or shifted from one ship to another at midday in order to spread our coverage. Barney checked out *Crevalle* and *Tinosa*, while *Flying Fish*, *Spadefish*, *Bonefish*, *Tunny*, *Skate*, and *Bowfin* all fell to my lot. They were old friends and, with Malcolm Henderson, I had checked them out before.

One late afternoon, while returning to port at the conclusion of *Bowfin*'s final runs, Captain Alec Tyree and I were having a quiet smoke on the cigarette deck, abaft the bridge, while the officer of the deck poured on the coal, as the expression was, to get us through the antisubmarine nets which closed inexorably at dark.

Suddenly the alert after lookout yelled, "Plane crash; bearing two one zero."

Instantly Tyree was calling orders for a reversal of course, while he and I scrambled up to the lookout platform whence he conned the ship back to a spot a couple of miles astern, where a Marine lieutenant fighter pilot was paddling toward us while his buddy, in another fighter, zoomed the spot to lead us in. He had hit the silk after his engine conked twenty miles out to sea. It was lucky for him we were out late that day, otherwise he might have spent some uncomfortable hours in shark- and barracuda-infested waters while awaiting rescue.

The newest member of the Hellcats—*Sea Dog*, Commander Earl F. Hydeman, had by that time received her transducer and other FMS gear from the badly beaten-up *Seahorse* where, according to report, it operated even better than in *Seahorse*. Barney evidently observed her trials, since she does not appear in my little black book. Her skipper was the senior officer of them all; hence upon him fell the mantle of command, the banner of Operation Barney, and the responsibility of leading the Hellcats into and out of the Sea of Japan. George Pierce was next in seniority and then followed Bob Risser, both veteran leaders in the Hell's bells symphony and excellently qualified to lead their respective subdivisions of three ships each, Pierce's Polecats and Bob's Bobcats—not to omit Hydeman's Hepcats.

Coming to our FMS group with a record of seven sinkings—plus his stellar performance of reporting the Jap Mobile Fleet as it swarmed out of San Bernadino Strait intent on overwhelming Admiral Spruance's Fifth Fleet then battling for Saipan—Commander Bob Risser had had no FMS experience against the real McCoy. However, he had had plenty of training in San Diego dummy mine fields and had cut his teeth under the able observation and direction of such experts as Harnwell, Henderson, Kurie, and Hayes, if, indeed, he ever got a look at the sonar scope during those hectic trials in April. With the mob he had in his conning tower, that would have been quite a feat.

Which brings up an observation of one of my C.O.'s, who said to Barney: "My FMS must be okay because the Admiral says it is. I've run plenty of trials with it, but I've never been able to get a look at the scope because Admiral Lockwood or Professor Henderson always gets there first."

Nevertheless, Bob Risser—in his quiet, unassuming, and always considerate way—was willing to give the FMS a trial. I do not believe he had complete confidence in it, but he did want to get into the Emperor's private lake, and if he had to carry an FMS along—fine! If it didn't work, he would run under the field. That, indeed, was pretty much the general feeling, as I have since learned.

But I wanted more than that. I wanted, for the Hellcats and for whose who would follow them, that extra factor of safety which an effective FMS with efficiently trained operators and well-indoctrinated skippers would provide; I wanted to chart those mine fields and the Hellpot orchards around the Empire for the use of our invasion fleet in Operation Olympic. Even then, Admiral Bill Halsey was demanding submarines to locate mine fields around Kyushu—our next objective.

As our team of deep-sea runners approached the starting line, my confidence in them deepened, as a result, no doubt, of daily contact with them, their ships and men. All of the Hellcat skippers had liquidation records which would have aroused the envy of Red MKVD's. All commanded proud ships which many times had sent out the equivalent of Commodore Oliver Hazard Perry's laconic message: "We have met the enemy and they are ours." Most of them had sounded their chimes against enemy mines at close range. One of our newest members, Larry Edge's *Bonefish*, was just in from running alongside the East China Sea barrier and counting the mines for miles.

Only *Sea Dog* was shy on length of service in the FMS navy, but her set had produced excellent results in *Seahorse* and had performed similarly in her own tests off Guam. And there was no question as to the ability and determination of her Captain, Earl Hydeman, to lead his Hellcats into the enemy's game preserve, come hell or high water.

To add to my feeling of elation and security, I knew that new boats were coming along—*Redfin, Runner, Sennett, Pogy, Pargo, Jallao, Torsk, Piper, Stickleback, Catfish,* and others that would furnish the succeeding waves into the Sea of Japan and destroy forever—or for the duration—the pipe lines through which our enemy channelled supplies from his last remaining overseas source.

However, to unsettle my very temporary smug feeling that we were abreast of—and perhaps a bit ahead of—the swift march of events, came a high priority demand from Admiral Bill Halsey for submarines to locate suspected mine fields in areas close to the shores of the Japanese home islands.

These areas would be required in mid-July by "Uncle" Bill's Third Fleet for bombardments of munitions-producing regions by carrier-battleship raids against the Empire. Our end of the job would not be difficult, since it demanded only that we establish the seaward boundaries of the mine fields. Penetration was unnecessary. The difficulty lay in not having sufficient mine-detector-equipped and trained submarines ready to operate. Certainly I could visualize no greater disaster to our morale at this tense period than to divert part of our Hellcats and thus lessen our coverage of the Sea of Japan. That Sea must be completely covered or not covered at all. Enemy supplies from Korea and Manchuria had to be stopped once and for all. And, once and for all, the Nips must know that we could cut their lines. A pulled punch at this point would do nothing but alert the enemy, warn him of our penetration of the Tsushima barrier, give him time to organize his anti-submarine forces—and cost us ships and lives. Revenge for Mush Morton and the *Wahoo* did not lie in that direction.

One sure way to avoid breaking up the Hellcats and sending them on pre-invasion missions to chart mine fields on the east coast of the Home Islands—an invasion that never took place and, thanks in large measure to the mortal blow to crumbling Jap confidence delivered by Hydeman's Hepcats, Pierce's Polecats, and Risser's Bobcats—was to get Operation Barney under way. Once off and away, the mission was secure. As for charting the mine fields on the proposed invasion coast, I was confident enough FMS sets would roll off our San Diego assembly line to meet Bill Halsey's needs as they arose.

Another consideration that counseled speed in delivering our attack was the international situation. The surrender of Germany had turned Russia's eyes eastward. I was informed that, at Potsdam, she had agreed to declare war on Japan three months after VE Day. Soon I was directed to submit a plan for dividing the Sea of Japan into operation areas for Russian and American submarines.

Naturally this idea did not appeal to me. The area in question could be covered adequately by our own submarines and the introduction of Russian boats, which had had practically no war experience, might easily result in fatal mistakes in identification. If we could not sufficiently educate our own trigger-happy air and surface forces to recognize American submarines and thus prevent the mounting toll of strafings, bombings, and shellings that we had to endure—what could we expect from allies who had never seen an American submarine? But, naturally, I immediately complied with my orders and asked for recognition signal codes to be exchanged. It is interesting to note that we never received any such codes from Russia.

As I have said, we took a dim view of the proposed Russian participation. Not only did I want to avoid the complications involved in having a new and strange ally share our patrol areas but also, based on what I had learned in England in 1941, I had no high opinion of the value of Red submarines as effective weapons.

In conversations with two British submarine captains who had acted as instructors and liaison officers, one of them summed up the situation by saying: "Their boats are clean and their crews are 'full of guts' but their knowledge of training and attack is about what ours was at the beginning of World War I."

Submarine operations in World War II had progressed to a point where experts were required; amateurs could add nothing to the picture but trouble.

Our mission had been to sink everything that floated under the Japanese Rising Sun. We wanted to complete that mission under our own steam, and we particularly wanted to clean out the Sea of Japan from which we had withdrawn in 1943 and in which Mush Morton and *Wahoo* had left their bones.

Daily training continued right up to the jump-off date and, with departure of the initial wave set for May 27, on the night of May 23 we held a conference of all the Captains and as many of their officers and FMS operators as we could pack into our Operations Room on the top deck of the *Holland*.

We ran a wonderful instruction film just received from the Laboratory at San Diego. It had been produced under the expert direction of the Harnwell, Henderson, and Kurie triumvirate and showed every phase of FMS training and operation. Every piece of gear was pictured and explained. As a grand finale we were shown the FMS screen with most realistic blobs and bell-like tones.

After the film was run, we excused all but the C.O.'s, their Exec's, and their Communications Officers and went into secret session. To prevent eavesdropping, orderlies were stationed at a distance outside with orders to admit nobody and to keep everyone away from the vicinity of the deckhouse. The night was one of Guam's hottest and muggiest, but blackout restrictions were still in effect in the harbor, so for a couple of hours we just had to sweat and bear it with covered doors and windows.

Dick Voge led off with an overall description of Operation Barney as we had laid it out, explaining the thinking and considerations which had entered into each decision. Copies of the operation order were issued to all skippers and they were invited to ask questions at any point. Dick explained that entry through Tsushima rather than La Perouse had been decided upon primarily because of the Kuroshiro (the Japanese Current) which sweeps up Tsushima Strait at about one knot speed, but pours out La Perouse with speeds up to three and a half knots. Entering with the current through Tsushima Strait would boost our speed through the mine fields and at the same time drift the mine cables in a direction parallel to our course. This would minimize the danger of fouling periscope shears, radar antennae, and bridges. The water through Tsushima is deep. In one undersea canyon it reaches more than one hundred fathoms, thus permitting the ships to run below the mine lines without danger of wiping off sound-heads and keel-mounted transducers against banks or rocks.

With large scale charts, he pointed out the principal ports in Japan and Korea which border on the Sea of Japan and indicated the expected routes between them. He also traced the Russian shipping lanes from Vladivostok to La Perouse enroute to and from the country which at that time was their Uncle Sugar, a valued friend and ally—the U.S.A.

Dick warned all hands to keep out of Japanese waters of less than fifty fathoms along the northerly coast line of the Sea of Japan. Also southwest of the Noto Peninsula—this because the Army Air Corps B-29s had been dropping magnetic and "oyster" mines therein.

Exit at the end of the Hellcat raid was to be via La Perouse where again we would have the aid of the current and use the routes followed by Russian shipping. Our information about La Perouse was to the effect that its mine fields were forty to forty-five feet down, out of respect for the safety of neutral Russian shipping, a lot of which went through the Strait.

As a final item, Dick said: "And if you get into such bad trouble that you can't make it out of the Sea of Japan, head for Vladivostok. There you will have the status of a man-of-war of a belligerent nation entering a neutral port. Maybe you can effect repairs and get out in time. At the worst you will be interned for the duration."

Next Barney Sieglaff took over. He presented details of organization of the Hellcats into three wolf packs, their sailing dates, starting points, starting times, area assignments, and, most important of all, the time and date of opening fire simultaneously.

Earl Hydeman's Hepcats—*Sea Dog*, *Crevalle*, and *Spadefish*—were to run through the mine barrier starting before daylight of June 4; George Pierce's Polecats—*Tunny*, *Bonefish*, and *Skate*—were to follow the next morning; and Bob Risser's Bobcats—*Flying Fish*, *Bowfin*, and *Tinosa*—were to make their entrance during similar hours of June 6. All boats were to reconnoiter their areas but to remain unseen until sunset of June 9—the hour for "Commence firing." All were to rendezvous on June 24 west of La Perouse and, under Hydeman's direction, make their exit that night.

"The mine field explorations conducted in Tsushima Strait by the *Spadefish*, *Seahorse*, and *Crevalle*," said Barney Sieglaff, "have given us the location of the southernmost mines. Intelligence information indicates that there may be three, even four strings of mines, with a distance of about one thousand yards between strings and about fifty yards between mines. Our best information places the mines in three depths—

three meters, thirteen meters, and twenty-three meters. In case of sonar failure, stay well down, not above 120 feet. As for the pressure and magnetic mines planted by B-29s, Captain Voge has warned you about keeping out of water of less than fifty fathoms along the northwest coast of Honshu to southward of Noto Peninsula. I repeat that warning; it's important.

"We have calculated your time of departure so as to permit time of arrival at Tsushima Strait at zero hour, based on a speed of advance of thirteen knots. If you want to take it more slowly, pack commanders are authorized to set their own time of departure."

Looking around the room, Sieglaff asked if there were any questions. None coming up, he made ready to adjourn the conference.

The scene that night in the old *Holland*'s Operations Room was unforgettable, one that will inspire me as long as I live. The intent faces of the Hellcat skippers and their officers, of Dick Voge and Barney Sieglaff, are etched in my memory forever.

"Gentlemen," I said to them, "I have been working with you on this project for quite a while. Tonight brings our plans to the climax. This is the day we have lived for. I have been impressed with your ships, their spotless condition, your efficient organizations, and your ship handling. But nothing in my life has impressed me as you yourselves have here tonight.

"Your questions show that you have given careful and critical study to this operation; your faces—your whole approach to the problem—show determination and deep down courage that is most inspiring. With this spirit, Operation Barney cannot fail. I want to ask one favor; I have been a submariner since 1914 and I have never fired a torpedo in anger. I hope that you will fire plenty of them for me in the Sea of Japan, for I would give a right hind leg to go with you. God bless you and good hunting!"

My notes, made that night, read: "It was really splendid to see. Bud (Captain Yeomans) wants to go but I can't spare him from Pearl Harbor. Barney and Bub Ward (Assistant Operations Officer) also want to go, so does our British Liaison Officer, Lt. Comdr. Barkley Lakin, and, lastly, I want to go.... Maybe Admiral Nimitz will soften his heart."—Which, however, he did not.

As I watched the busy scene that followed the conference—pack groups, juniors and seniors making their plans for cooperation, special signals, private arrangements, rendezvous for exchange of movie films, etc., etc., I was amazed, as we elders often are, by the resilience and resourcefulness—the sheer love of adventure—of youth.

Here were men going on a mission from which they might not return. True, all missions carried that grim possibility and these were battle-tested men, even though their average age ran only into the lower twenties. But to them this was all routine.

After the meeting broke up, I returned to my cabin and for the umpth time read and reread a well-thumbed letter I had received no longer ago than that morning. It came from those members of my staff I had left at Pearl Harbor Submarine Base when I moved forward to Guam. It was an answer to our request for an evaluation of Operation Barney. I called this unit my "Braintrusters" because one of their jobs was to coordinate my planning with top level braintrusters who did indeed dwell in high mental marble towers. These were the civilian scientists and analysts of the Submarine Operational Research Group originally organized in Washington but later transferred with an IBM machine to Comsubpac H.Q. at Pearl Harbor. Their evaluations carried great weight with us.

The often-read letter—reducing many paragraphs to a few lines—warned me that great hazards were involved in Operation Barney; that unusually heavy losses of men and ships could be expected. Further, the letter ventured the opinion that the mission did not appear to be warranted by the probable damage it could inflict upon the enemy; and finally, that unless the strategic situation demanded its execution, *Operation Barney should not be launched*.

The question which I kept turning over and over in my mind was: Should I accept this estimate of the situation by high staff officers whom I had selected by virtue of their capacity to think clearly and straight? (Incidentally, one of these officers was so eager to make the run that he had pressured me quite constantly.) Naturally, I was reluctant to put aside or disregard the counsel of my trusted advisers. Throughout the day I had studied their estimate with great care.

As to the harvest which we hoped to reap, the original figures on the volume of shipping in the Sea of Japan came from another Washington brain trust. It was based upon the volumes given in consular shipping reports.

As to the hazards involved in the wholesale underrunning of a mine field by a fleet of subs, I was fully cognizant of their gravity. However, I felt that only those who had practically lived with FM Sonar—as had Barney, Professor Henderson, and myself—could possibly realize the capabilities and wizardry of this new equipment so lightly branded Hellsbells in the American tradition of making light of even the deadliest things. A wonderful tradition, by the way.

As for going. . . . God, how I wished I could go along with those Hellcats of the Sea.

I reread the letter once more that night after the conference. And, again, I decided against following its well-intended advice. Wars were not won that way. This was one of those unknown factors that so often weighed heavily in the scales of victory. Operation Barney was *on*. It would stay *on*. In my inner ear it was as if I heard the voices of Mush Morton and other lads who had gone down in their submarines rise in a swelling chorus of approval. I had kept faith.

14

"BARNEY" ON THE ROAD

The sun stood hot and high over the island of Guam and slim white lines of foam etched the surface of the gently heaving sea as the first section of Hydeman's Hellcats made ready to slip through the narrow gate in the torpedo net that protected Apra harbor against underwater sneak attack.

From the deck of the *Holland* rang laughter and light voices—familiar features of a "despedida," a time-honored Navy way of speeding embarking friends. As the day of departure for the Hellcats approached, it was natural that we should plan a bit of "despedida" along the lines we used to arrange in Manila in the old days when monthly transports sailed for God's Country—a small party to bid farewell to friends and shipmates going on distant missions.

To this end, the Flag Secretary, Lt. Comdr. E. L. (Ed) Hynes, and the Flag Lieutenant, Lt. Comdr. Bob Kaufmann, had manned the phones a few days before the Hepcats led the outgoing procession. After considerable argument and use of the blarney, they had managed to secure promises to attend from half a dozen girls. Getting away for a luncheon party was difficult because nearly all of them had full-time duties during the daylight hours. Still, it was to celebrate the departure of the first echelon Hepcats to dare the Hellpots of Tsushima.

Nature smiled on us that day and both my cabin and the Captain's cabin were thrown open to the gentle tradewind airs while chatting groups of Hellcat skippers and uniformed girls gathered on deck or sat around tables to partake of the excellent buffet lunch the cabin steward had prepared. It was a scene I shall long remember—the keen young faces, the blue of the Red Cross uniform mingling with the white and blue of the nurses and the khaki of our submariners.

The ladies were at their best, gracious, gay, and ready to laugh at even the shadow of a joke. The Red Cross representative was Miss Leota Kelly, while the Navy was represented by Lieutenants Edith Fielder, Virginia Vahey, Bert Larkin, Jean Giddings and Marge Roberts.

But working hours are working hours and ships have to sail on schedule even during a "despedida." Eventually the officers of the Hepcats made their farewells and, while we watched from the *Holland*'s boat deck, mooring lines were taken in, crews mustered on deck, and the Hepcats backed away amid last-minute calls of "Good luck," "See you on Market Street," "Don't forget to duck," and the old traditional "Good hunting."

The day was May 27. The year was 1945. The hour was seventeen minutes past three o'clock. One by one in close column and led by an escort, the Hepcats threaded their way through ships anchored in the harbor, through the gap in the torpedo net, and out to sea. Three long, slim and low silhouettes of gray painted steel—strong, swift, and powerful. Leading the three-boat wolf pack was Earl Hydeman's *Sea Dog*. Close in his wake came "Steiny" Steinmetz's *Crevalle* and lastly Bill Germerhausen's *Spadefish*. Free of the port, they swung into scouting formation and dropped their escort. Line abreast and five miles apart, they pressed northwestward to their targets some two thousand miles away at a crusing speed of thirteen knots.

According to plans drawn for Operation Barney, the vessels were to leave in three sections of three ships each on three successive days, starting on May 27. They were to arrive at the west entrance of Tsushima Strait (Nishi Suido), a run of sixteen hundred miles from Guam, about sunset—also on three successive days, starting June 3, so as to submerge at daylight of the next day and feel their way north and east through the Strait under the mine field into the Sea of Japan. Next to leave on successive days, after Hydeman's Hepcats were Pierce's Polecats and lastly Bob Risser's Bobcats.

Chances are that thousands of people watched the three submarines as they stood out of the harbor that May day without giving a second thought to their mission. Vessels of their kind came and went so steadily to and from Guam in those days that they ran thirteen to the dozen. There was nothing about their appearance to indicate any unusual objectives. True, they were painted in the darkish gray that reduced their visibility in northern waters as against the lighter gray that is the best camouflage in tropical seas. But that in itself was not unusual. Submarine operations were more and more swinging northward into the homewaters of Tojo and his gang.

From my position on the deck of the *Holland* I followed them with eyes and ears and heart—followed them until I could no longer hear the muffled roar of their engines; until the sun glare on the water washed out the forms of their steadily dwindling hulls. All about me people stood in silent or talking clusters and yet I felt peculiarly alone—alone with the spirit of "Mush" Morton, the submariner whose courage and tragic death with every soul aboard the *Wahoo* were the inspiration which set so many men and minds and machinery into motion for the highly important purpose of bringing relentless and aggressive war to a body of water which the enemy regarded as the Mikado's own.

Two long years, short a few months, had passed since Morton and his gallant crew submerged for the last time. At long last, I felt quite certain, we had the electronic key that would unlock the heavily mined doors into the Sea of Japan. I knew that the FMS was neither foolproof nor perfect; I knew that many high-level naval planners did not share my confidence in this new secret weapon; I knew that even among the skippers of the submarines that constituted the Hellcats, there were men who had but small faith in sonar's ability to single out and point out the mines that dipped and swung like deadly seaweeds on the ends of cables anchored in the waters of Tsushima Strait.

On the other hand, there was no dearth of men, scientists as well as submariners, who shared my belief that Hellsbells would do a fine job of chiming in the Sea of Japan. With but few exceptions, the skippers of the Hellcat submarines belonged to that school of thought.

I turned my back to the sea and headed for my office. There I ran into Barney Sieglaff who gave me a quick grin. "Well, boss, the chips are in and the cards are drawn!" he said.

"Yep," I replied, "and a lot of people think I'm drawing to an inside straight."

Barney gave a short laugh. "Instead of that, you've got a royal flush, Mikado high. Just wait till the showdown starts a couple of weeks from now."

A simple thing to say—"Just wait!" But waiting can be a heavy hod to carry. And, somehow, its weight increased the next day when I stood rooted to the same spot of the *Holland*'s deck and watched George Pierce and his Polecats set a westerly course at eighteen knots into a spanking breeze that whipped up rows of dancing whitecaps. More men, more ships, more hopes, more precious blue chips thrown into the game in full faith that we held the high cards and the winning hand. More of the same on the third day, May 29. Wind-driven clouds would now and then blot out the sun as the Bobcats, led by "Bob" Risser and his *Flying Fish*, made knots for the western horizon.

And thus they sailed. Nine big, powerful fleet-type submarines, each equipped with a brand new secret electronic weapon, promising in tests but so far untried in grueling, nerve-snapping tests such as those that lay ahead. A formidable wolf pack manned by about eight hundred competent submarine sailors. Only the officers knew the plans for Operation Barney. But, while crew-members did not know about the project, they were fully aware that something extra-special was being dished up, and every soul aboard was ready and eager for the dish, whatever it might be. There was not a single instance of malingering. On Guam miracles of recovery had been wrought among Hellcats on the sick list as the sailing dates became known. One torpedoman aboard the *Crevalle* was hospitalized following minor surgery. He was

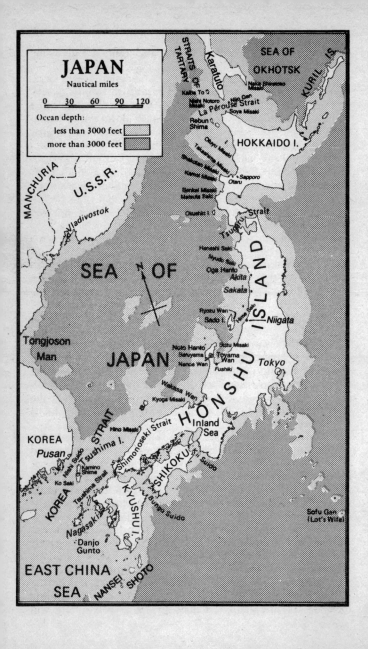

returned to his ship a bit prematurely because of his vehement insistence.

In announcing the nature of the mission, each Commander set his own pattern, but nearly all of them took Operation Barney out of wraps while Guam still hung in the middle distance. As each Hellcat settled down on its northwesterly track—lookouts at their places, observers at their screens, crewmen at their stations—the Captain of the vessel lifted the talker's microphone. Slowly and carefully, he drew for his men a complete picture of the entire mission after the first familiar and inescapable: "Now hear this..."

To be sure, none of these brief, informal, and to-the-point speeches were greeted by ringing cheers. But somehow the mood of its crew has a way of penetrating the atmosphere of a ship. The chief effect of the announcement to the men was the removal of the suspense which always saturates ships that sail under sealed orders. Like their skippers, the crews of submarines want to bring home the bacon, and the way the war was running just then—northward to Japan's home islands together with a sharp decline in Nipponese shipping—tended to make a productive submarine patrol a thing of the past.

My submariners had worked so well at sinking whole fleets of Marus that they had virtually torpedoed themselves out of business. Therefore the prospect of entering virgin hunting grounds, even at the risk of being blown higher than a sounding balloon in the Mikado's mine field, was deemed a proper potential price of admission to the tonnage paradise of Maruland.

Although the primary rule of the run from Guam to the southern entrance of Tsushima Strait was to make knots and keep schedule, the commanders of the nine ships put in as much time as possible on training dives, radar tracking on surface ships and airplanes, gunnery practice on floating mines, and sonar runs on almost everything and anything that offered a target.

On one occasion, Commander William J. Germershausen was putting the sonar crew of his *Spadefish* through its paces. The ship was running submerged and well below periscope depth when the sonarman sang out with a lusty ejaculation of unsimulated surprise. At the same time, the sonar scope lit up like a moonless sky full of flying saucers and the conning tower of the *Spadefish* was filled by the sweet, round, and dulcet notes of tolling bells—a veritable concert. Captain Bill and his technicians estimated that the sonar screen showed at least twenty contacts, and each contact registered the light disc and the sound quality a mine should and would register. It was almost incredible, yet mines apparently surrounded the *Spadefish* at every point of the compass. With mines before and behind, on bow and quarter, and with the bottom of the sea below, Germershausen decided that there was but one place for him to go in order to solve the deadly but fascinating mystery that confronted him.

"Take her up," he ordered. "Fast! Blow bow buoyancy—blow main ballasts."

The deceivingly smooth maze of movements that bring a submarine to the surface were performed by men at wheels and levers in a few seconds. Presently the *Spadefish* was bobbing on the sea, her propelling machinery at a dead stop. Alert lookouts jumped to their places while the Officer of the Deck took his station on the bridge. Without muttering the Skipper's standard request to the Officer of the Deck for permission to enter the windswept bridge, Germershausen shot up through the main hatch. No second-hand report for him on that brood of mines revealed by his FM Sonar! His sharp glance swept the sea on both sides of the submarine.

No mines in sight. Not a single one. Nothing. The mystery was never solved. Likeliest explanation: a school of fish.

On another occasion the *Spadefish* was exercising at periscope depth when the FMS picked up a clear contact at close range. "On observation through the periscope," said Captain Germershausen, "it proved to be the empty half-shell of a grapefruit floating on the surface."

Shortly after noon on June 1, the *Sea Dog* informed the *Crevalle* that something had gone wrong with her radar and that—if repairs were not made in time—she would have to depend upon the *Crevalle* to guide her through the not-so-distant Nansei Shoto island group. The transit was made south of Akuseki Shima at four-engine speed because those islands were crawling with Japs and none of the subs had the slightest desire to meet up with a resident patrol boat. Fortunately, from the standpoint of visibility, the vessels ran into violent squalls with much thunder and lightning. An hour after midnight the transit had been accomplished in driving rain with Steinmetz coaching Hydeman along via

B-29

voice radio. The following night the *Crevalle* had to do some more sheepherding. All of this made the crew of the *Crevalle* feel that they had a vested interest in Hydeman's little flagship—and they never let the *Sea Dog*'s crew forget it.

As planned, the Hepcats reached the place of rendezvous south of Tsushima Strait the night before the dawn they were to run under the mine field into the Sea of Japan. They reached this important jumping-off place without incidents of any kind.

Similarly, Pierce's Polecats made the run to the waters south of Nishi Suido—the west channel of Tsushima Strait, and the one selected for transit—without running into any adventures. The only break in their routine happened in mid-morning of June 1 when a B-29, evidently in distress, circled the small flotilla a couple of times. The pilot of the super-bomber radioed that he was considering ditching his plane to seek refuge aboard one of the three submarines. But when he learned that they were westward bound on a mission that could not be deferred or delayed, he decided against ditching and headed toward his base in the hope his plane would hang together until he got there.

The Polecats broke formation long enough to transit the Nansei Shoto independently at 1400 on June 2, and that night—about midnight—the submarines of this group heard the first of the long line of enemy radars. The skipper of the *Skate* observed that the "Japanese have built radars in many, many places"—an observation to which Henry Greer of the *Seahorse* would give wholehearted concurrence. That night, too, the Polecats' skippers saw their first Japanese planes on this particular mission. From then on, until they reached the point of entrance to the Sea of Japan, it was an endless chain of diving evasions to escape being seen by enemy aircraft or vessels.

Live Japs did not trouble the *Tunny* on this trip, but one who was not alive made it take a second look. In logging this incident, Commander Pierce wrote: "3 June. Sighted good Jap in water. Not a fresh one!"

15

TINOSA SAVES DITCHED AIRMEN

More lively were the adventures of Bob Risser's Bobcats. The trio, although fairly well separated, staged a highly competitive hunt for a lifeboat full of B-29 fliers whose plane had become disabled while enroute back from the Empire after a bombing mission. Here is the story direct from Dick Latham, skipper of the *Tinosa*, as he presented it to me:

"In the radioshack in the after-end of the control room my radiomen were standing their usual watches and in addition had a receiver tuned in to the frequency of the pilots of a B-29 unit returning from a raid on Japan. Suddenly the radiomen were startled out of their usual gumchewing complacency when they heard one of the pilots report to one of his formation mates that he had suffered considerable flak damage and might have to ditch. I was notified of this conversation at once and arrived at the radioshack to find that an exact log was already being kept on the flyboys' conversation. A smart move on the part of my operators.

"Shortly after this, the pilot announced that he was ordering his crew to hit the parachutes and that he was ditching his plane at a certain position so that a Dumbo plane with a dropable lifeboat could be sent to the scene. The time was about 1300. This position was immediately plotted on the *Tinosa*'s chart and was found to be approximately two hundred miles almost due north of *Tinosa*'s present position and in the vicinity of a towering pile of rocks, the Japanese Island of Sofu-gan, also known as 'Lot's Wife.' At once the roar of four huge diesels throbbed through the *Tinosa* as I ordered the speed increased to nineteen knots, the maximum in that rather high sea. Fortunately the sea moderated and the bridge remained dry even with the increase in speed. Four hours later the *Tinosa* received a message, along with several other submarines in the area, to proceed to the aid of the downed aviators. By continuing to man the aviators' frequency we knew that by now a Dumbo had dropped a Higgins rescue craft for the fliers and that they were all apparently in the Higgins boat. *Tinosa* had a good jump on getting to the spot. She arrived on station about midnight, but could find no trace of the lifeboat.

"About 0130 a fog set in which reduced visibility to about one hundred yards. *Tinosa* cruised back and forth searching. During the night about four other submarines arrived in the vicinity and also took up the search. Dawn brought no relief from the fog—in fact it seemed to get thicker. By about 0900 several aircraft were on station with the submarines and *Tinosa* was soon in communication with them.

"About this time the aviators spotted the lifeboat through a patch in the fog, which by this time was being burned off by the sun so that, although visibility on the surface was still about one hundred yards, there was clear blue just a few feet above the *Tinosa*. The position report, as given out with the latest aircraft contact, was some fifteen miles from *Tinosa*'s position, and she dashed off to this new spot with renewed hope, only to find no trace of the lifeboat. The downed aviators had a Gibson Gal Transmitter which sent out an automatic SOS on 500 KCS when the crank was turned. The submarines had no direction-finders and could not obtain a bearing on this signal but could merely tell that they were getting hot or cold by the intensity of the SOS received.

"By now it was 2 June and the *Tinosa*'s navigator was convinced that the aviators' dead reckoning position was probably many miles in error. We on the *Tinosa* knew the aviators had a direction-finder and could get a bearing on their Gibson Gal Transmitter. It seemed possible that if the search planes that were circling overhead could locate the position of the lifeboat, they would be able to dive that position and the *Tinosa* might be able to get a bearing with her surface search radar on the low-flying planes. So we sent a message to the planes asking them to dive on the position of the lifeboat. They replied to the effect that the survivors had gotten tired of cranking the Gibson Gal, but, as soon as they resumed, the planes would be able to carry out this assignment."

At this point the *Tinosa* crew had the uncomfortable sensation of being within a few miles of Japanese shores while they steamed in circles on the surface, blowing their whistle constantly to alert the survivors. It worked. The survivors heard the whistle and cranked the Gibson Girl with renewed energy. The planes got the bearing and dived on the appropriate spot. *Tinosa* got a bearing on the low-flying planes with her surface radar and steamed directly toward the lifeboat. Soon the lifeboat was sighted one point on the starboard bow and about a hundred yards distance. In no time, eager submariners hauled the aviators aboard. Ten men, all but one of the crew, were hauled to safety. The parachute of the Chief Engineer of the plane had failed to open and his buddies had seen him plunge to his death.

"The *Tinosa* resumed her journey toward the Sea of Japan with all hands confident that the rescue was an omen of good luck," continued Dick Latham. "There is a peculiar thrill in the rescue of a human being which fills the rescuer with a feeling of satisfaction that must at least be comparable to or even surpass the feeling of those rescued. In this case, not one of the aviators was injured and the happiness which pervaded *Tinosa* was felt by every soul aboard. The submariners took great pride in demonstrating that submarine chow was the best in the Fleet.

"The aviators were properly impressed as they consumed their pie à la mode with each meal, and their faces were beaming until they found out our destination—after which they were most anxious to transfer to a submarine headed in the other direction."

In fact, the story went around that when Dick Latham informed the survivors that he was enroute to break through the mine fields that protect the Sea of Japan, they were unanimous in their desire to climb back into their lifeboat to wait for another submarine to come along!

As *Tinosa* plowed westward toward the Straits south of Kyushu, she received another message from a downed aviator. On a pitch black but clear night, while various Japanese patrol planes flew low overhead, she searched diligently for the lost aviator, but with no success.

"This search had to be called off in order that *Tinosa* could rendezvous with *Scabbardfish* on the following night for the purpose of transferring the aviators to the homeward-bound submarine. At the appointed time, *Tinosa* picked up friendly radar interference from the *Scabbardfish*. The submarines hove to about fifty feet apart while a rubber liferaft was put in the water and a heaving line was used to haul it back and forth between the subs and thus transfer the aviators."

Again the night was black and clear and those aboard the *Tinosa* felt little apprehension about this meeting within a few miles of Nagasaki.

As Dick Latham took stock of his whereabouts in the dark morning hours of June 4, he was feeling pretty good. Although he had been at full on four engines most of the time in the past two days and had burned a lot of fuel, he would be nearly on schedule.

The *Tinosa* was cruising on the surface when one of the two starboard look-outs sang out: "A dark object, looks like a raft on starboard quarter! About fifty yards."

Instantly suspicious, since no aviator had been reported missing in that region, Dick ordered a couple of men with Tommy guns on deck and backed up slowly. On Okinawa there had been talk of suicide-rafts manned by Kamikaze Japs. Those rafts, loaded with explosives, were propelled by swimmers and exploded on contact. He had just transited Nansei Shoto, so dared not throw a searchlight on the dark and still-distant mass, but he ordered his men to shoot at the first sign of movement aboard it. As he came closer, he saw the raft was a couple of floating logs. Dick's feelings were well expressed in this log entry: "Felt sort of ridiculous lying to in the middle of the strait, hailing a bunch of logs, with a Tommy gun ready. No one visible and logs would not answer. Continued on."

At this stage of World War II in the Pacific, lifeguarding, of which Comdr. Dick Latham and his *Tinosa* gave such an excellent demonstration, was big business—big in fostering comradeship and cooperation between aviators and sailormen, big in developing devices and procedures for improving our score, big in morale building for all concerned, and big in the end result—lives saved.

By the end of the war, we had rescued some 504 dunked aviators. The record haul of thirty-one during a single patrol was held by the *Tigrone*. The lifeguarding submarines were open constantly to attack by enemy planes and submarines. In fact, some ventured so close to the coast that they came under the fire of shore batteries. The list of heroic rescues was very long, and treasured in our Submarine Force archives are letters or dispatches voicing the gratitude of most of the Pacific Commanders of Forces—MacArthur, Halsey, Spruance, Mitcher, Giles, and Spaatz, to mention a few.

The logs of the *Bowfin* and the *Flying Fish*—remaining members of the Hellcats' Bobcats—sprouted young orchards of sour apples because their efforts to rescue the aviators had not been successful. There is a friendly, but none the less keen, rivalry among subs who are doing lifeguard duty, and although it was a side issue on this occasion, the rivalry still held sway. As they neared the Japanese islands, the Bobcats also encountered extensive enemy activity. On the very last morning, one of the Bobcats believed that it had been spotted near the strait by a Jap patrol vessel. This compelled her to submerge and use almost an hour's worth of precious battery, every bit of which might be needed during the long sixteen-hour submerged run through Tsushima Strait that same day. But, as things turned out, all ships had all the juice they needed to make this greatest of all under-mine-field runs in submarine history.

16

HEPCATS IN TSUSHIMA STRAIT

Where the swells of the East China Sea search like long green fingers among the hard cold rocks that fringe the thinly inhabited southeast coast of Korea as well as the stony shore of Kyushu Island of Japan, there is a water gap of some ninety miles called Korea Strait. In the very center of that Strait, heading almost north and south, lies long, narrow, and mountainous Tsushima Island like a mighty battleship anchored in mid-channel. On its right runs the fairly shallow eastern channel, cluttered with islands and teeming with small-ship traffic, called Tsushima Strait. On its left stretches the deeper but fairly narrow western channel. It is known as Nishi Suido.

The presence of more than a dozen lighthouses in the Tsushima area is ample evidence that these are tricky waters to negotiate. But in times of war, when none of the lights were blinking their warning messages and when mine fields forbade all surface traffic except to those who were equipped with mine charts, the submerged transit of either channel by enemy subs into the Sea of Japan past Tsushima Island called for steady nerves, master-seamanship, and topnotch ship-handling.

We had selected the western channel for our penetration mission because it was in all respects the safer of the two. Both were mined, but from our observations we had reason to believe that Nishi Suido had fewer patrols, and the charts showed deeper waters and better current conditions. As previously explained, it was important that our subs should have a straight, steady, and not too swift current which would sway the mine cables parallel to the course of the submarines and yet would not dip the mine cases so deep into the sea as to seriously obstruct passage under them.

Nishi Suido was about sixty miles long, thirty miles wide, and from fifty to one hundred fathoms deep.

In the top fringe of the East China Sea, from a starting place some sixty miles east of unlit Komundo Lighthouse on the Korean coast and some forty miles southwest of Ko Saki Light on Tsushima Island, the Hellcats would run submerged from just before dark on a steadily increasing northeasterly course—fairly close to the coast of Tsushima Island—until they had the mine fields far astern as they surfaced in the up-to-then peaceful and secure waters of the Sea of Japan.

Once inside the mine barriers, the Hellcats, doing their utmost to avoid detection, would proceed to their respective areas of operation. Hydeman's Hepcats would go to the northeast sector of the Sea of Japan to destroy all shipping encountered and inflict damage on the west coast of the islands of Honshu and Hokkaido, from the busy port of Niigata up to the southwestern part of Sakhalin Island, where floating fish canneries had been reported. Ports such as Tomarioru and Otomari on Sakhalin and Otaru on Hokkaido were likely producers of targets. Hakodate on the Tsugaru Strait would not be approached because of mine fields and swift currents, but it could be expected to contribute its quota of shipping.

The invisible and unmarked underwater paths beneath the mine fields of Tsushima Strait as our Hepcats followed them on that June 4 morning bore to the northeastward. The Cats' pace was so moderate that a person walking at a good steady gait would have beat them to the finish lines with time for a breathing spell to spare—about three knots, which is almost creeping speed. This speed had been selected for the passage of all the Hellcats because, at a rate so moderate, propeller noises would be low while steering control would still be good. Last, but not least, if a mine were sighted dead ahead and close, backing the motors at full speed would kill the ship's headway almost instantly.

Just before dawn—about four o'clock—the Hepcats swung into formation. First the *Sea Dog*. Three miles abeam of it, the *Crevalle*, and four miles astern of the *Sea Dog*, the *Spadefish*. There were no signal flags lashing in the wind, no signal lights blinking commands as the small flotilla headed into Tsushima Strait. The *Sea Dog* did a routine disappearing act. Its two companions followed suit and kept stations below just as they had on surface.

According to the log of the *Spadefish*, it came to the surface some sixteen hours later—at 2050 according to the ship's clock—in the Sea of Japan. In trying to describe his own feelings and those of his men, Bill Germershausen made these concise but illuminating comments: "Regarding the mine fields—the most important part of the patrol, I am afraid, was hair-rising but uneventful.

"When our FMS picked up a mine—and we picked up a lot as we went along, with many long waits in between—there was no doubt about it.

"When you heard Hellsbells ringing, it did not sound like a tri-plane practice target, a school of fish, or even like a dummy mine. You knew it was the real thing. And it gave you the creeps.

"The feeling those sounds gave us baffles description. But what can one say—except that it made the mouth dry and ran prickles up and down your spine as a piano player might run the scales."

As for Maruland—when the *Spadefish* surfaced smoothly in the Sea of Japan—Bill Germershausen had this to say: "It was hard to believe that there was a war on. The Japanese ships were blithely sailing back and forth without air or surface escorts. They steered straight courses and burned running lights—something I had not seen in three and a half years. 'But,' I said to myself, 'we'll fix that!' And we sure did.

"The passage itself was taken by all hands rather fatalistically. I don't think anyone was very trustful of the FM sonar gear, particularly since the mines we detected were picked up at such short ranges that we would not have been able to maneuver around them. We made the passage at 180 feet, at which depth we apparently under-ran the moored mines.

"During the transit we heard at least two very loud explosions which we were tempted to attribute to the *Sea Dog* and *Crevalle* having met their fate, but, upon surfacing late on June 4, we happily made contact."

While I am not in complete agreement with Bill Germershausen that the mines were registered on the sonar too late to take evasive action, I do think his observation makes interesting reading in view of the varying opinions among his companion skippers. Running at 180 feet, unless his ship were trimmed up at an angle of 5 or 6 degrees, his keel-mounted transducer might be shadowed by the submarine's bow before a mine dead ahead came within pick-up range.

Aboard the *Sea Dog* the situation was different. From

the very first hour, when it submerged, to the very last after sunset when it rose to the surface, the FMS on the *Sea Dog* was blandly noncommittal. If there were any Hellpots in Tsushima Strait, they did not cast reflections on the sonar's screen. Nor did they give voice to any kind of noises—from bells to scratches.

The vessel was more than half through the Strait before all hands came to the realization that the ill luck that had forced collapse of the ship's radar two nights running had befallen the ship's sonar set. Under the circumstances, there was nothing to do about it but run deep at slow speed. This Hydeman had done, adding a few extra feet of depth to allow for the dip of the mines caused by the current. At any rate, Earl's passage through the mine field was smooth to the point of boredom.

Steiny Steinmetz' doubts about the workability of the FMS aboard his *Crevalle* underwent a drastic change as he passed under the mine field. FMS had to sell itself to him the hard way, but sell itself it did. This is what Steiny said to me on the subject:

"I think you had far more confidence in the FM Sonar than any of the skippers involved. The *Crevalle* training at Pearl didn't allay our doubts. At Guam the results were far better but still inconsistent. Our first patrol with it was characterized by so many 'clear, bell-like tones' that I reported I couldn't make any pattern out of the contacts and therefore assumed we had not yet reached the mine fields.

"However, when we did penetrate, there was no question in anyone's mind that the gear was working. Also, as I recall, we did not have any upkeep troubles.

"The day of the breakthrough was of course a tense one for all hands. We were forced to submerge early due to a close and persistent plane contact. Our passage was not marked by cables scraping down the side like Ozzie Lynch had. We did hear a lot of very loud explosions throughout the day, which we could not figure out.

"When it came time to surface, we found ourselves in the midst of a traffic pattern and consequently were forced to surface with several small ships a bit too close for comfort. However none of these gave any indication of being aware of our presence."

17

HELLSBELLS RING FOR POLECATS

Among those who loved the Hellsbells was Commander George E. Pierce of Tullahoma, Tennessee, skipper of the redoubtable *Tunny* and boss of the Polecats.

"For my money," he said in his unadulterated Southern accent, "I would be happy to do that patrol again. With but one reservation, in that I would put in a bid for better luck with respect to targets for my torpedoes. As I reported at the time, the FMS worked beautifully and gave us a few tense moments as we neared the center of the Strait.

"The FMS sounded like the Philharmonic warming up and then the mines started showing up on the screen. We were pointing fair between two mines in the first row, and as we approached the line, the FM gave off with the Philharmonic tuning-up effect again. We had the second line on the screen before we lost the first line. I really *loved* that FM gear."

Mortal man will never know if the blobs and bells that kept Commander Ozzie Lynch and his exec, Lt. Comndr. Robert C. Huston, on their toes were rocks, as they suspected, or mines, as they feared. In recalling the eventful hours of that underwater penetration aboard the *Skate*, Ozzie said:

"On the trip through the mine fields I decided that the thing to do was split the job with the exec in conning the ship through the mines. He was being as charitable as possible, permitting me to get some sleep until about the coffee hour (about 0800) as I remember, but sent for me finally.

"I arrived in the conning tower and found him fully occupied dodging sonar contacts that we both considered in our best judgment as rocks, but at the same time we could not afford to deliberately run over a contact. Sort of like the previous patrol in which we set the clocks ahead a day in Midway in order to avoid sailing on Friday the thirteenth. We were not superstitious, but there was no use in taking unnecessary chances.

"The FMS equipment was working fine, and very soon we got some contacts which were very definitely on mines. We finally hit an area with so many on the screen that it looked impossible to get through. We managed to scrape a mine mooring cable down the side of the ship. Soon the reports of the effects of this filtered up from the pressure hull beneath. The general trend of the reports seems to be that the mine cable sort of held reveille in succession from the bow.

"Right after this very positive indication of mines I took a chance on the intelligence you had gotten for us with regard to the spacing of the mine lines, and came up to periscope depth for a quick look with the periscope in order to get a visual fix on the mountain peaks on either side of the Strait. I felt that I was taking a chance, since, although the gear could find the mines, there was no assurance that another accidental grouping like the previous one would be encountered. I got the news that we were through the mine fields when the listening sonar operator reported that he heard propellers. We came up and found a reasonably good-sized craft headed across the Strait. I presume he had been briefed as to where he could cross."

The reactions to FMS aboard the *Bonefish*, skippered by Comndr. Larry L. Edge, will never be known because his patrol report vanished into the same untraceable blue that closed over Larry, his men, and his gallant ship a couple of days before Operation Barney had run its course. On that last occasion, when Larry and Ozzie Lynch had a chance to speak, Larry was more interested in hunting trouble than in escaping it. There will be more to say about Commander Edge later on.

18

MINE CABLE RUFFLES BOBCAT

Last to penetrate the mine field were Bob Risser's Bobcats. For two days running, six submarines in groups of three had accepted the challenge of the barrier of high explosives. Was a third penetration on the third day a case of taking the pitcher to the well once too often?

There was but one way to find out—to do it.

At the outset the auspices for the venture seemed not too favorable because of the intense Japanese air and sea activity in the entrance to the Strait. It was as if the Japs knew that something was brewing close to the bottom of Tsushima. And, of course, neither of the two remaining Bobcats—the *Tinosa* with Commander Latham in command and the *Bowfin* with Commander Tyree as captain—had any way of knowing whether the penetrations by the Hepcats and the Polecats had been completely successful or not.

Instead of a dawn rendezvous, Bob Risser in *Flying Fish* led his fellow Bobcats down into the depths at 0301. During the first hour they picked up a great deal of pinging, even explosions, on their instruments.

With the exception of Lt. H. J. Smith, Jr., the Executive Officer, all the *Tinosa* officers were reservists and excellent specimens of the courage and skill which non-career sailors bring into the Navy when the Hellsbells of our enemies summon them for service. As Commander Dick Latham, her C.O., put it: "There was a deceptive passiveness about the crew at this time which would have fooled an inexperienced observer but which to her commanding officer indicated a perfect psychological attitude toward the approaching assignment."

When it came time for the Bobcats to line up and penetrate the mine field, the *Tinosa* was given the center track. This position made her the vessel farthest from either shore. In advance, Latham and his officers decided not to bring the *Tinosa* up to periscope depth for observations but to make the transit at a keel depth of 120 feet, checking their position by dead reckoning and fathometer soundings. They were afraid the periscope might be sighted and thus warn the Japs that submarines were transiting the Strait. The keel depth of 120 feet was chosen because it was estimated that the deepest Japanese mine would be set at about seventy feet. With the periscope in the lowered position, the *Tinosa* would just clear the deepest mine if this were true.

What with the successful and unsuccessful search for downed aviators and the rendezvous with a submarine on the preceding night, Dick Latham was tired as the hour for making the transit approached. Having the utmost confidence in his executive officer, Snuffy Smith, the skipper decided that he and the executive officer would stand watches on a four on, four off basis during the transit. Dick was to take the first watch. The *Tinosa* dived at the break of dawn at 0400. She went to 120-foot keel depth on the prescribed northeast-erly course and at the prescribed speed of three knots while the executive officer turned in and the skipper took his station in the conning tower to watch the FM sonar.

"We had had considerable experience with mine fields by this time," recalled Captain Latham, "and none of us was the least bit fooled by the false contacts obtained on fish. These sometimes produced the bell-like tone on the sonar and they sounded very much like an actual mine.

"But when it came to picking up mines during that first four-hour watch, there were absolutely none of that breed of cats. If we had had a Hollywood script-writer aboard, he might have found something special in the atmosphere of the ship or in the bearing of the men that would indicate an overhanging menace—a parallel between the Hellpots that hung over our heads and the well-known sword of Damocles suspended by a hair over the balding dome of some ancient Athenian sage.

"However, if that atmosphere existed, I saw no trace of it from 0400 to 0800. To veterans in combat, death is purely a matter of degree—a something that may lie waiting just around the corner. And since the human being is the most adjustable living thing on earth, he soon learns that there is no profit in peeking around corners. I should say that the nature of this operation keyed the men to the highest pitch. They were like prospectors in a hostile country looking for pay dirt and expecting to find it in big chunks. The enthusiasm and eagerness to raise hell in Hirohito's backyard was shared by all hands. The performance of duty by every man was typical of good submariners."

When Dick's turn of duty was up, about 0800, Snuffy Smith relieved him. The skipper made a beeline for the wardroom where he consumed a hefty breakfast of fruit juice, scrambled eggs, and steak. After that, he turned in and fell into sound slumbers. He was roused out of those about 1130 when a messenger called him: "The Executive Officer says that if you would like to see some mines, please come up to the conning tower."

The messenger, a boy in his late teens, delivered this interesting news with an air of suppressed excitement. After all, the situation was a bit out of the ordinary.

At the time he was called, Dick was so groggy with sleep that he does not remember to this day whether he failed to get up when called or whether the mine show just happened to be short and sweet. At any rate, the blobs and bells had vanished by the time he got there. Explained Snuffy Smith: "I picked up a mine about one point on the port bow. The moment I saw the blob on the screen—a fraction of a second after the bell sound rang out—I yelled, 'Right full rudder.' And believe you me, I got it. Wonderful helmsman that fellow! Never saw such service."

"Only one mine?" asked Latham with an air of disbelief.

"Oh, no—just wait," answered Snuffy. "Shortly after she started swinging, I picked up another mine. This time about two points on the starboard bow. A fine kettle of fish. It was like looking at an ultra-slow motion picture, the way the *Tinosa*'s bow swung toward the second mine with a slow but seemingly unalterable determination to ram it. I quickly called for left rudder. And again I got prompt action."

It is fairly easy for anyone who has been in a tight corner of any kind to gauge the tension among the men in the conning tower—throughout the ship, in fact. Because the *Tinosa*'s talker—standing above the control room hatch talking into his microphone as cool as a sidewalk engineer—relayed the tight little sonar drama to the crew in all parts of the ship in minute detail but without any dramatic huffings and puffings.

With Smith's order "Left full rudder," all had been done that human hands could accomplish. From there on, it was strictly up to the Lord.

World War II saw the development of a very extensive submarine language—words and phrases that had no meaning outside the world of submarines. One of the words in this unique glossary was the "J-Factor." This expression indicated a benevolent influence and loving spirit that held its protective arm around the shoulders of submariners. It was a deeply reverent word. Translated it meant the "Jesus-Factor" —the protecting influence of the Son of our Lord.

And that morning, aboard the *Tinosa*, the J-Factor truly exercised its lifesaving influence as the men in the conning tower stood momentarily in silent apprehension. The blob on the screen grew larger, firmer, and brighter. The bell tone that rang through the conning tower increased in volume and clarity.

Outside, in the dark cold waters of 120 feet below the surface, a Hellpot studded with death-activating horns that would break at a slight touch and explode the seven hundred pounds of high explosives packed away in the minecase bobbed menacingly at the end of its anchor cable. A touch on one of those many projecting horns and nothing in our earthly world could save the *Tinosa*.

There are moments when men pray with words that only the heart can speak and only God can hear—prayers so deep that they do not find reflection in murmurs or even moving lips, and yet prayers of electrifying force.

Slowly, ever so slowly, the menace of the mine increased— so painfully slowly that it seemed to twist and squeeze the innards of the watching, listening men. In the conning tower no one said a word. No one but the talker. Smoothly, quietly, he performed his job of describing the action taking place on the FMS screen: "We are getting close to the mine now. As we get closer, the blob on the screen starts to melt away—and the bell sound is getting weaker. This is because the hull of our boat lies between the mine above us and the sonar-picker-upper in the keel. That's the way it is, boys." A pause. Then: "If you've been holding your breath, relax. The screen is clear now."

In the after torpedo room where men on duty were at their stations and men off duty rested on their kapok mattressed pipe bunks, thoughts were concentrated on the mines. The boys were not sure of the chances of survival of crewmen in any other part of the vessel, but they did know that if a mine banged off near the stern of the ship, they would have had it. The four torpedoes in the stern tubes, not to mention the spare torpedoes stowed outboard alongside the frames of the ship, promised the men in this section of the *Tinosa* a quick exit from the mortal scene.

The compartment was so quiet that the clink of a torpedo tool on the deck would have sounded like a depth charge. At their low speed through the ocean's depths, even the accustomed gurgle of water through the superstructure and deck gratings was stilled. The only sounds audible were the faint whisper of the screws and the subdued whirring of the ventilating fans. These were punctuated now and then by the low whine of the steering motor as the helmsman in the conning tower shifted the rudder.

Into the tenseness of their thoughts broke the voice of the talker: "The exec just ordered full right rudder to bring us back on course."

Then they heard it—a new sound, stealthy and sinister coming from the outside, from below and abaft the conning tower. It sounded like the scraping rattle of a scaly monster. Slow and hideous, it emanated from the hull—a squealing as though the very skin of the ship were in pain. A sound as though a huge sea serpent rising from the bottom slime were slithering along the welded steel plates that sealed the submarine's people and her vitals from the sea.

The sound brought the hackles of every man to stand stiff as brushes. Currents of gooseflesh swept their bodies. Sweat poured from glands that date back to eras of primitive fears and rages. Hearts thumped and jugular veins pulsed like living things. The cable of the vanished mine had contacted the *Tinosa* on the starboard side just abaft the conning tower. And now as the vessel crept ahead, the cable was scraping her side.

Throats were so tight that no one could speak had he wanted to. Not even the talker.

The mine cable continued its squealing, scraping course along the entire hull of the vessel. The exec and his conning tower gang—who first heard the sound—muttered silent prayers that rope guards installed around the stern planes and propellers would prevent the mine cable from catching on.

U.S.S. Tinosa

Moments merged silently. After centuries of tension, the scraping sound stopped and Stuffy knew that the *Tinosa* had cleared that particular mine and its cable. He fished a none too clean handkerchief from a hip-pocket and wiped his cold and clammy brow.

At this moment, blithe as the proverbial meadowlark, although still a bit sleepy, Dick Latham came up the control room hatch into the conning tower. On his way up from the cabin, if one may dignify a five- by eight-foot cubby hole with the name of cabin, he had thought the men were sort of quiet but had paid no particular attention to it. After all, under-running mine fields was brand new to them.

Glancing at the sonar screen and finding it free from blobs, not hearing any bells and knowing nothing about scraping mine cables, Dick said jocularly, "Well, Snuffy, I see that everything is normal!"

"Huh!" ejaculated Smith as he ran a lightning review of the last few eternal seconds before his inner vision. "Yep, all but a few mines, Captain, and one of them just saluted the quarter deck."

Since it was about a quarter to twelve, almost time to relieve the conning tower watch, Latham nodded to his exec and said, as generations of officers-of-the-deck have said, "I relieve you, sir," and took over the watch.

Snuffy Smith, however, was too full of the morning's happenings and too excited and elated about his successful evasion of sudden death to have thoughts of sleep. This under-running a mine field did not happen too often in a lifetime—in fact might not happen even once—so he elected to remain in the conning tower and supervise the plotting while the *Tinosa* made her way through three more distinct lines of mines. So far as Latham could tell, the *Tinosa* hit the gaps right in the middle on the remaining three rows of Hellpots and scraped no more cables.

The mine fields in Tsushima Strait consisted of four very definite lines of mines, each line separated from the next by about one thousand yards. The mines within each line were about fifty yards apart. The sonar gear was working excellently and it was possible to see and plot four or five of the mines in each line.

The *Bowfin*'s transit was unspectacular. During the night and early morning before she staged her day-long Tsushima dive, Skipper Alec Tyree was deeply concerned with a surface ASW patrol on the south side of the strait. Fortunately he was able to work his way around the enemy snooper—get north of him—so that the *Bowfin* did not have to dive too early and thus add a couple of extra submerged hours to a trip which Tyree already considered long enough.

In recounting the tale of his Tsushima run, Commander Tyree said: "After diving, I calculated the approximate time we should encounter mines. Without being boastful, I knew that I—along with a sonarman whose name I remember as Benson—were the most skilled in detecting mines on the gear. So I scheduled Benson for the 08-12 watch which I estimated to be the watch when mines would be encountered.

"About 0700, I had a chair brought to the conning tower. There I parked in the port after corner where I could hear and listen for the bell tones, and there I remained until sometime in the late afternoon or about dinnertime.

"I had decided before we started through the Strait that we would run deep. It was 150 or 180 feet, I can't remember which. At any rate, it was my feeling that *deep* was our best bet, since even if our sonar gear were not working, we'd still have a better than even chance. I still vividly remember jumping up from my chair when we made our first contact on mines about 1000. They appeared to be thickly bunched clusters and without an opening. We had time to change course about 25° to 30°, then put the rudder over in the opposite direction to start a swing back to the course of the current.

"Nothing happened and we breathed a sigh of relief. No cables scraping down the side. But we knew we had passed a line of mines. And about twenty minutes later, another of the same.

"When nothing happened after another thirty minutes, Benson was ready to take a blow after an already long session for one sonarman. He was about all in. I had him relieved; so of course it wasn't too long before the entire crew knew we had passed a couple of hurdles. The tension remained great for the remainder of the day, but nothing else of note occurred.

"About 1900, I knew we were through and came below for something to eat. As I remember, we surfaced about 2045-2100, and shortly after getting to the bridge, I got soaked by an unexpectedly choppy sea. Since we were to avoid action while enroute to our assigned area, I went down that night, took a shower, put on pajamas—the only time I ever did that on a war patrol—and, being thoroughly exhausted, had a good night's sleep. At diving time in the morning, still being really tired, I didn't even go to the bridge, just ordered the dive and turned over to sleep until nearly noon.

"To say that we were not scared during the transit would be at least inaccurate. We were. I am sure that I said a prayer of thankfulness when we crossed the first hurdle on the way in and another after we reached deep water in the Sea of Japan. The FM sonar seemed to work well and we were blessed with fewer false targets than we had normally encountered in training and off Tsugaru."

The only Hellcat besides Ozzie Lynch to bring his submarine to periscope depth in Tsushima Strait and take a quick look on the seascape above the mine fields was Commander Bob Risser. The transit of his *Flying Fish* as he describes it was a tense experience for all hands.

"My exec, Julian Burke, and I alternated at the conn. We dived at 0401 that morning and our first mine contact came at about 0840. This developed into several contacts—one very close aboard to starboard. A second group of contacts came at 1014. From 1138 to 1150 some scattered contacts were made.

"At 1728 we came to periscope depth to obtain a fix on Kami No Shima. About one hour later a small freighter, smoking heavily, stood across our track from NW to SE but after crossing ahead of us, suddenly turned 180 degrees and eventually disappeared over the hill.

"We surfaced at 2050 that night in a rising gale—well into the Sea of Japan. Looking back now on the whole experience, that day seems rather remote and it is indeed poorly remembered. Perhaps it was the newness of the experience—in any event, for me it was far from the most exciting day of war in *Flying Fish*."

Risser's closing comment on the transit of Tsushima Strait brings us again into hailing distance of the J-Factor. And I present it here because it reveals the strong but often hidden influence of God on the acts and the thinking of our submariners.

"I would like to make a sort of unrelated point," said Captain Risser, "although it has nothing directly to do with Operation Barney. I'm far from being a religious type and I never led my crew in prayer or at hymns, but I do not recall a single night that I did not ask His help.

"The after lookout must have often wondered what the Captain was doing back there—pacing up and down, fore and aft, every night. He didn't know and I wouldn't have told him that I was praying for my officers, my crew, and my ship.

"Somehow, on the cigarette deck of a submarine in enemy waters thousands of miles from home, one feels awfully close to God."

Yes, Risser is right. The so-called cigarette deck on a submarine is an after extension of the bridge, a platform that covers the main engine induction pipe and is surrounded by a railing. Because it is partially sheltered by the periscope super-structure, this place had become a favorite spot for the skipper to do some solid thinking and perhaps a bit of communion while he caught a quick cigarette or two. Hence the name cigarette deck. In fact, it looks quite a lot like a pulpit—with machine guns on it.

19

HELLCATS IN HIROHITO'S SEA

The principal length of the Sea of Japan stretches some nine hundred miles from Tsushima Strait in the southwest to La Perouse Strait in the northeast. At its widest, between the island of Honshu in Japan to Valadivostok in Siberia, it measures about 250 miles. In shape and size, this watery area bears fairly close resemblance to the western end of the Mediterranean from Gibraltar to the toe in the boot in Italy. The principal differences between these two important bodies of water lie in the relatively few islands, coastal and otherwise, in the Sea of Japan and in the great variations in depth. Whereas the Mediterranean is generally shallow, the Sea of Japan has a minimum depth of about nine hundred feet.

Over the centuries, Japan has learned to look upon this well-protected and well-situated land-framed sea as its exclusive ocean made to order for the Maru-boats of Nippon—a veritable Maru Nostrum that provides important life lines from the Asiatic mainland for essentials which Japan is unable to provide for the huge population on its main islands. Life lines for rice and other important food; for coal, ore, and other vital industrial raw materials. To the Sea of Japan itself, the Japanese populace looked for its principal culinary item—fish and other sea food.

Leading into this private oceanic preserve are five narrow and extremely difficult doors in the form of straits that provide passage to and from the East China Sea, the North

Pacific Ocean, and the Sea of Okhotsk. Running from south to north, they are: Tsushima Strait, heavily mined. Shimonoseki Strait, a narrow channel thread that runs west from Japan's famous Inland Sea. (During the war, this shipping link was so thoroughly mined and fortified by Nippon that no enemy traffic would be so foolhardy as to attempt its passage. Under this Strait the Japanese had dug a tunnel connecting the industrially rich sections of Honshu and Kyushu Islands.) Next, Tsugaru Strait between Honshu and Hokkaido, also heavily mined and protected by shore batteries to prevent any possibility of entry. La Perouse Strait, running between Hokkaido and Karafuto Islands, narrow and heavily mined with a slender corridor for neutral Russian shipping. And, at the very tip of the Japanese islands, northwest of Sakhalin, the chill and tortuous channel of the Strait of Tartary.

Those were the doors behind which Japan operated with bold, contemptuous insolence.

At the risk of being perhaps a bit too repetitious, it may be desirable to repeat here that the principal object of the Hellcat invasion was not only to disrupt life lines and sink as many Japanese ships—large and small—as possible, but also, in fact, chiefly—to destroy Japanese confidence in the ability of its military leaders to maintain those supply lines against American or other Allied attacks. It was no secret to the rank and file of Japanese that the uninterrupted operation of the trans-Sea-of-Japan shipping lines meant the difference between food and no food; between survival and starvation, victory and defeat.

The basic factor in warfare is the spirit of combat, the will to fight, on the part of the populace. Once public morale has been undermined, all the saber-rattling in the world by military leaders will not restore that intangible factor. Therefore, if we—through harassing the shipping on the life lines across the Sea of Japan or along the coast lines of the home islands—could convince the Japanese that their food intake was insecure, a long start would have been made toward the moment when they would want to throw up the sponge and call it a day.

For that reason, the Hellcat commanders had been instructed to torpedo everything that came on their periscope cross-wires. All freighters—big and small—were top priority targets. The same went for sea trucks, trawlers, even fishing sampans and other vessels that could be sunk by gun fire.

The object was quantity not quality—not a gentle belly scare but sheer starvation terror.

"Sink 'em all! Shoot 'em all!" was the order of the day.

To the skippers of the Hepcats—the first of the three invading wolf packs—the Sea of Japan had a dream-like quality when they, on the night of June 4, surfaced at the end of their all-day submerged run and set course northeast for the coastlines of Honshu, Hokkaido, and Karafuto. There to await the long, slow five-day lapse before the June 9 hour of sunset when they could begin their attacks. Meanwhile, the sight of well-lighted vessels steaming steady courses—and without armed escorts—toward coasts rimmed by garlands of light and other visual aids to navigation that flashed their friendly beams was so tempting to the Hepcat skippers that they developed permanently itchy trigger fingers.

On June 8—after four days of this, to him, inhuman torture—Steiny Steinmetz of the *Crevalle* wrote in his log book: "Sighted still another ship through my scope. A fine big one. Of all contacts, this was the toughest to throw back into the pond. I was strongly tempted to swing left, shoot, and then use as an excuse: 'Sorry, Admiral Lockwood, I was just cleaning my torpedo and it went off.'"

Incidentally, the theme song of the *Crevalle* was "Don't Fence Me In!" At no time during the sixteen days it spent cruising some 2557 miles in the Sea of Japan was the *Crevalle* ever really and truly fenced in, but it came a bit too close to it for comfort on June 14. A thrill-studded tale hangs on that incident and it will be told here, as will the story of the *Flying Fish* when it came much too close for comfort to being really walled in. All at its proper time.

20

SEA DOG BARGES INTO BUSHES

If a Hollywood motion picture producer were to cast a three-in-one combination of adventurous explorer, steel-nerved marksman, and relentless manhunter it would never—repeat:

never—occur to him to select Earl T. Hydeman, Commander, USN, and a spectacularly successful submarine sailor virtually since his Annapolis days, for the role. The reason the movie maker would pass Hydeman over is that the real thing in the line of superior marksmanship, hunting, and exploring seldom if ever follows the concept we paint on the canvas of our imagination.

Earl Hydeman—medium-tall, square-set, slow-spoken, and measured in his actions—in uniform as well as out of uniform and minus his well-earned decorations looks like any successful man who could be anything from an architect to a zoologist. There is nothing in his outward appearance to suggest that he has all the qualities of rough and tumble seamanship plus the high daring and deep contempt for the orthodox required in a man who was not only to command the *Sea Dog* in a bold and protracted invasion into the very heart-waters of the enemy but also to direct the three Hepcat boats in the nine-ship Hellcat group of which he was the task group commander. I was lucky, Operation Barney was lucky, and the Navy was lucky that a combat sailor of Earl's stature was available for that job after serious depth-charge damage to the *Seahorse*, which was to have been one of the Hellcats, caused hurried last-minute changes.

In developing his plan of campaign on the broad pattern presented at my May 23 conference aboard the *Holland* in Guam, Earl proceeded on the solid theory that, after the first stunning blow of surprise had caused wide cessation of shipping activities in the Sea of Japan, the enemy would confine as much as he could of his shipping to coastal waters well within the Hundred Fathom Curve because inshore-waters are notoriously unappetizing to submariners. This for the simple reason that the safety factor in diving is present or absent in absolute ratio to the amount of sea water on hand to dive in.

But while shoal water areas in the Sea of Japan could be dangerous to submarines from an operational standpoint, they offered, on the other hand, rich awards to the submerging hunter who had the guts to play the high cards and ante up the big blue chips that are called for in a game where death is the scorekeeper and where the stakes are for keeps. Too many of our submarines had played this game along the shallow China Coast to be alarmed about the ante.

Commander Hydeman entered the Sea of Japan commit-

ted to a bold plan. It called for giving the harbors and
coastwise steamer tracks in his territory along the shores of
Hokkaido and Honshu not only thorough but tenacious and
aggressively vigorous coverage. The *Sea Dog* and the other
two Hepcats, the *Crevalle* and the *Spadefish*, could be
depended upon to give their respective districts devastating
attention.

From June 4, his day of entry, to sunset of June 9—the
day and hour of M-Day (the time for open season on shipping), the *Sea Dog* engaged in practice runs on unwary
Japanese skippers. And there were a lot of them. Trouble was
that once the shooting started, these fat little boats would
scatter and disappear like coveys of quail before the hunter's
gun. In other words, as that tough old submariner Captain
Tex McLean, my operations officer at Perth, Australia, used
to drawl, "Damn it, Admiral, we've got to go in and beat
them out of the bushes." Hydeman was perhaps an admirer
and a disciple of the veteran Tex. In any event, beating them
out of the bushes was one of his favorite sports. The sun set
early in World War II on submarine skippers who believed
that they took unwarranted chances with their ships when
they ventured into waters of less than twenty fathoms—or
120 feet.

Undoubtedly they were right. But many good men have
gotten away with submarining on slim margins and a few have
not. In the then-current situation, hunters like Hydeman
would have to explore well within the Hundred Fathom
Curve and venture into treacherous waters where shipping
lanes are so narrow and so shallow that vessels like the *Sea
Dog* really stuck their proverbial necks out when they steamed
into them. To engage in combat in shallow waters with
anything like an even chance, a submarine must have at least
three hundred feet of water under its keel. To have less can
be fatal. And on one occasion, with an outlook that was
decidedly unfavorable, Earl was to find himself in exactly that
kind of a situation.

It was 0512—about the hour of sunrise—on June 19
when the *Sea Dog* registered its thirty-eighth, thirty-ninth,
and fortieth ship-contacts in the Sea of Japan, a full ten days
from M-hour when it fired its first torpedo and sank its first
ship under the banner of Operation Barney.

As the curtain rises on this particular stage setting, a
light haze drifts over land and sea and obscures the scene

with its milk-white fluff. For purposes of locale identification, the *Sea Dog* lies submerged some four thousand yards off the beach that skirts the sea front between Benkei Misaki and Kamoi Misaki on Hokkaido Island. Within a short distance from the gently breaking surf, the land rises into green foothills that quickly grow into rugged, medium-high mountain ranges. These are cut at irregular intervals by valleys that widen out into small, fertile coastal plains and estuaries which look westward. The face of the dawning sun seemed to take a cautious peek as it rose above the mountain tops, as if old Mr. Sol expected to see something slightly unexpected. Such as—of all things an American submarine in his Nipponese Nibs's oceanette. But if the sun did take a preliminary look, all it could have seen of the *Sea Dog* would have been its rare and quick up-and-down periscope movements, because the vessel itself lurked at periscope depth at exactly fifty-nine feet below the sea's glassy spread. Not 58.9 feet. Nor 59.1 feet. But exactly fifty-nine feet on the nose.

For that was the way Earl always ran his show. Not a little too long; not a little too short. But on the nose. Still, there are noses and noses. Some a little short. Some a little long. And at times they get pinched in too narrow a crack as we shall presently see.

Aware that he was heading from shallow into even shallower waters, Earl took a final sounding as he stopped all motors and coasted along into a fathometer recording of forty-five fathoms, or 270 feet. Nothing to brag about, but enough to meet the demands of the forseeable future. This position, according to Earl's hunch, was about where coastwise traffic would be running.

Bite by bite, the round red sun ate its way through the morning haze. And in the rapidly thinning fog, the officer on periscope watch saw three AK's loom up like ghost ships on a phantom sea. Just like that. One moment there was nothing. Then there were three.

As the intercom sang out the news, Hydeman came up the conning tower ladder on the jump. Three AK's! Pay dirt in the golden dawn. In a flash he was at the scope. Battle stations were sounded by the talker and on the gong. All hands answered the call at breakneck speed. The three targets were steaming up the coast from the south. At the time of sighting, the distance was about four thousand yards.

The orderly confusion of men scrambling to battle stations and casting loose their equipment ended. Everyone and everything was where he and it was supposed to be. The element of time was exactly right. Not a little long. Not a little short. But on the nose!

Now the periscope waltz began. Because of the short range, Earl had to work fast. He ordered all tubes forward brought to the ready. Next the *Sea Dog's* bow was swung toward the targets in order to bring the more numerous bow tubes to bear upon them. (Six forward; only four aft.) Two torpedoes, he felt, would be plenty for the leading ship.

Nine minutes after the first sighting: "Fire one!"

One . . . three . . . seven . . . eight: "Fire two!"

Thus in jig time two fish were speeding toward the first AK.

Even as the fish left the tubes, Hydeman was getting a quick set-up on the No. 2 AK and the TDC operator was grinding away furiously to get gyro angles set on the next three torpedoes. On the gyro angle depends the direction of the torpedo run when it leaves the tube. Hence, it means the difference between a hit and a miss.

The situation was not too good because large gyro angles had to be used, and to make matters worse, No. 1 torpedo crashed into the first AK before the torpedoes aimed at the second were launched. Their intended target meanwhile got her helm hard over, and a thick column of sooty smoke poured out of her stacks as the black gang in her furnace room poured on the coal. One torpedo explosion was heard from this second salvo, but the damage could not be observed.

A periscope sneak-peek and Earl, always a realist, bade No. 3 a regretful farewell. Out of range. But No. 1 needed his attention. It was now north of the *Sea Dog* and sinking fast. The ship's stern was under and some of the crew were scrambling into a lifeboat from the amidships island just abaft the bridge which, as Earl watched, reached the water level.

So far so good for No. 1. But what about No. 2? . . . Just then Hydeman spotted a single-engine plane approaching from behind the sinking freighter.

Holy smoke! This could be very bad indeed. Earl knew that his approach on the AK's must have brought him into pretty shallow water and to be caught there by a plane could be fatal, even if the fly-boy carried only a couple of depth charges. A thin water blanket is neither protection against observation nor cover under which to evade the deadly "ash cans."

So far as Hydeman was concerned, the scene with the three targets was shot and the show was over. It was time to strike the set and get to hell-and-gone away from the locale. In this business, one war-bird in the sky usually means more coming out of the bush. That single-engined bird could have bombs under its wings. And at the beck and call of the pilot's radio were speedy bombers and fast patrol boats.

Out! Out! Earl needed out. But how?

The *Sea Dog* was pointed toward the beach on an 060 heading. The skipper took a quick range on the sinking AK. About four hundred yards. Enough room? No! What with the northerly current and the decreasing depth within the distances involved, he would not be able to turn in the direction of No. 1 for the *Sea Dog*'s get-a-way. There were no selective exits. No choice but Hobson's—a turn to the right. So ordered.

Next, Hydeman directed that his QB listening head be rigged in. Simultaneously he called for a sounding and ordered the *Sea Dog* taken down to 150 feet. He based this decision on the forty-five-fathom sounding taken early in his approach, with allowance made for having entered more shallow water in nearing the beach in his turns toward the targets—150 feet should still be okay.

That was it. Not 149.9 feet or 150.1 feet—but 150 feet on the nose. Still, as before mentioned, there are noses and noses. Some long. Some short. But unfortunately Neptune had not been consulted about noses at this particular spot off the island of Hokkaido.

Before the QB listening device could be rigged in—before a new sounding could be obtained—the *Sea Dog*'s descent came to a sudden and somewhat jarring stop. And its depth gauges read neither forty-five fathoms nor 150 feet. They registered a heart-stopping 116 feet with the ship resting on the very floor of the sea on an 065 course still headed for the beach.

Overhead an enemy airplane. All around, enemy shipping.

"If we were fly-boys, they would bawl us out for not letting the wheels down," spoofed Hydeman who, among other things, had the magic formula for producing a laugh when it was most needed.

The *Sea Dog* was as far down as it could go without a bulldozer bow. But the cool head and quick thinking that have always been Hydeman's outstanding characteristics did not fail him this time. In addition, he had a set of superior operators on the diving controls. One of Hydeman's practices was not to permit his plane operators to become specialists in operating either the bow planes or the stern planes. They had to be equally expert in both operations, and that interchange-ability stood the *Sea Dog* in good stead that morning.

Investigation revealed that the ship was grounded very lightly forward. For some fifteen minutes the vessel's fate rested in the able hands of the Diving Officer and his skilled planesmen. As a team they did a splendid job of backing the *Sea Dog* off and swinging her stern southward. When at long last she was free of the bottom and heading north, there was ample room for turning left to clear the beach.

During those fifteen minutes, there had been bitter apprehensions beneath the outward calm of the crew members. First, would the hostile plane drop its eggs? And with what depth set on the exploders? Next, how long would it be before other planes would show up with their high explosive loads? How long before patrol boats would start their unrelenting pinging search?

How long?

At the outset, a few of the men aboard the sub would not have given a plugged nickel for their chances of survival. They had been caught red-handed trying to raid the henhouse and were in a mighty ticklish situation. But Hydeman was not a man to be stampeded into hasty action. From a navigational standpoint, there was nothing alarming in the situation. The *Sea Dog* could always be lightened and gotten off the bottom. The tricky part was to get off the bottom and out to deep water without coming to the surface or wrecking the sub's propellers.

But then as time slipped by—five minutes, ten, fifteen; half an hour, an hour—hope took the place of stolid resignation. In his log Earl Hydeman wrote: "Surprisingly, there was no attack. None the less, we went deep for a while and opened out to gather our wits and survey the damage which, fortunately, consisted only of a smashed QB head and a bent shaft."

In retrospect, Earl—always judicial and analytical—observed: "The whole attack was misdirected by a greedy desire to empty all the bow tubes at three beautiful unescorted AK's. This merely resulted in a hurried attack and firing at too short a range for effective multiple fire. By the time we were ready for action again, there were several patrol craft pinging up and down the coast. And a DE showed up in the late morning for a thorough search of the area, and the search lasted all day."

My own reaction to Earl's observation is that he takes too much the short end of it. The submarine is a weapon of swift aggression—a flashing foil rather than a studious sabre. When you are beating the bushes it is natural to expect that you may stumble among the roots. One of my own bosses back in the days when I was a youngster in submarines forgave one of my operational casualties with the observation: "Well, you can't make an omelette without breaking a few eggshells."

When the expected counterattack failed to develop—and all hands, somewhat fatigued following the day's long and heavy pressures, needed rest and relaxation—Hydeman took his ship to 150 feet. As he turned the watch over to Lt. James P. Lynch, his exec, Earl's quickly scanning, keenly observant eyes made a running check of the various controls and indicators in the conning tower and the control room. All the boys were on their toes and the depth gauges read 150 feet. Not 149.9. Nor 150.1—but 150. Right on the nose.

Things were shipshape and Bristol-fashion aboard the *Sea Dog* and presently its skipper slept the sweet slumbers of those who are "on the nose."

As the fates of war would have it, this June 19 attack—which caused the scratching of one AK and might have resulted in more but for the sudden and untimely appearance of a scouting plane—turned out to be the *Sea Dog*'s last opportunity to line up an enemy ship on her periscope crosswires. In ten days of operation, the Hepcats had worked with such a will and to such good effect that the enemy had locked the henhouse doors tight. No ships were moving with the exception of destroyers and patrol boats sent out to hunt and sink the subs that had raised such havoc in the Sea of Japan and caused nationwide consternation throughout the empire of the Son of Heaven. Japanese newspapers, Japanese radio, and Japanese gossip brimmed over with official and semi-official explanations of what was going on in the nation's private ocean. Among these frantic explanations and face-

savings were reports to the effect that submarines had been
"smuggled into the Sea of Japan." How we were supposed to
have done that smuggling was not explained. Probably with
parachutes!

Intermingled with stupid explanations of what had
happened and how were not-so-stupid threats and promises
of putting a stop to the activities of the invaders. With the
best they had, which unfortunately for them was not much—
because their losses had been heavy and their ability to make
replacements was nearly exhausted—the Japanese set out on
an air and seaborne cleanup campaign. At the same time, it
seemed that only the most essential shipments were made
and then only in bottoms which already had one foot in the
maritime graveyard through sheer decrepitude. Most of the
traffic now moved at night, but without running lights and
with lookouts and escorts.

Thus the *Sea Dog* reaped its initial rich harvest during
the first two weeks after it rounded the northern end of Sado
Island—about dawn on June 9, M-Day—and moved inside
Ryozu Wan to have a look at the harbor at the eastern bulge
of the bay. After having conducted a submerged inspection of
the port of Ryozu, and found nothing there, the *Sea Dog*
headed northeast at 1455 and eventually prepared to surface
ten miles off Sado Island's Hime Saki Light which, like others
of its kind along this supposedly safe coast of Japan, was
burning brightly.

How military leaders, who had the deceit to plan the
wiping out of Pearl Harbor while they conducted diplomatic
peace negotiations in Washington, could be so childishly
trusting as to leave all the lights turned on at the terminal
points of their trans-Japan Sea life lines, was more than
Hydeman and his companions in arms could figure out.

At 2000—well after sunset on June 9—just as Hydeman
was about to give the order to surface in the slot, some
twenty miles wide, that runs between the east coast of Sado
and the shores of Honshu, the sonarman reported: "Medium
screws."

The bearing was 040 true. Hydeman swung his periscope and sighted the target almost immediately. It was a
small freighter of about 2500 tons. It ran serenely along on a
steady course of 205 true at eight knots. Her sidelights were
burning brightly. Earl had only to bring his ST night peri-

scope into action, get a good solution with four observations, and swing to a course for a 90 track.

"This is really too easy, like shooting fish in a rain barrel. One torpedo should be plenty," mused Earl.

"Stand by!"

2015-18 "Fire one!"

With a range of only seven hundred yards, the crash of the torpedo hit came almost instantly and the submarine shook with the concussion.

2015-45: "We hit him forward," sang out Earl as excited faces turned toward him. "And look at him dive!"

Down went the target in a neat sixty seconds—good diving time even for a submarine! Scratch one freighter and at a cost of only one torpedo.

2023-00: "Surface." In seconds the *Sea Dog* surfaced into good visibility.

2023-15: "S-J contact. Bearing 060 true . . . 10,000 yards. Wow—oh, boy . . . a saturation pip, Captain," said the radarman.

Earl jumped down the ladder for a peep at the radar screen. A smile as bright as a sunrise lighted his cheerful face. Big stuff. "Bring her round to course 135," shouted Earl. "Keep the ranges coming in. Tell forward torpedo room to make ready all tubes."

From the bridge, at a range of 3400 yards, Hydeman had seen a monster of a ship loom out of the night. She was at least 550 feet long and towered skyward like the wall around the Emperor's Tokyo palace. A tanker of at least 10,500 gross tons in Earl's book of ship silhouettes. In fact a dead ringer for one of the Nissyo Maru class—and a submariner did not get a crack at anything like that too often in those days of increasingly lean hunting.

Problem: How to sink him? This was bound to be a long shot and tankers sometimes take a lot of sinking.

Solution of problem: Three torpedoes from the bow tubes. Spread, two hundred feet between torpedoes. Set torpedo depth, six feet. Interval, eight seconds. Range at firing, 2600 yards.

2044: "Commence firing."

2045-38: One hit aft. Two misses.

The *Sea Dog* pulled away from the target and watched it for a while. Huge columns of fire spewed skyward in the after part of the vessel. They were streaked with white steam and black smoke. Invisible figures dashed madly about topside with flashing lights. They looked like gargantuan glowworms flittering in the dark. As Earl looked on, it became evident that the ship's crew had bested the flames. The fires were extinguished. The ship got under way at five knots on reverse course.

2112-40: "Fire five!". . . Missed.

2113-45: "Fire six!" . . . A hit! Forward of amidships.

A beautiful explosion. The foremast toppled. The bow broke off and sank. The stern assumed a steep down angle. It burned brightly for a while. Sank.

Again complete darkness reigned over the sea. That is, but for the continued flashings of Hime Saki Light on Sado Island. The glare of the city lights of Niigata was plainly visible against the sky to the southeastward, with the occasional beam of a searchlight. Earl wondered how soon the Japanese would realize that something which was not according to the books of their honorable ancestors was going on.

The next day produced sightings of freighters that were out of reach or fishing smacks too unimportant this early in the game. Following that, the day of June 11 was too thick with fog to permit the easy pursuit of a 4000-ton AK. From 1307 to 1555 the chase ran its humdrum course. First submerged, until 1335, when the Sea Dog lost its target in a mountain of snow-white fog. The range, eight thousand yards. Shortly after surfacing, the victim was rediscovered and kept in sight at ranges that ran from eleven thousand to fourteen thousand yards.

The hoodoo that had played havoc with the Sea Dog's electronic equipment during the run to Tsushima Strait, and again during the day when the vessel under-ran the Emperor's mine field, was on watch once more this June 11. Time and again the ship's radar would lose its contact at distances beyond thirteen thousand yards. Fortunately the fog would lift now and then and permit visual pursuit. There were moments when Earl wondered why the enemy did not sight the submarine and turn away, because the vessels were in plain sight of each other at distances no greater than fourteen thousand yards. Hydeman could only figure that one of his torpedoes must have the name of the pursued vessel written on it by the hand of Kismet itself. This reassuring suspicion was confirmed at 1510 when a fortunate rain enabled him to turn in to close the track at just the right moment. At 1519 he dove and spent the next half hour closing the track slowly; he came to a good position at 1555 and fired one torpedo at 1280 yards.

1555-43: A big, juicy MOT bull's eye.

Having landed in the Middle Of the Target, this first torpedo needed no follow-up assistance. MOT is submarine marksmanship of the highest order. One fish. One ship. On the nose.

As he watched through his periscope, surrounded by grinning crew members and regaling the talker with what he saw through the eye piece—so that all hands would be kept up to date on happenings—the target broke in two, up-ending both the bow and the stern. The *Sea Dog* resumed its patrol to southward. Two hours later it sighted a destroyer to northwestward and apparently on a southwesterly course. He was pinging on long scale and soon disappeared below the horizon.

Another successful attack was staged during the breakfast hour of June 12 even as the men were congratulating themselves on the good work performed the previous afternoon. The call to battle stations went bonging at 0635.

"All ashore who's going ashore!" shouted one crewman.

"No passengers on this bucket!" gurgled another of the ship's wits as he made a one-gulp job of his third cup of coffee.

Through the periscope, Earl saw four ships well spread out in a rough box formation. They had just rounded Nyudo Saki and were pointed fairly well into shallow waters along the coast between that cape and its near-twin, Henashi Saki. All were medium AK's. After some quickly executed calculations, Earl decided to go for the nearest vessel in the left-hand column. True, he faced a fairly long shot. But Hydeman thought he would chance a three torpedo spread. This because the enemy craft seemed to be on the large side and, in addition, there was at least a fair chance of slamming into the far AK of the four with a remaining torpedo from the spread. Crowding his luck? Maybe.

0822: The *Sea Dog* fired three torpedoes. Spread, 150 feet apart along a 130 port track. Torpedo run, 3200 yards. This was a long chance and the two minute and ten-second interval of waiting seemed interminable to the tense listeners.

0824-10: One hit.

"Lady Luck was sure riding that one," breathed the

TDC operator who realized how little dope his sharpshooting skipper had to go on. Some may call it luck, but to me it was another Hydeman Special. On the nose. MOT stuff. The torpedo landed slightly abaft midships. The target broke in two and sank within two minutes. That torpedo surely did its job. As for the target's three friends, they were headed into even shallower water along the coast in a mad rush for sanctuary against our avenging submarines. But Hydeman let them go; there was nothing else to do. His submerged crawl could never match their terrified dash for safety. To follow them on surface gave too many odds to an enemy with air or sea pursuit within much too easy call.

To some people, thirteen is unlucky or, perversely, lucky. To Hydeman it is just another day in the month when it falls on the thirteenth. Therefore, June 13 had no special significance for Earl. If anything, this particular June 13 was completely unproductive. At least until 2010 when a superstitious person might have concluded that Old Lady Luck had packed up bag and baggage and kissed the *Sea Dog* goodbye.

The vessel had just come to surface after her day-long submerged run when a report came up from the after torpedo room that a loud noise, which sounded like an explosion, had been heard on the starboard side while the ship was surfacing. At the same instant, it became obvious to all hands that the starboard propeller and shaft were making excessive noises and vibrations.

"Our hearts sank into our boots," wrote Hydeman in his Log. "This pretty definitely indicated that the starboard clearing wire—one of those just installed in Guam, running from the starboard propeller guard to the hull just forward of the stern tube bearing—had parted and fouled the starboard screw. This is 1¼-inch steel cable and could really do some damage."

The *Sea Dog*'s skipper rang up "All Stop" so fast that the engine room annunciators quivered. No submarine was allowed to go to sea with a noise level of more than seventy-two decibels, but here was the *Sea Dog*, 2500 miles from home, in enemy waters, with an engine room that sounded like a boiler shop. During the next hour, by cautious testing at various speeds, it was found that the starboard propeller had a fairly loud thump at slow speeds. Also, there was an irregular clanking noise on the hull itself just forward of the propeller.

Undoubtedly the clearing wire was wrapped around the propellor shaft and striking the hull every time the shaft revolved. To operate under such conditions could be just plain suicide if counterattacked by destroyers.

For some strange reason, at high speeds the shaft thump could not be heard on the surface, although the ship vibration seemed to be slightly heavier.

What to do? And . . . how to do it?

All through the ship, sleeping men had come awake and all hands were doing some heavy Monday morning quarter-backing but with a noticeable absence of heavy-handed humor. There are means of handling breakdowns anywhere within the hull of a submarine, but there are very few ways of making repairs in those portions of the ship that are outside the hull and below the water line.

Presently, by a process of elimination of possible causes of breakdown, it was decided that the starboard clearing wire and that alone could be at the bottom of the trouble.

While the search for the cause of the explosive noise was at its peak, a message came in from the *Crevalle* reporting its sinkings of targets, its escape from three DD's off Henashi Saki, the gunning of two sampans that morning, and the blankety-blank absence of a blankety-blank target since Monday. The *Crevalle* pleaded to be sent where there were more targets. On the same pack frequency came one from the *Spadefish* reporting four AK's and four sampans sunk and prospects of more if she could remain four more days in the section she then occupied.

The answers were Yes! and No!

At midnight, having pulled clear of the coast, the *Sea Dog* stopped and lay to. While under way, Hydeman had completed preparations for shallow water diving and for various methods of removing or securing the parted mine clearing cable. The project of shallow water diving—in the dark hours of midnight, almost under the shadow of a hostile coast, and in a sea that ran high and could at any moment produce one or more enemy searchers—was made possible through the ready willingness of several men who volunteered to undertake the job. From this group of volunteers, Captain Hydeman selected Lt. Edward W. Duckworth and Andy

Dell, Chief of the Boat, because of prior experience as skindivers. Dell was a barnacled veteran with nine war patrols under his belt; Duckworth a youngster with but one previous combat venture to cut his battle-teeth on.

In the absence of any other equipment, the job had to be done by means of a shallow water diving outfit. But all attempts to reach and trim off the dangerously dangling ends of the starboard clearing wire were unsuccessful because the rubber face mask proved useless. As soon as the diver went under the surface and headed for the keel, sea water would leak in around the face mask and fill it with water. For more than an hour—most of which Duckworth and Dell spent in icy water that often threatened to smash them against the *Sea Dog*'s hull—the fruitless attempts to reach the damage were continued.

Then Hydeman, feeling that he had courted fate long enough by keeping the *Sea Dog* in a terribly exposed position, gave up. With two men over the side and others tending them way aft on the waveswept deck, the *Sea Dog* was a sitting duck for a surprise attack. In case of trouble, Hydeman would have his hands full getting his people down the hatch and his ship under water. Enough was enough. At 0140, forced to admit failure, the *Sea Dog* got under way.

In a situation like that, the scuttlebut aboard a ship contains a high percentage of guessing that can reach unbelievable absurdities. The *Sea Dog* was no exception; all hands began to speculate on the ship's next move.

Among the young bloods and the lighthearted adventurers, there were probably some wishful thinkers who concluded that the *Sea Dog* would have to beat it for Vladivostok. For her the war was over. With thoughts centered on investigation of vodka and buxom Russian girls they could not see how internment for the duration would be such a bad dish.

To the pessimists—and they are ever present—the old *Dog* was dead. She'd never make it anywhere, Vladivostok or home, with that anvil chorus in the engine room. Tomorrow, or next day at latest, a lousy Jap tincan would corner her and force her to the surface with ash cans; the skipper would open the sea valves and set off the built-in demolition charges to wreck her secret equipment. And the crew, what might be left of it, would climb aboard rafts that would lead to a Japanese prison camp unless their captors decided to perforate their rafts with bullets—as had been done.

To some of the older men who had faced tough situations before, the *Sea Dog* was far from being a dead dog, but Operation Barney was finished for her. The Old Man would radio the next senior Hellcat skipper to take charge and then high-tail it for deep water and up to La Perouse. There he'd trail some Russky ship, eastbound, and once through the mine fields pour on the coal for Gooneyville.

The old scuttlebut is a venerated institution—and a valuable one. After all, it furnishes a relief valve and it provides, without benefit of formally worded paragraphs, an estimate of the situation over which the skipper and the exec might spend hours. All this brew of *Sea Dog* scuttlebut lacked to make it effective was the authority that makes the decisions. That rested with the Captain, and I doubt that any of this scuttlebut ever reached Hydeman. Also, I doubt that the thought of giving up the *Sea Dog*'s role in Operation Barney ever entered Hydeman's head. In his opinion the *Sea Dog* could complete its mission. It would roll out of La Perouse Strait with the other Hellcats after the sunset hour on Sonar Day. Not before it. Not after it. But on the nose.

As things turned out, the skipper's way of thinking was on the right course. The scuttlebut, as is usually the case, was off the beam. Once the *Sea Dog* was under way, it was immediately noted that the starboard shaft thump occurred only for short periods at low speeds. Also, performance at high speeds—up to eighteen knots—was quite satisfactory.

"But," mused Hydeman in solitary conference with himself, "it could be that the cable ends are still dangling loose. If that is so, then they could cause a lot of further trouble."

Meanwhile the *Sea Dog* set course to southwestward for day surface patrol across western approaches to Akita, Sakata, and Niigata. . . . Sufficient to each day were the evils thereof.

By the time Operation Barney ended, the *Sea Dog* had sent six enemy vessels, with a total of 29,500 tons, to the junkyard of dead ships where Davey Jones keeps his locker. Most important of these was the 10,500-ton Nissyo Maru type scuttled by Hydeman in his second and third attacks.

In his report on the *Sea Dog*'s patrol, Captain Hydeman declared that all his officers and leading petty officers displayed great degrees of skill, resourcefulness, and tenacity: "The material difficulties encountered were quite troublesome, enroute to and in the area, and the strain imposed by the naturally difficult entrance and exit to the area had noticeable effects, especially on the officers. Efficiency of the personnel was always high, even after continuous days and nights of repairing machinery and radar gear, looking for oil leaks, working with a suspected fouled propeller, evading patrol craft, and making approaches.

"Of the many officers and men who contributed very substantially, it is desired to mention the two whose work was most outstanding: Lieutenant James P. Lynch, USN, the executive officer, whose leadership qualities, ability as assistant approach officer, and good old Irish pugnacity were an inspiration to the ship, and Lieutenant Kelly B. Reed, (DE) USNR, whose work as torpedo officer and TDC operator was largely responsible for putting a few Jap ships where they belong. When these two got their heads together over the TDC, the Japs didn't have a chance."

21

CREVALLE DEFIES ASH CANS

It had been a dull forenoon aboard the *Crevalle*. Earlier in the morning, Steiny had set a patrol course that originated two and a half miles off Ranutappe Saki and ended two miles off the cape called Suneko Saki. All told, this beat was about fifty miles long and skirted the very edge of the Hundred Fathom Curve. That is the line where shelving, gray-green, shallow-bottom coast waters change into the rich blue of the real deep-water sea. And if any men have a yen for waters that run deep, they are your submarine sailors in wartime. Where there is depth, there is safety. That is, relatively speaking.

Among the *Crevalle*'s most appreciated treasures on this particular mission was a slim, tall, athletic-looking Englishman with a pleasantly modulated British accent. His brown hair brushed to mirror smoothness over his high unfurrowed brow, he was the only supercargo among the Hellcats, namely Lieutenant Commander Barclay Lakin, Royal Navy. Lakin was the only self-invited guest whose application for passage with Operation Barney—my own included—had been granted by the higher powers. He was a real submariner with many Mediterranean patrols to his credit, which had gained for him, among other decorations, the highly prized DSO. Lakin had come to us as a liaison officer in 1944 to replace the redoubtable Comdr. Tony Miers, R.N., who wore the Victoria Cross, also won in Mediterranean patrols. Barclay was an able, jolly, easy-to-get-along-with, but keen-eyed type, who was at home and made friends wherever he hung his hat. He was aboard the *Crevalle* simply because Steiny had won him in a High Spade game participated in by all the Hellcat skippers, every one of whom was anxious to have Lakin aboard his own particular vessel.

While a guest of the ship, Lakin made himself usefully available whenever possible. He had established his "office"—a folding campstool—in a corner of the *Crevalle's* conning tower near the plotting table.

As this June 14 day grew older, the routine of the submerged vessel ran its normal course. Watches were changed at four-hour intervals. At 1440 the observer at the scope sang out: "Masts bearing zero-one-five!"

At the same instant the operator at the hydrophones reported: "Pingings, not too close on same bearing."

The ship's talker, at his ship-wide microphone, repeated the news. As such, it did not set the *Crevalle* afire with sparks of agitation. Five minutes clicked by. Then the officer at the scope: "Merchant ship. Bearing one-three-zero!"

Seven minutes, and the *Crevalle* speeded to five knots in order to close the target. But at 1452, the picture and the situation changed: "Three AK's heading south hugging the coast," was the news from the periscope. "Wait a minute!" —as the Exec swung his periscope around the full circle of the horizon—"Here are two escorts on our starboard bow, heading north. We are between the AK's and the tincans."

Through the loudspeaker in his cabin, Steiny—who had been putting in some well-earned sack time—heard the report. By telephone he spoke to Lt. G. F. Morin, USNR, his exec, in the conning tower one deck above him: "Battle stations. Submerged. Torpedo."

A split second later, the *Crevalle's* interior reverberated to the tuneful but always exciting call of the general alarm: "Bong, Bong, Bong, Bong. . . ."

With well-rehearsed and smooth speed, all hands went

to their assigned stations. "Battle stations. Submerged. Torpedo," repeated the ship's talker, a pharmacist's mate. He had been selected for that job because of his ready ad-libs, resonant voice, and clarity of speech.

Silently or exchanging soft-voiced banter, men filled the various combat posts—singly or in groups. Men who had been asleep got into their clothes at top speed. The eternal acey-deucy, pinochle, and cribbage games in the messroom were broken up. Half-written letters were stuffed back into lockers and, in the galley, the cooks secured their gear against the possibility of crashing on steep dives. Or they checked to see that the supply of coffee in the big coffee maker was adequate.

A submarine is two things. It is, secondarily, a ship that draws its motive power from four powerful diesel engines while on surface and from 240 huge electric storage battery cells when submerged. Primarily it is a highly mobile and flexible weapon that aims and discharges missiles in the form of torpedoes with 750-pound, high-explosive war heads. The call for battle stations brought that primary purpose of the *Crevalle* into prominent focus.

In the forward and after torpedo rooms, chief torpedomen and their crews centered their attention upon the nests of torpedo tubes whose gleaming bronze breech doors were the centerpieces for a seemingly endless array of polished valve wheels and vent levers which surrounded them. The torpedo tubes were arranged in two tiers—six tubes in the forward, four in the after torpedo room. Between these tiers was a narrow working space at the far end of which sat a torpedoman hunched over the repeater from the TDC in the conning tower, by means of whose data he was able to keep the steering gyros of all his torpedoes continuously aimed at the target. As the crew took their battle stations that June afternoon off the island of Hokkaido, all tubes were already loaded but not ready to fire. Those grimly final preparations awaited orders from the conning tower. In the racks along the sides of the torpedo room lay the sleek, bright steel bodies of reload torpedoes which, after the first salvo had been fired, would, with the aid of tackles and a brief ten minutes of deceptively frantic effort by a sweating crew of well-trained hands, be loaded into the maws of the gaping tube doors.

Under the vigilant eye of the chief torpedomen in charge, the forward and after impulse tanks were brought up to an air pressure of four hundred pounds, the amount required to start the three-thousand-pound torpedo on its oceanic way; gyro setting spindles, by which the course of the torpedo is directed, were engaged in their sockets. Men stood by to flood the torpedo tubes with water from the WRT (Water Round Torpedo) tanks, after which the tube outer doors would be opened and the torpedoes would be ready for their missions of death and destruction.

All awaited the Captain's order: "Make ready all tubes" or "Make ready such and such tubes." When that message came, the final steps would be taken, the torpedo room talker would report "Torpedo room ready" to the conning tower, and the "ready" light switch would be turned on. After that the crews relaxed except for two torpedomen who stood by the hand firing valves in the event that the electric firing circuit from the conning tower might fail.

The ready switch, which I have mentioned, lights a green light in the torpedo firing panel in the conning tower. There are ten such lights on that panel, one for each torpedo tube. When a tube is fired or not ready, the light shows red; when the tubes are ready, the lights are green. The firing panel is presided over by a carefully selected, non-trigger-happy man who, at the attack officer's command, presses buttons to fire all or a designated number of tubes. In his left hand he holds a stop watch with which to space his shots a certain number of seconds so that the explosion of one torpedo will not detonate the one immediately following it.

Torpedo crews have a traditional custom of dedicating each torpedo fired to some particular person. Usually they write on the war head the names of their wives or best girls. Sometimes they would write "Merry Christmas to Hirohito," or "This one is for you, Mr. Tojo." In a historic attack when *Sealion II* sank the battleship *Kongo*, four of the torpedoes bore the names of the four men killed by Japanese bombs at Cavite on December 8, 1941, when the first *Sealion* was destroyed.

The air of business as usual that pervaded the conning tower and the control room had vanished by the time Skipper Steinmetz had shot through the hatch from the control room to assume his battle role—that of Attack Officer. Comdr. Lakin was right at his heels.

"What's the situation, George?" he demanded of Morin.

"Looked good at first, sir. Three AK's are about to cross

our stern, but now we've got two damned tincans on the
starboard bow," answered the exec as he yielded his position
at the attack periscope to the Old Man. Eyes and ears sharp
as razors, the lad at the periscope button was ready to shoot
the instrument up to the surface at the lifting of an eyebrow.
In making periscope observations, every second counts. A
peek that consumes ten seconds has reached the saturation
point. Six seconds is better. Periscopes, carefully camouflaged
though they are, especially if the sun catches the lens at the
right angle, are more easily spotted than most people believe.

"Up periscope," grinned Steiny. He squatted on the
deck and as the eyepiece rose above the well, he extended
the training handles and followed the scope up till it broke
water, where, by a gesture to the lad at the controller, he
stopped its ascent. Steiny swung quickly to the AK's on the
starboard quarter. Morin was squatting on the deck, eyes
glued to the bearing circle on the periscope sleeve.

"Bearing, mark," sang out Steiny.

"One-three-five," answered the exec.

"Range, mark!"

"Three-one-double zero," reported Morin.

"Down periscope. Angle on the bow, twenty starboard."

Range, bearing, and angle on the bow were repeated by
the TDC officer as he fed them into his dials, and were
recorded by the plotters on their chart.

Before the scope was half-way down, the Captain ordered: "Up periscope." As before, he seized the handles and
swung the scope swiftly to the starboard bow, centering on
the leading destroyer.

"Bearing, mark!"

"Zero-two-zero."

"Range, mark!"

"Two-zero-double zero."

"Down periscope. Angle on the bow, fifty starboard,"
said the skipper quietly. Then, turning toward the talker,
continued, "Make ready all tubes."

"Make ready all tubes," bawled the talker into his mike.
This was getting hot.

"It's a tricky set-up," said Steiny. "We'll fire first with the
stern tubes at the two leading AK's and hold our bow tubes
for the tincans in case they pass within range."

Then, for the benefit not only of the operating personnel
in the tightly crammed little conning tower, but so that all

aboard the ship might know what was going on by way of the talker, the Captain explained: "Those two escort vessels look like Matsu Class destroyers. They have two widely separated smoke stacks with white bands painted around them. And guns. Plenty of guns."

Rubbing his square, determined chin briefly with the broad thumb of his left hand, Steiny leaned over the plotting table and briefly studied the situation. Grinning into the sparkling eyes of Barclay Lakin, he said, "Yeah, Limey, we might get a sample of each. Right?"

"Quite all right," laughed back Lakin. "Let's have a go at it."

The smiling silence of the enthusiastic conning tower group signified their approval.

But, alas, even a Matsu Class destroyer can disrupt the plans of the Captain of one of Uncle Sam's submarines. It so happened that, as he spoke, the two unsuspecting DD's had worked to the northward of the *Crevalle* and cut in so that they were heading between it and the trio of equally unsuspecting freighters.

1519-03: "Up periscope. . . . Damn," ejaculated Steiny as he squinted through the eye piece.

1519-06: "Down periscope. . . . Damn their eyes, they are lousing the whole thing up," growled the Skipper with bitter and personal resentment toward the pilots of his targets. "Those stinking escorts have reversed course and will pass between us and the AK's. They will be right on top of us just about the time we fire the stern tubes." A brief pause. Then, with quick and resolute decision: "We will have to attack the escorts first and tackle the others later."

1522-31: "Up periscope."

With quick, smooth, well-practiced speed, ranges and angles were fed into the TDC and to the plotting team.

1522-34: "Down periscope. . . . The nearest DD is fairly close," remarked Steiny. "So close that the bands around the stacks show a dirty gray rather than white."

From the periscope he cast a quick glance on the firing panel on the port side of the tower. He saw the ten large silver-dollar sized firing buttons. All ten lights were green. "That nearest escort has made a 180-degree swing," continued the Captain. "As of now he should present a five-degree starboard angle. Not much. But our main chance." For the length of a flash, he stood in intense concentration. "Get

ready for a down-the-throat shot. Stand by forward," he
shouted. "Stand by one, two, and three. Steady on course
275," he added.

Rapidly the final set-up was ground into the TDC.
Swiftly the plotting officer projected the courses of the *Crevalle* and its target. Human and mechanical computers had
done their best with the hurried information the Captain had
fed to them. From here on in it was up to the torpedoes.

The firing data was: Torpedo runs, about 1200 yards;
track angle, 12 starboard; gyros, 009; depth setting, 4 feet;
torpedoes, three MK 18-2 electric; torpedo spread, ¼ left-0-¼
right; firing intervals, 10 seconds.

To intertwine these strands into a single thread, Steiny
snapped hasty observations through his periscope. The sound
men did not have to report pings of the DD's sonar gear—
those unpleasant sounds could be heard through the hull but
they did not seem to be steadied on the submarine. This was
encouraging. The sound of fast screws became louder and
louder. This because the distance to the nearest destroyer
had now narrowed down to less than fifteen hundred yards.
The action was fast and thinking likewise but not too fast for
Steinmetz to realize more and more keenly the extremely
ticklish position in which he stood. If a pop-eyed Jap lookout
spotted that periscope or if a solid echo came back to an
enemy sonarman, there lay the *Crevalle*, squarely in the path
of those onrushing destroyers, a sitting duck target for their
depth charges with no time left to change course or go deep.

The youthful Captain, in whose hands rested sole responsibility for the lives of four-score men, flashed a prayer to
the Lord: "O blessed J-Factor, be with us now."

Seconds dragged like hours. The TDC showed the range
still too great. Steiny could not wait any longer.

1525-10: "Up, periscope. . . . Close, ugly, and big as a
house—but who's afraid of the big Jap wolf," chuckled Steiny
partly to himself.

1525-13: "Down periscope."

At a moment like that, even the ablest and most experienced submarine captain may be permitted to whistle up his
courage in the dark recesses of loneliness that surrounds a
submarine commander at the moment of decision. It is the
loneliest spot on earth. So lonely that one would welcome the
company of even a pirate's ghost. Down-the-throat—the most
difficult shot in the bag. A small sub with a towering destroy-

er bearing down on it. David and Goliath. As seen through the periscope, the onrushing warship—even though it was making only a comfortable eleven knots—loomed over the sea like a giant. And close. But that nearness was deceptive. For a semi-sure shot, the gap between the man-o'-war and the *Crevalle* was still too great. After all, what was range? Nothing but distance. Yards of air and yards of water—distance steadily shrinking with death riding high in between.

Steiny's prayer was that he next look would show the target on a steady course not pointed directly at the *Crevalle*.

1525-51: "Up periscope."

Less than thirteen hundred yards, but still not close enough. The DD had steadied on a course about five degrees to the right of the sub—thank God for that! That target sure looked big!

1525-54: "Down periscope."

A swift glance around the tower, the tense faces showing white in the semi-darkness. Well! Here goes!

"Fire one!" sang out Steiny.

At the firing panel the man on duty smacked the firing button solidly with the palm of his right hand. In his left, with his thumb, he set the timing sweep of a stop watch going. On the instant he hit the firing button the light switched from green to red. Down in the forward torpedo room, the tube crew heard the order repeated by the talker. Torpedomen stood ready to slam the hand firing key if the firing circuit from the conning tower should fail to function. But it did function. Their ears caught the powerful thud of air rushing into the tube and the submarine quivered slightly as the departing fish sped out through the muzzle door.

"Number one fired," shouted the chief torpedoman.

"Number one fired," repeated the talker.

The man at the firing panel had his eyes glued on the second sweep of the stop watch in his left palm. Five— seven—nine—

"Ten seconds," he shouted.

"Fire two!" ordered the skipper. And the fish in Number Two Tube was on its brief swim to potential glory.

"Ten seconds," came the third and last call.

"Fire three!"

Again lights flashed and air thudded into the tube as the third torpedo headed for its goal.

Steiny switched his attention to the sonar-man whose

instrument was following the sound set up in the sea by the tiny propellers that speeded the deadly war head toward its target at fifty-one miles per hour. The technician, listening intently, glanced up with a grin: "Yes, sir, Captain; hot, straight, and normal."

Three heavenly words all skippers and torpedomen love to hear. They mean that their fish are behaving as good torpedoes should. Steiny nodded and shifted his attention to getting out of the destroyer's way. Any second now all kinds of hell would be apt to break loose. Even if his torpedoes blew the first destroyer to smithereens, there was still another one to reckon with.

"Swing left," he directed. "Steady on course 270. Take her down fast. Catch her at three hundred. Rig for depth charge; rig for silent running. Let's go while the going's good. This won't last long."

With the graceful speed of a shark the *Crevalle* turned her snout westward. At the same time, she stuck her nose down till things started sliding around on the galley shelves. Her trip to extreme depth was made in just about the time it takes an express elevator to drop from top to bottom of a thirty-story building. The men leaned back to keep their balance and steadied loose gear that threatened to slide.

But all these adjustments were automatic. Every man's thoughts were centered on the three torpedoes that had just left the *Crevalle's* forward tubes. Would they hit? Would they eliminate one pursuer from the murderous counterattack that was bound to follow?

The sonar operator hunched over his instrument: Torpedo propeller sounds were dimming, but the drumbeat of destroyer screws was thunderous overhead.

As seconds lengthened into one minute, every man aboard the *Crevalle* knew that the attack had failed. In a torpedo attack, where ears await the blast of 750 pounds of high explosive war head, no news is bad news. The longer the lapse between firing and blasting, over a given distance, the surer the submarine is of failure.

They also serve who only stand and sweat as they wait to catch a gruesome kind of hell! The Japs must have seen some of those shallow-running torpedoes, and if they had not, there would be the end-of-run explosions to alert them.

Meanwhile the output of her giant batteries pushed the *Crevalle* deep into blue water while, throughout the ship, all sound-producing gear and activities were brought to a stop. This so that the keen ears of hydrophones could not pick up a single sound of moving parts or a whisper of propellers that could bring sudden death and disaster to the *Crevalle*.

The sonar-man with ears glued to his headphones, keeping close track of the enemy propellers, listened for the after-effects of the three torpedoes. At 1532, seven eternal minutes after it was fired, came the boom of the first fish. But instead of the lusty whang of a war head socking into steel, it was the mournful hollow whoom of an end-of-run explosion. All noise but no score. A miss. Thirty seconds later came the second torpedo. Same thing. A miss. The third torpedo was never heard from.

But the absence of its whoom was compensated for at 1537 when the Japs dropped the first four of the cloudburst of depth charges that was to follow. Retaliation usually comes quickly in A/S warfare, but this pair of escorts was evidently of the home guards or had served too long in these waters where live targets had heretofore not been available for training.

Another factor in the *Crevalle*'s favor was the sharp eight-degree jog in the temperature curve of the sea water, as revealed by the bathythermograph, through which she had passed in her headlong dive. Those sharp jogs, we had learned, always disconcerted the pursuers because they deflected the pings of the supersonic echo-ranging gear and thereby gave our enemies false information.

As Steiny and his crew followed the sound of enemy propellers and awaited the downpour, the pinging, pinging, pinging of the searchers could be heard throughout the ship. Everything had been done to protect the *Crevalle* that could be done. The rest was in the hands of the gods. To take his mind off those grim, gray shapes racing above him and seeking to destroy him, Steiny engaged in snatches of conversation with Lakin who started the ball rolling by asking what the skipper thought had happened to his attack.

"Your guess is as good as mine," said Steiny. "What do you think happened?"

"Could be that one of the torpedoes broached in time for the Japs to see it and change course," ventured Lakin.

"Yes," observed Lt. Morin, "or the DD heard the fish coming."

"No," said the skipper, "there was hardly time for

maneuvering with less than a minute to work in. With that tincan making eleven and the fish making forty-six the combined speed of approach was a terrific fifty-seven knots (sixty-five miles per hour). Either our estimate of his speed was badly off or he made a radical change of course just before we fired."

Steiny took time out to take a couple of dry pulls on his unlit pipe and continued: "It might have been better if I had not fired when I did. That's the trouble with those damn down-the-throat shots. That high, sharp bow of a destroyer looms like the blade of a guillotine coming down to chop your head off. Mush Morton had the right idea."

"And that was?" asked Lakin.

"He let his exec—Dick O'Kane, it was—waltz around with the periscope. That left him free to evaluate the situation coldly and only on data from the plotting board and the TDC—no razor-sharp bows to cut into his judgment.

"The average run of these three torpedoes was about twelve hundred yards. And that was much too much. In fact, seven hundred yards in recommended for this type of shot."

"That's easy to say when you are not aboard a submarine with a destroyer bearing down on you at express-train speed," offered Lakin.

"Guess you've got something there," agreed Steiny. "He looked awfully big and I wanted to shoot and get off his track. I believe now that if I had held fire, he would have gone by and we might have been able to get a crack at the last AK without the DD's knowing we were there until they heard the torpedo explosions. I reckon my ingrowing hate of Jap tincans was my undoing."

"Well, don't let it worry you too much," said Lakin. "You have still a high batting average, as you Yankees say." He laughed and extemporized with appropriate motions: "The sub that shoots and dives away will rise to shoot some other day."

"Quite the poet, aren't you, Old Limey," spoofed Steiny just as the first four Jap depth charges threatened to tear the seas apart.

"Oh, you haven't heard anything yet, old boy. You know, I am addicted to poetry. And there may be more."

At that moment—one minute after the first four depth bombs exploded—came six really big ones.

"More what?' asked Steinmetz. "Poetry or depth charges?"

"Both, I venture to say," replied Lakin with a chuckle and retired to his "office," the campstool in the starboard after corner of the conning tower. There he pulled forth a pencil, a notebook, and a package of cigarettes. "What are the smoking rules?" he asked.

"One cigarette on the hour. As you know, the conning tower is the stuffiest part of the ship." Which is true—a small space crowded by a dozen men, all of whom must breathe air from the same air-conditioner.

At the outset, the depth charges that exploded all around the ship were not close. In fact, the long count—between the metalic click of the pressure wave and the cr-rrump! of the explosion with its accompanying sibilant swish of water in violent motion through the vessel's superstructure—indicated that they were dropped at a distance that was quite harmless as far as the *Crevalle* was concerned. While these hounds of TNT were not close enough to bite, their barks revealed that they were of block-buster size. They probably weighed some six hundred pounds as against half that weight for the older type of depth charge. The former could be lethal at thirty feet; the latter, at twenty feet.

During the next five hours, the *Crevalle*—except for a few daring periscope glimpses—held her course to seaward, reduced noises to an absolute minimum, and kept her fingers crossed. The first two hours were the worst—a seemingly endless mixture of booms, rushes of tortured waters, and ceaseless echo-ranging pings—the everlasting, inescapable pingings—now close, now far off, but never absent. One thing was fairly certain however: the Japs never really had the *Crevalle* bracketed in their patterns, a J-Factor for which her crew was devoutly thankful.

As the hours went by at the slow pace of the beads of a rosary in the fingers of a praying supplicant, two men were busy writing in the *Crevalle's* conning tower.

Outside, a super-duper depth charge set loose an eruption that shook the submarine so that cork dust from the hull insulation fell to the deck in a fine drizzle.

Wrote Steinmetz:

1539: Condition as previous. One charge. Not close. No damage.

Wrote Lakin:

> *Methought my ear was not far wrong,*
> *When soon I heard the doleful song*
> *Of him who must prognosticate*
> *Upon our miserable fate*
> *Since we've become the powerless dupe*
> *Of Hirohito's killer group.*

Wrote Steinmetz:

1545: Four charges in quick succession. All fifteen charges released up to now were to port and above us according to Depth Charge Direction Indicator.

Wrote Lakin:

> *The killer group! The killer group!*
> *The awful Hunter-Killer group:*
> *O pity us beneath the sea*
> *Too terrified e'en to flee!*

Wrote Steinmetz:

1626: 2 charges, distant. We ran as deeply as we dared—60 rpm gradually working to seaward. We were under an 8° negative layer. Pinging is still in evidence. We have one on each quarter.

Wrote Lakin:

> *The rudder's jammed! Whatever next?*
> *My aunt in Brooklyn will be vexed*
> *To learn her nephew's now become*
> *Dodger of the Rising Sun;*
> *Whose evil electronic eye*
> *Our futile antics can descry.*

Wrote Steinmetz:

1843: Echo ranging getting weaker, both on starboard side, so we changed course to 210°T. Rigged for normal running.

Wrote Lakin:

> *The hunter group! The killer group!*
> *The dreaded team is on the snoop.*
> *O grant us, Neptune, just one layer*
> *In answer to our constant prayer.*

Wrote Steinmetz:
1900: At periscope depth, all clear but pinging still heard over sound gear, one pinger only.

Wrote Lakin:
> *Relentless in their hostile quest,*
> *Myoptic Nips with crafty zest*
> *Are dimly probing undersea*
> *With beams of sonic frequency;*
> *Patiently seeking to locate*
> *The submarine unfortunate.*

Wrote Steinmetz:
1922: Pinging getting louder. Sun has set and it is beginning to get dark.

Wrote Lakin:
> *You skulking group! You vulpine group!*
> *You slinking, stinking, savage troop!*
> *Your victim's safer than you know*
> *Entombed six-hundred feet below!*

Wrote Steinmetz:
1935: DD seen through scope. He bears about 155° rel. and has a large starboard angle.

Wrote Lakin:
> *These slogans made to terrorize,*
> *Are Axis propaganda lies.*
> *The Blitzkrieg is a busted flush;*
> *And Aryan purity is mush;*
> *Kamikazes are only names*
> *For gaudy fools in ancient planes.*

Wrote Steinmetz:
1954: Had been concentrating on pinger, watching his movements in the gathering darkness when sound reported screws at 130° rel. Took a look and just able to make out the other DD. He was not pinging. Eased deep again.

Wrote Lakin:

> *The fumbling group! The bungling group!*
>   *The Emperor's comic circus troop.*
> *If anyone's to hunt and kill,*
>   Crevalle *is the one who will!*

Wrote Steinmetz:
2115: Surfaced and headed toward sea. No radar contacts.

Among the entries of the *Crevalle's* log covering that day's incident of torpedoes, depth charges, and frustration is one that appears under the heading of *"Anti-Submarine,"* the verse which Lakin wrote about sweating it out while the depth charges raise merry hell all around you. The depth charging and pinging came to an end shortly after 2100. Fifteen minutes later Steinmetz surfaced and headed to seaward. There were no radar contacts. There was nothing. Only the big and beautifully empty sea, the big and star-strewn sky. But in the hearts of those aboard the *Crevalle* there were souls brim-full of gratitude because it was good to be alive.

But it is high time to backtrack with the *Crevalle* to M-Day and the hours immediately before sunset on June 9. Troubles with mine-clearing cables had hit the vessel just as it arrived on station at Henashi Saki during the night of June 8. Most of the June 9 morning had been spent putting the bow planes in working order. The cables installed at Guam to guard against snagging the planes on mine cables had fouled on deck cleats, a situation that, as explained elsewhere, could be serious if the planes were jammed while diving. Steinmetz recommended abolishing the mine-clearing cables and rigging in bow planes when in mined waters—which is entirely feasible. In the course of the day, officers on the *Crevalle's* periscope watch sighted several ships, most of them small freighters.

With nightfall came conditions highly favorable to the *Crevalle* and its mission: good visibility, sky overcast, no moon, sea calm.

At 2121, the radar tracking party, stationed earlier in the evening, reported a contact to the northeast at 13,200 yards. On further investigation, the contact turned out to be a

2300-ton freighter of the type called Sugar Charlie Love. Using his stern tubes, Steiny fired Tubes 9 and 10. The run was 2250 yards and both torpedoes were beautiful M O T (Middle of the Target) hits that sent columns of fire and debris high into the night sky.

These two bull's-eye hits, the *Crevalle's* first attack in Operation Barney, showed the Skipper's shooting eye to be right on the beam and were taken as good omens by all hands. The results on June 10 were, however, somewhat mixed. At 0900, the O.O.D. (Officer of the Deck) at the periscope sighted an old-fashioned tug pulling a heavy raft of logs. One torpedo. No hit. The fish broached and the target avoided. About noon on the same day, a Sugar Charlie Love hove into periscope view. Three pickles settled his hash with two hits at 650 yards that rolled the ship over to leave about twenty-five survivors scrambling for the life rafts in the water.

During the small hours of June 11, the *Crevalle* sighted several sailing ships but let them pass as not worth the powder it would take to blow them skyward. Later it ran into an engine-aft AK which, unhappily, saw the torpedo before it found its mark. Its whistle screaming to the high heavens like a stuck pig, the steamer backed away from the missile and made off at boiler-busting speed. The *Crevalle*, on the surface, gave chase and, after gaining position ahead, dived and swung onto a firing course. At fourteen hundred yards, Steiny let go from Tubes 3 and 4. Both torpedoes were hits.

Through his periscope, Steiny had the target in easy sight. As the enemy ship started to turn over, there was a mad scramble to clear a lifeboat.

"The target," he said for the benefit of the talker, "has a forty-degree list. It is now righting itself. But she has much less freeboard than Lloyd's would insure. . . . Here's a ripe one," he snorted. "Although it looks as if the bow section is about to break off at the foremast, some of the crew have opened up with machine guns from the bow, the bridge, and the stern."

"They are a game lot," observed Lakin from his 'office'.

"You can say that again," agreed Steiny. "The shooting is fast and furious, but a periscope is pretty hard to hit at any distance. It is a pretty sight, though! . . . The long, fiery trails of tracer bullets weaving through the night. . . . It's an awful waste of bullets, but they won't need them much longer."

A few minutes later—stern high in the air—the ship nosed into the sea. . . . "One less SCL," wrote Steinmetz in his log.

Five hours after this incident, the *Crevalle* saw the enemy expose his teeth in a grimace that was not a grin. At 0810, warned by constant pingings, Steinmetz remained well wrapped up in his watery blanket. Keeping close watch, he saw first one destroyer escort, then another, and lastly a third put in their appearance. The trio was strung out in a line of bearing about two thousand yards apart. The nearest DE was about eight thousand yards from the *Crevalle*. Concluding that his foes had classified him as an undesirable citizen and decided to wipe him off the books, Steiny headed out from the coast at a depth of two hundred feet and under a sheltering eight-degree layer.

As the pinging faded away, he decided to go north in search of greener pastures. The three DE's, he noted in the log, did not influence his decision. "Not much!" he added as an afterthought.

Shortly before midnight of June 13, Steiny went through Okushiri Kaikyo to comb the waters off Matsuta Saki. The weather was thick with rain squalls and heavy fog. At 0323 and on the surface, he was five miles off his objective waiting for the fog to lift. Just after daylight, and as if halted by the throwing of a switch, the fog bank stopped short and the *Crevalle* found itself in a clear area—visibility: unlimited. Behind the submarine stood the snow-white wall of fog from which it had just emerged. In front of the ship, almost within stone's throw, rode two cargo luggers—ugly little scows but beautiful targets for gunnery practice, the largest seventy-five, the smallest twenty-five tons. But was this the proper moment?

"Left full rudder," snapped the Skipper, "all ahead full. Let's get back into that cotton wool and take stock."

Back in the fog blanket Steiny slowed down and looked the situation over. Those luggers might report him—if they carried radios—but they were tempting targets loaded to the gunwales. Gun crews were standing by, as always when surfaced, right below the gun-hatch ready for immediate action with the *Crevalle*'s five-inch gun and the two quick-firing forty-millimeters mounted on the cigarette deck or forward of the bridge. But—and this was the tickler—a quick view had shown Steiny that the coast was only about three and a half miles away. Close enough for gunfire to be heard ashore—that is, if there were people ashore to hear it. This was a fairly wild and desolate section of the west coast of the home islands, thinly populated and, probably, with inferior lines of communication. By the time the shooting was over and the news got around, the *Crevalle* would be long-gone. Also—and this was important—action on the surface would be a stimulating change to men who for days on end had spent much of their time submerged. If for no other reason, engaging the enemy luggers would be good for morale.

"Ahead standard," ordered Steinmetz. "Battle surface."

Cheers rose up through the open hatches. Gun crews loved to shoot and they were right on their toes. Ammunition was brought up on deck from below by being passed from hand to hand. In less than a minute all three guns were manned. Seconds later they were spraying steel and fire as the *Crevalle* swept out of the fog and found the luggers still in full view. Largest of the two was the nearest, so it bore, momentarily, the full brunt of the fire. On seeing that the smaller sampan was heading for the beach as fast as he could leg it, Steinmetz shifted fire to the would-be escapee and literally tore him apart with shells.

At breakfast a little later that morning, there was an ample supply of new conversation in the mess room and ward room. As the Skipper had thought, the incident had an excellent effect on the *Crevalle*'s morale and broke the monotony of long hours submerged.

No vessels were sighted during the rest of that day by the sub, and Steinmetz concluded that the enemy was holding all shipping in port until he had had a chance to muster forces to meet this submarine war which had so suddenly erupted all over the Sea of Japan. Proof of this new vigilance came the following day, June 14, when the *Crevalle* received her previously described depth charge drubbing from two enemy destroyers. After that incident, the *Crevalle* went north to try to intercept cross-sea traffic between Korea and Tsugaru Kaikyo. In the course of June 15, as he ran submerged during daylight hours, Steinmetz sighted and avoided several destroyers. One of these was painted not the usual gray but yellow-brown with large black splotches. Evidently it was camouflaged to work close to shore so as to blend with the rugged mountain background. Fortunately the *Crevalle* radar was color-blind and therefore not fooled by that sort of trickery.

That evening, near midnight, the sub came dangerously close to stepping into a deadly pitfall. About 2030, it surfaced to head for the joint patrol area designated on the Hepcat schedules. While underway, the *Crevalle* began to pick up radar interference that remained with it off and on throughout the rest of the night. It was the same kind of 10-CM radar that had tricked the *Seahorse* into a vulnerable position a few weeks earlier in the East China Sea. Once again, the belief that it was friendly radar came close to putting an American sub and its crew out of business for keeps.

For a time, Steiny thought that this deadly hocus-pocus was bonafide, a natural conclusion because Hellcat submarines were expected to be in those waters for the Hepcat rendezvous. Just as Steiny was on the point of deciding that the interference came from a nearby Hepcat, the signal changed its quality. It became ragged and took on more and more similarity to the Jap 10-CM obtained on earlier patrols. The friendly mask was dropped and revealed a grinning enemy face. As if he had sighted Beelzebub himself, Steiny slipped beneath the surface and away from the evil interference as rapidly as he could so as not to draw the masquerader down upon the *Sea Dog* and the *Spadefish*.

As his vessel slid into its deep, dark element with almost lightning speed, Steiny could not help but wonder if the *Crevalle*, in making such an express submergence, would ever repeat the tragic performance it staged on the morning of September 11, 1944. While passing north of the Postiljon Islands to enter Makassar Strait, she made a trim dive. At 0624 she surfaced. Fifteen seconds later the ship took a sharp down angle and resubmerged with upper and lower conning tower hatches open. The officer of the Deck, Lt. Howard J. Blind, and Quartermaster W. L. Fritchen were left on the surface as the *Crevalle* went down. The former was lost. Fritchen was rescued.

The ship was making standard speed on the surface and as she went under, her momentum drove her down at a rapidly increasing angle. Water poured into the conning tower and down the hatch to the control room and pump room. The noise of the roaring torrent drowned out all orders and communications. There was strong evidence that as the

Crevalle started down, Lt. Blind sacrificed his life by staying with the hatch until he had unlatched it. At 150 feet the upper hatch seated. Meanwhile the *Crevalle* had taken a 42° down angle and Robert L. Yeager, Machinist's Mate, who was in the crew's space, had the initiative and presence of mind to man the telephone. Being unable to get in communication with any officer and ascertaining that standard speed was still rung up, he ordered "All back full." This action would most quickly check the *Crevalle*'s downward plunge and remove the terrifying angle on the boat. Yeager's action was correct and in giving that one command he probably saved his ship. His experience as battle station stern planesman since the *Crevalle* was commissioned had probably qualified him better than any man aboard to make such a decision.

The *Crevalle* had reached 190 feet before she started up, and with the maximum down angle, water in the control room was above the forward battery door and the pump room was completely flooded. Water in the conning tower was up to the armpits. At 0626 the *Crevalle* popped to the surface backing full. Lookout positions were manned immediately and search commenced for the missing men. Fritchen was soon recovered, but although Blind's head was seen on surfacing, he disappeared while being approached and was never sighted again.

The *Crevalle* remained in the vicinity on the surface the rest of the day. Everything was grounded out in the conning tower, control room, and pump room, including the radio transmitters. A bucket brigade was put to work bailing out the pump room. Meanwhile the *Crevalle* stood by to dive in hand power. Fortunately nothing was sighted and she was able to continue with repairs on the surface. That night the *Crevalle* headed for Darwin, diving by day using hand-controls until clear of the Barrier. Four days after her casualty she passed the *Bonefish* who relayed information of her estimated time of arrival at Darwin.

Information is not available to determine what caused the *Crevalle* to suddenly submerge. Probably she surfaced with vents open and after the escape of the initial blow of air, settled. The rush of water prevented men in the conning tower from pulling the hatch lanyard and presumably it was only after Lt. Blind had unlatched it from topside that the flow of water finally closed it.

The mid-sea meeting of the Hepcats was staged on the

night of June 17 as planned. After exchanging data and swapping experiences and good luck wishes, the three subs parted. The *Crevalle* set course for Oga Hanto where she— soon after arrival—sighted four small vessels that were too far off for action. Four attacks upon several cargo vessels and one destroyer escort on June 18, 19, 20, and 21 were fruitless. Various reasons—from evasive action to unfavorable firing position—were given in the analysis of the *Crevalle*'s report. They were four soul-searing days that gave high hopes and zero results. Time was slipping by. Here it was June 22 and only one more day before the nine Hellcats would meet west of La Perouse Strait and "set course 090" as the expression ran—meaning "head east for home." Who would have the largest bag?

The *Crevalle* had already just about shot her wad. Only two torpedoes—both in the stern tubes—were left out of the twenty-four she had brought along. One attack that Steinmetz had made was so close inshore that his torpedoes, which evidently under-ran the shallow-draft target, exploded on the beach, probably giving the goggle eyed inhabitants the scare of their lives. Those two remaining fish Steiny wanted to save for some special celebration. Off and on during the past few days, an enemy destroyer—now and then in company with

Fubuki Class Destroyer

enemy airplanes and patrol boats—had snooped around him and made a nuisance of itself. Not near enough to cause depth-charge damage, it was nevertheless close enough to be rather annoying. Now, as midnight of June 21-22 approached, this DD seemed to have aggressive ideas again. Heavy screws were heard by Steiny's sonar. And the pingings were back, now close, now far off. But always around.

At 2306, June 21, following radar contact at 12,300 yards, Steiny began tracking the Japanese destroyer. At 0008, June 22, the range was nine thousand yards. The deadly target took no chances on a straight shot. It kept zigging right and left between 060 true and 120 true. Speed, eleven and one-half knots. Being up ahead of the target at that time, Steiny went to battle stations. Submerged. Torpedoes.

"That damned DD," said Steiny softly, "is living on borrowed time."

At 0047, the *Crevalle* finally caught the target steadied down on a left zig. It was another down-the-throat shot— angle on the bow, zero! The last two torpedoes were launched, both from stern tubes and at periscope depth. The enemy's pinging and the sound of his propellers could be heard all over the sub. Range, only one thousand yards.

0047: "Fire Nine!"

0047-10: "Fire Ten!"

"Left full rudder, take her to three hundred feet; flood negative," ordered the Captain.

Seconds piled up in long silent layers as those aboard the *Crevalle* listened for the telltale repercussion of a mortal hit.

0047-42: "First torpedo hit," shouted the sonar man.

Wild cheering throughout the *Crevalle*. Men did jigsteps and pounded each other on the back as they stood before their stations, dancing with joy but with their eyes on their dials.

"All ahead one third," ordered Steiny. "Hold her at her present depth."

A strange silence pervaded the vessel as propeller beats and pingings came to an end. Somewhere outside the submarine, on the surface of the Sea of Japan, those sounds had died with the ship that gave them life. Soon loud clanking noises, as of an old-fashioned anvil, came from the stricken warship's bearing.

0054: A long and enormously loud explosion shuddered through the sea as if the Jap's boilers blew up in concert with the depth charges aboard it. Five minutes later Steiny took a peek from periscope depth. In the darkness he saw the target. It was either lying on its side or it had turned completely over. No lights were showing, just a flat surface with no superstructure in evidence. Ten minutes later the moon went behind a cloud and the *Crevalle* surfaced. When the sub's diesel's were started up, they smoked heavily. this could have given the *Crevalle*'s position away. However, there was no answering gunfire. To Steiny this was additional proof that the enemy ship had rolled over. From past experience, he knew that his never-say-die opponents would fire if they had a gun or a platform to fire from. In the *Crevalle*'s log the sunken enemy destroyer was listed as being of the Yugumo or Fubuki class with the after stack removed.

At 0320 on June 23, Steiny started for the La Perouse rendezvous on the surface. Several hours later, having charged his batteries to the brim, he submerged and prepared to catch up on lost sleep.

"These last few days have been busy," was his understatement in the Log. "After all these misses, this morning's episode served to raise morale about 1000 per cent."

The *Crevalle*'s total sinkings during 2557 miles of cruising in the Sea of Japan were three AK's, one 1500-ton destroyer and two luggers, a total of 8500 tons. Even as the morale aboard Steiny's ship rose 1000 per cent at the time of its departure, so it is safe to say that Japanese morale—because of his visitation—had fallen a similar 1000 per cent by the time the *Crevalle* headed home.

22

SPADEFISH TORPEDOES SCORE

Commander Bill Germershausen leaned across the sprayshield of his *Spadefish's* bridge with binoculars pressed tight to his eyes. The tenseness of his pose indicated plainly that he was not there to enjoy the beauty of this starlit June night or to philosophize about the beam of the lighthouse which flashed its warning from some miles ahead. Subconsciously he strained forward, evidently trying to bring his eyes closer to the object of his search. His left hand brushed impatiently at the smoke which rose from his pipe and interfered with the work of bringing into focus the wide-open harbor of Otaru, Japan, which in the gloom ahead was beginning to separate itself from the background of hills that loomed behind it.

Presently, when his eyes had attained the desired degree of visual sharpness, Bill began to examine the outlines of ships to determine which were within and which were beyond the safety afforded by the breakwater that separated the inner harbor from the outer roadstead. As the examination proceeded, the young skipper's face assumed the professional but impersonal air of an orthodontist staring into the mouth of a patient who is about to receive the unpleasant news that he must lose an important number of teeth. Only there would be no laughing gas in Bill's contemplated operation to assuage the pain. The only anesthetic known to those who extract ships from the enemy's jaws is the absolute painlessness of complete extinction.

In line with Commander Earl Hydeman's idea that the richest harvest of Japanese shipping would be under the

protecting shadow of the coast, the *Spadefish* had proceeded
to Ishikari Wan, a bay that makes a sizeable dent in the
western coast line of the Island of Hokkaido. "Beat 'em out of
the bushes" was Hydeman's slogan. At the deepest indenta-
tion of the bay nestled the port of Otaru, protected from
unruly seas by a cape known on the charts as Takashima
Misaki. Its bluff extremity was adorned by a lighthouse which
shone with peacetime brightness. At the time of his arrival in
the area, shortly before dawn on June 8, Bill had engaged in
some gentle and super-careful reconnoitering in preparation
for M-Day. Aboard the *Spadefish* the crew spent the major
part of the eighth tracking ships and putting final touches to
battle station arrangements. In the course of the day, there
had been enough shipping in and out—but mostly out—of
Otaru harbor to make Bill and his crew drool with happy
anticipation. Hardly an hour went by without producing
several different types of freighters. Shortly after lunch, when
two magnificent carogomen passed within easy torpedo range,
Lt. R. M. Wright, Germershausen's executive officer, gave
his boss a look so pleading that it would have melted the
heart of a cast-iron deer. But Bill shook his head sadly and
reminded him: "I know how you feel, but patrol orders say:
No attacks before sunset tomorrow."

Whereupon he sighed. And so did Wright. Orders are
orders.

At 2015, the *Spadefish* surfaced to charge her batteries
and give the crew a chance to stretch and fill their lungs with
fresh air. At midnight, when all seemed quiet, the sub made
a rehearsal run for the next night's entry into the port of
Otaru which brought her close to the entrance of that port.
No patrol boats were in evidence, no aircraft searchers, no
radar beams bouncing in the blue of the beautiful night.
What a shock this peaceful community would receive on the
morrow!

The *Spadefish* remained submerged throughout the daylight hours of June 9. To most of those on board, this was the
longest day in the year. However, there was a yarn that one of
the hands, a bouncer in a dance hall in civilian life, remarked,
"I'm all for this quiet life. I came into subs to get caught up
on sleep. I'll get enough excitement when I get back to
tossing bums out of barrooms."

At 1640, the sixth Maru of the day passed within ten
thousand yards of the submarine which again made a practice

approach. A sample of the impatience aboard the *Spadefish* is reflected in the following log entry at 1705: "In attack position, but we still have two hours before shooting time. Almost let go at this one, but thought better of it in the last minute."

At long last did that evening sun go down. And no sooner had darkness drawn its obscuring cover over land and sea than Bill brought his ship up from periscope depth. At that time, the sub was some fifteen miles from Otaru harbor. The moment for action had come and the *Spadefish* headed shoreward at fifteen knots. . . . Past the long and short flashes of Takashima Light. . . . Past the short and long flashes of Ishikari Light.

Ten miles from the harbor, Bill stopped all engines and, while his vessel coasted along, stepped up to the skipper's favorite station, the little fold-up platform on the starboard side of the bridge. With the aid of his binoculars, supplemented by reports from the night periscope and the radar, he began to take inventory of the ships in the harbor to determine how many would be within reach of his Mark 14 steam torpedoes.

It is interesting to note that most of the Hellcat skippers had elected to load up with the old Mark 14 torpedoes for this foray into the Sea of Japan. This torpedo was the same one which gave Mush Morton heartbreaking trouble in this same sea because it either failed to explode or exploded prematurely. Now that we had equipped it with the new type of firing pin, the Mark 14 was restored to favor. And, in fact, it was preferred over the new electric Mark 18 because the latter had a speed of only about thirty-four miles an hour as against the Mark 14's fifty plus miles per hour.

As he took inventory, Bill was glad that he had had opportunity the previous night to orient himself for the day of reckoning. He planned to slip into the outer roadstead, unseen and unheard, and attack shipping anchored outside the breakwater. To penetrate inside this thick stone wall would, under the circumstances, be a risk not to be warranted by the potential results. He was not afraid of enemy patrols discovering him, because there were no patrols. Bills's principal fears were directed toward the station ship that rode at anchor quite close to the entrance to the breakwater. If its lookouts were vigilant, there could be trouble not only from the sea but from the air. Near the city was Sapporo airport where a considerable number of four-engined military planes, mostly transports, were active around the clock. It would be a simple routine for the station ship to radio or phone the airfield and ask for planes to drop bombs on the *Spadefish*.

From the volume of traffic he had seen since his arrival in the region, Commander Germershausen expected to find many ships at anchor both inside and outside the breakwater.

At 2215, Bill turned to his exec, Lt. Wright, and said, "Okay, Dick, let's head in."

A moment later, two of the *Spadefish*'s four diesels purred into low-humming life and, so gently that her progress made no sound, she stole over the surface toward the easily identifiable lights of the station ship. A light rain had set in. This was all to the good since rains dampen both hearing and vision. True, the harbor lights were now barely distinguishable, but everything else was in the *Spadefish*'s favor. Now and then the eastern sky would light up as Sapporo airfield turned on its landing beams and planes would be seen circling above the field, their powerful headlights cutting knife-sharp wedges through the dark.

Presently the *Spadefish*'s radar picked up three ship contacts dead ahead at thirteen thousand yards. They plotted-in as being inside that section of Otaru harbor known as Tarukawa basin. Drawing nearer, at almost tip-toeing speed, various white harbor lights and multicolored town lights became visible. The breakwater could also be identified on the radar screen. Some seven minutes later Bill sighted the entrance lights to the breakwater on both bows. At the same time the probing fingers of the sub's radar picked up and identified three ships at ranges of 9,100, 6,800, and 6,250 yards.

"Make ready all tubes." The order came in a whisper, lest some unexpectedly nearby ears should catch it. "Damn that plane!" No whisper this time, but Bill's fine, resounding bass. This was his greeting to a huge four-engined Japanese plane that—with headlights glaring and motors burping as the pilot retarded throttles and let down flaps to reduce landing speed—swept at dangerously low altitude out from the coast and over the harbor. The *Spadefish* was smack in the center of the path of its glaring landing lights.

For seeming eternities the twin beams held Germershausen, his bridge personnel, and his look-outs pinned down like butterflies on needles. Everyone ducked—first, to escape having his night vision ruined by the glare of the landing lights; next, out of sheer instinct to escape whatever threat was imposed by the presence of the plane.

"Holy Moses! He almost took my cap off," exclaimed Bill, after the aircraft had roared from overhead and swung into a wide circle that would bring it to an into-the-wind position on its approach to the field. "I wonder if those pilots saw us. They had enough light on us to make movies."

"Don't think so," said Wright. "They are still heading for the field. You'll go ahead as planned, I presume?"

"Yes, yes, Dr-r-r what's-your-name?—oh, Livingston! The presumed Dr. Livingston!" chided Bill. "Exactly as planned. If anybody wants to start something, we'll shoot it out with them. You've got a gun crew standing by below?"

"Yes, sir," replied Dick.

At the time this little drama was staged, Bill was not aware that he had a ship-wide audience. The 1-MC microphone on the bridge was close enough for the entire dialogue to be broadcast throughout the ship. Thus Bill was doubling in the role of talker, and all hands heard the discussion. To them, at battle stations, it was far from reassuring. A day or two later, when the thrilling side of the incident had replaced the chill of danger that it first aroused, one of Bill's old hands suggested that it might be a good idea to snap that bridge mike off when sticking the old *Spadefish*'s neck too far out. Said he: "We sure had ringside seats for that bout, Captain. It sounded like that so-and-so was about to lay an egg on us and me—with thirteen patrols behind me—I thought maybe I should have stood at home. It was pretty strong medicine for the new hands and I reckon there were some wet spots around the deck."

Bill approached the breakwater entrance slowly. It was a narrow gap marked in the dark by two rather feeble white lights. Why white, Bill wondered. One should have been green, the other red. Special instructions to keep their eyes on the station ship had been issued to the two forward lookouts. It was well within spotting range of the sub's low, dark hull or even of the faint white ripple made by the vessel's bow as it munched away at the tiniest of wave-born bones.

But as the *Spadefish* was about to enter this ship-studded shelter of Maruland, the payoff expectations changed from greenbacks and gold into pennies and dimes. All but one ship were disappointingly small. And that one vessel, having just left its anchorage, was standing out to sea. Germershausen turned his attention to the station ship. It was lying about fifteen hundred yards off near the edge of a spread of fishing nets. He decided to attack it even though it was fairly small. . . . He would catch up with the departing AK later. At one thousand yards, the station ship's hull was invisible behind the curtain of rain, but Bill whanged away with two pickles. They probably underran the target's shallow hull. At any rate, neither exploded. Thoroughly disgusted, Germershausen cleared the harbor at flank speed, unknown, unseen, and unmourned. His objective now was the AK that had slipped away. He caught up with it exactly ninety minutes later.

0130 on the morning of June 10 began a series of sensationally productive operations for the *Spadefish*. At that hour, still on the surface and from a distance of 1350 yards, she attacked the AK that almost got away from Otaru harbor. The heavily loaded target was in plain view through the TBT (Target Bearing Transmitter) binoculars when the *Spadefish* released three torpedoes from the bow tubes. In one, two, three order, Germershausen saw and heard the torpedoes explode. So well placed were the hits that the target disintegrated and disappeared in less than a minute. Reload! As usual, the boys wrote their names and the season's greetings on the three new torpedoes before they were slid into the empty bow tubes as the sub steamed on.

Ten minutes later to the dot, the radar made a contact at eighteen thousand yards and the ship began tracking with the eagerness of a keg-bearing St. Bernard in a blizzard. At 0230, the target (another freighter) was caught in the *Spadefish*'s sights. It had just rounded the bulging point of Shakotan Misaki and was headed for Otaru. It never reached port. Three fish, two of which exploded as intended, were dispatched toward the enemy freighter. It blew up and sank almost instantly.

Germershausen now began to feel that the frustrations he had encountered earlier in the evening were being compensated for. This belief was confirmed at 0244, ten minutes after the last trio of torpedoes were launched, when the *Spadefish* made still another contact at ten thousand yards. The first streaks of dawn were showing as Bill whittled the range down. The game was another medium freighter. The objective was to sink it before daylight; otherwise it might escape. According to the radar pips, the distance was 6,900 yards at 0253. Bill got his dope as he stood huddled in the shelter of the bridge. The day was cold and windy, but clear.

"Clear the bridge! Take her down," he ordered. "Periscope depth. Battle stations. Torpedo. And make it snappy. Don't want to lose this one."

Came the bonging of the battle station gong. Like shadows suddenly emerging into life, the four lookouts slid quickly and silently down from their posts on the periscope shears and through the conning tower hatch. Other bridge personnel followed. The Captain came last. Water was already surging up to swallow the ship as the quartermaster, standing ready under the conning tower hatch, slammed the heavy hatch cover shut and secured it. Used to the morning twilight, Bill's eyes had no problem adjusting to the softly toned bulbs that lit the conning tower. He headed for the periscope which was shot upward by the alert hoist-boy before his Skipper could complete the "Up periscope" order.

"Got to get a quick setup this time," he told everyone in general. "We'll close at flank speed."

"All ahead flank," repeated the steersman as he swung the engine telegraphs ahead.

Precisely at 0300, Bill brought the sub up to forty-five feet to check his periscope radar range against his old reliable ST surface radar. They checked right on the nose. The range was a little longer than Bill liked, but the target was getting away. Already the torpedo track was 120 degrees port, which placed the *Spadefish* well abaft the target's port beam. This would have to be fast or not at all.

"Make ready three tubes forward," he ordered and strained toward the firing panel as though by sheer concentration and will power he could make the ready lights flash on more quickly. Minutes slid by on velvet. No sound as men stood ready at their stations. No motion.

As ready lights of 1, 2, and 3 Tubes flashed on after what seemed interminable waiting, Bill, already squatting at the periscope, sang out, "Up scope. Check bearing and fire. . . . Stand by."

0310: "Fire one. Use ten-second intervals."

0311: First torpedo hit. Target settled about ten feet on an even keel. Ten seconds later, the second torpedo hit. Target broke in two and sank immediately.

Third torpedo—robbed. Nothing left for it to explode on.

"Reload!... Dick, check our position and set a course for Shakotan Misaki. That area is hot. We'll patrol submerged there today."

"Nice shooting, Captain," said Wright. "Better hit the sack."

Following a hearty breakfast, Germershausen sought the welcome comfort of his bunk and reviewed the night's events: three ships down and one cold miss. Not too bad, but the targets were disappointingly small. The question was how much damage had the night's work done to his prospect of inflicting further damage in the Otaru area? Could the Japs have heard the explosions? Doubtful, because the attacks had been staged well out to sea. Could they have seen the flares of the explosions? Perhaps, but that, too, was doubtful because they would be very low on the horizon. Lastly, all three ships sank so rapidly and the attacks were staged with such complete surprise that they had had no chance to use their radios to give the alarm.

No, Bill concluded. He was, accordingly, all set to do business on the same old corner whenever a target showed up.

Alas, the day was uneventful and unproductive. When he surfaced about sunset, nothing was in sight. Sometime afterward he had a radar contact at twelve thousand yards and commenced an attack approach on a target that seemed to be of the same size as the freighters he had sunk the night before. Five minutes later something tipped the enemy off to the danger. But what? At any rate, the Japanese reversed course and headed for Ofuyu Misaki. Half an hour later, as he tried to bring the range closer than the gap of eight thousand yards then separating the two vessels, Bill got a shock of intense surprise: radar interference from the target. Now what?

This meant that the vessel was not a harmless little freighter but a fighter—probably an armed patrol boat. Bill had no way of finding out because visibility was bad beyond one thousand yards. With all tubes ready, the *Spadefish* bored in at flank speed. Germershausen was prepared for any stunt his opponent might pull. There was something plenty smelly in the situation. It was not garbage and it was not in Denmark. But it smelled to high heaven right here off

Japan—the smell of a mankilling trap studded with depth charges.

Just as the *Spadefish* got into firing position—ready for a three-fish MOT salvo—the target swung around with a wide swathe of wake behind it and headed straight for the *Spadefish* at top speed.

Swish—swish—swish went three torpedoes from the bow tubes for a down-the-throater at thirteen hundred yards. Too long, but it had to be tried.

With the third fish gone, Bill reversed course at full speed, and the *Spadefish* began to kick up her long bridal veil of foaming spume. Now the darkness was punctuated by the red slashes of gunfire. Missiles whistled overhead. Nothing big—probably only forty-millimeters. But soon they began to straddle the *Spadefish*. Good shooting. . . . And the sub was in no position to shoot it out. With a sizeable sea running, a gun's crew might be lost overboard before it could cast loose and fire the five-inch gun.

The sub might have been able to evade on the surface, but the shots were getting too close. Bill rang for the "down" elevator and sent the sub below in one quick running stride. Down to three hundred feet. There he rigged for depth charges—and just in time. The first charge exploded at 2320. The eighteenth and last boomed at 2323. Bill stood out to westward at eighty rpm. No damage. No more shooting. But lots of pinging. That, too, came to an end at 0115 when the *Spadefish* surfaced to charge her depleted batteries. The crew, except for those whose duties kept them alert, seized the opportunity to build up their reserves of sack time.

And so it went—day after day, night after night—target contacts, approach runs, torpedoes that hit freighters or torpedoes that missed freighters, gun attacks on trawlers and sampans, and last-minute identifications of Russian freighters that, as neutral vessels, had the free use of Japanese waters.

Those Russians! Ah, they became thorns in poor Bill Germershausen's side. They were improperly lighted and in other respects failed to obey rules for neutral vessels in combat waters. At least twice Bill sneaked up on a rich-looking target only to discover at the very last moment before the man at the firing panel smacked the button that his intended victim was a Muscovite.

But there was one occasion when the fat got really singed in the fire. The *Spadefish* was patrolling about fifty miles west of La Perouse Strait on the night of June 12-13. Shortly after midnight a radar contact was made at 22,000 yards on a ship which proved to be lying to. Meanwhile a moving contact was picked up at 19,700 yards and approach commenced. The weather was unsettled. Mists alternating with rain and fog reduced visibility to from fifteen hundred to eight thousand yards.

The night was very dark and the sea was calm. At last a favorable firing position was obtained but firing withheld because of doubt concerning the nationality of the target. Finally the target was closed on the starboard beam and two torpedoes fired from a range of thirteen hundred yards at 0133 on June 13. Two hits were registered and the target sank in eighteen minutes.

Before the torpedoes hit, the *Spadefish* had closed to eleven hundred yards, yet neither hull nor lights could be seen. The target had been unescorted and on a steady southwesterly course. This course headed the ship for Vladivostok, but information available to the *Spadefish* showed that Soviet shipping bound from La Perouse Strait to Vladivostok was routed due west. At least fifteen unescorted Japanese ships had previously been sighted in the vicinity stearing steady courses, so that being unescorted on a steady course had been no clue to the target's identity. Furthermore the southwesterly course could have been the Karafuto or the Empire-Korean route.

At 0209 the same morning a target, subsequently identified as Russian, showed lights which were visible at eight thousand yards and the attack was broken off. Later in the morning another Russian was seen whose white lights were sighted through the periscope at three thousand yards and colored identification lights at fifteen hundred yards.

According to a Tokyo broadcast on June 17, the Russian ship *Transbalt* was sunk at a spot thirty miles south of the position in which the *Spadefish* made the attack I have described. If it was the *Transbalt*, according to the broadcast, the majority of the crew had been rescued by a Japanese patrol boat. Subsequent information received from the U.S. Naval Attaché at Moscow confirmed the sinking of the *Transbalt* on June 13 but gave no hour of sinking or other particulars except that Rebun Island bore 237 degrees distant fifteen miles from her position.

It appears that if it was the *Transbalt* which the *Spade-*

fish sank, she was either displaying no identification lights or lights of insufficient intensity. Furthermore she was steering a course at variance with the information furnished the United States regarding routings of Soviet vessels.

By the time the patrol drew to a close, Commander Germershausen and his crew aboard the *Spadefish* on its fifth war patrol had sunk four 4000-ton AK's for a total of 16,000 tons, one large AK of 5400 tons, and one 4000-ton UN. These estimates, plus one motor sampan and three trawlers, added up to a total of 26,050 tons—a fine wolf pack's work in any enemy's ocean. The Post-war Joint Army-Navy Assessment Committee cut these estimates in tonnage; even so, the total was impressive. But above and beyond that fine score is the blow inflicted on Japanese morale by this aggressive campaign in waters believed to be safe.

With typical modesty, Commander Bill Germershausen ended his patrol report with: "Much of the credit for the success of this patrol is due to the devotion to duty and unquenchable fighting spirit of the executive officer, Lieutenant R. M. Wright, USN. Lieutenant Wright possesses to a high degree that quality which is necessary for success in submarine warfare—an overwhelming desire to destroy Japs. He is recommended for early command of a fleet submarine."

23

SKATE BAGS SITTING DUCKS

Noto Peninsula lies about halfway up along the west coast of Honshu Island. It has the dog-leg shape of a boomerang, and a rather squatty mountain range runs down its spine. On the eastern side of the tongue of land that runs some thirty miles from its base to its tip are two bays with excellent harbor facilities and several coves. The tip is called Suzu Misaki. This was known to the Hellcats as "Windy Corner," not only because of the stiff breezes that whipped around it, but also because of the amount of Korea-bound and coastal shipping which, in ordinary times, slips past its bare and rocky snout. As it turned out, the sinkings of ships which took place there might almost entitle it to rank with the famous windy corner at the Battle of Jutland in World War I.

The two bays east of the Peninsula are called Nanoa Wan and Toyama Wan and each shelters several harbors, two of which are outstanding, namely the ancient seaport of Nanoa and the newer port of industrial Fushiki. Unfortunately for Japan—and likewise for the three-submarine Polecat pack of the Hellcats assigned to the Noto Peninsula region—these prominent harbors were closed territory to shipping and to submarines. This because they had been extensively planted with magnetic mines dropped by flights of B-29's. Since mines know neither friend nor foe, it would have been highly dangerous for the Polecats to venture into such ports as Nanoa and Fushiki or other harbors in the region that had been sprinkled with highly explosive seeds. But being clever fellows, our enemies had diverted their coastwise shipping into the several coves and other natural anchorages provided by a generous Mother Nature. There were several of these on the Toyama Wan side of Noto Peninsula and at least one excellent sheltering cove on the seaward side of the land mass. This latter cove—about five miles long and some two miles deep—was protected by a mountain-clad point that served as a fine wind-breaker. The name of this inlet is Matsugashita Byochi. The cove's main handicap from a Hellcat standpoint was that on the coast, a short distance above this slick little anchorage, stood Saruyama Lighthouse, home of the only shore-based radar station on that part of Honshu Island. Another potential disadvantage was that this particular section of Noto Peninsula is only some ten miles wide from shore to shore, and Commander Richard B. (Ozzie) Lynch, skipper of the Polecat *Skate*, hoped that mine planting B-29's had not, through error or over-enthusiasm, dropped their deadly calling cards on the Matsugashita side of Noto Peninsula. Like all Hellcat skippers, he had been carefully briefed during the Holland conference in Guam as to the whereabouts of magnetic mines dropped from B-29's.

At dawn of June 9, the *Skate* dived for an all-day patrol just north of "Windy Corner," but evidently the winds of fortune were not blowing in Ozzie Lynch's direction. At any rate, he did not sight a single vessel all that day. About breakfast time on June 10, he sighted a small vessel that turned out to be a minesweeper. Perhaps he thought that a minesweeper's lot is hard enough without being torpedoed; anyway, he let the vessel pass and remained on his southerly course which presently took him down the Fifty Fathom Curve past the eastern tip of Suzu Misaki.

At 1120, as he was running submerged, Ozzie sighted a peculiar squareshaped object on the horizon. He scratched his head under the rim of his cap—a queer kind of a duck. What could it be? Since the sea was glassy calm, he could easily give his presence away by excessive use of his periscope. But carefully he stole another look. Now he noted that the darn thing had a gun on it.

"Battle stations. Submerged," ordered Lynch. "We've got a submarine. He's steaming serenely on the surface. A Nip submarine and no mistake about it. Quick and careful, boys! We can't let this fish slip out of our hands. I'll bet my bottom dollar that it's one of those new I-121's, as big as our own Fleet Submarine. Like us. About 1470 tons."

1130: Ozzie took another peep at his target. "It is coming out of a fifteen- to twenty-degree zig. Give me right full rudder. I think that should just about cut us a nice piece of cake."

Thirteen minutes later, another peep. "Yes-siree," gloated Lynch with a quick glance at the TDC dials, "came out just even! The range is now eight hundred yards and the gyro angle is less than forty-five degrees."

At 1144, the *Skate* let go a salvo of four torpedoes. At 1145, the enemy submarine, which turned out to be the I-122, sank, hit squarely amidships.

It was gone before the smoke and debris cleared away. The second torpedo exploded amidst the wreckage, but the third and fourth were, as the boys said, "robbed." A few minutes later the *Skate* heard breaking-up noises and hissing air in the direction of the sinking. As Lynch watched, a large air bubble burst on the glassy sea leaving the telltale iridescence of an oil film. That was all—just an oil slick to mark the spot where a submarine had made its last dive.

Well, maybe that was the way Mush Morton and the *Wahoo* went. Swiftly and suddenly. Without warning. Without pain.

Many hours later, Lynch noticed a low-flying float plane winging back and forth over the area of the sinking. "Looking for survivors, or for us?" wrote Ozzie in his Log.

Shortly after dark that evening the *Skate* had its next

ship contact, a small vessel which it chased for half an hour until the target gained the doubtful security of the Fifty Fathom Curve of waters that were very close to an area that had been mined by B-29's. Lynch cut off the pursuit; he had no yen to take chances with magnetic mines.

During the night of June 10-11, the *Skate* stood north around Suzu Misaki and south along the peninsula's seacoast in the direction of Matsugashita Cove. To avoid taking chances on being located by the Saruyama Light station's ever-sweeping radar set, Lynch dove as he approached this point and remained submerged during most of the daylight hours. Again an empty day. Not a contact until half-past five in the afternoon, when he sighted smoke to the southward. The vessel, whatever it was, steamed northward close to the coast, unpleasantly near the shallow Twenty Fathom Curve. Despite the dangers of entering shallow waters, Ozzie bored in to head off the approaching vessel.

By now, he could see that it was a heavily loaded AK of about 4000 tons and threfore well worth bagging. At the same time, the *Skate* had problems on her own hands. She had been patrolling submerged all day, and as a result the batteries were near the low-voltage limit. In other words, unless Lynch succeeded in knocking out his target within the hour, he would run out of juice and be forced to sit on bottom until darkness permitted him to surface and charge batteries. To surface and turn on his diesels in order to close the range and attack with gun or torpedo was out of the question, for, even if he got the freighter and was not counterattacked by planes, the hunting would be spoiled in this very promising locality.

In a quick conference with his exec, Lt. Commander Robert C. Huston, supplemented by hasty information from the Chief Engineer as to the exact state of the battery, the skipper decided to pour on the juice and worry about a flat battery afterward. He really liked the steam Mark 14 torpedoes with their high speed and I would be willing to bet the genial Ozzie was at that moment doing some plain and fancy cussing about not having some of them in those forward tubes and damning all Force Commanders who urged the use of Mark 18 electrics because of their wakeless feature, which provided greater safety for the submarine.

Be that as it may, the *Skate*'s best sustained submerged speed of about seven miles per hour was insufficient to close to a sure-fire hitting range, and painfully she had to accept 3500 yards as the minimum she could obtain.

Attempting to make the most of a poor set-up, Lynch, at 1834, fired a spread of four torpedoes and hoped for the best. . . . They missed. "Extreme range shots," wrote Ozzie in his Log, "are the weeds!"

At any rate, Lynch had one lucky break. Because of shoal waters there were no end-of-run explosions to reveal his presence. All four fish vanished into the falling night with the silence of Boojums, than which there is supposed to be nothing more silent, unless it be Snarks.

In the late twilight and on the surface, Lynch saw the target enter Matsugishita cove. Taking a closer look, he did a double-take of happy surprise. At anchor in the cove, were two other ships, a small and a medium cargo vessel.

It did not take Ozzie long to figure out his immediate course: wait for full darkness; surface and charge his batteries; then nose the *Skate* into the rich little treasure chest called Matsugashita Byochi. After that some fine and fancy shooting. Therefore, promptly at 2245, when the batteries were topped off, Lynch headed into the cove to see about sinking the three ships that had sought shelter there. But fifteen minutes later it began to rain in downpours so heavy that Lynch could hardly see his hand before his face. Earlier that evening, there had been repeated visits by a plane or planes equipped with radar, or perhaps even the new magnetic anti-submarine detector called Jitan. To avoid discovery Lynch would dive to three hundred feet if depth of water permitted. Throughout the night the *Skate* patrolled close to shore to out-fox radar planes by losing himself against the shore background or making them believe he was a belated Japanese fisherman working his way back to his home and a warm cup of sake.

At 0310, Ozzie thought that the early dawn light would be adequate to enter the cove. Instead, the rain continued and he submerged until 0845. By that time the rain had stopped. As the *Skate* bored silently into the cove, her crew was called to "Battle Stations. Submerged." Lynch knew from his charts, such as they were, that he was going into ultra-shallow waters—ten to twenty fathoms. The *Skate* would really need wheels for this one. As he entered the cove, Lynch discovered a fourth ship, a small 1000-ton tanker, riding at anchor with the three vessels he had observed the previous night.

Taking cautious peeks through the periscope, Ozzie was grinning like a Cheshire cat. "Boy, oh boy, what a shooting gallery!... Here, have a look, Bob. Did you ever see such a row of sitting ducks?"

"Like shooting clay pipes at Coney Island. What luck, what luck!" breathed Huston with awe in his voice. "But don't forget, Cap'n, they'll have to be long shots. We can't go much closer; there's only three fathoms under the keel now. And they'll have to be fast so we can git while the gittin's good."

"Check," said Ozzie. "Stand by all tubes."

Then as the talker passed him the mike, he added, "Now, all hands, on your toes. This has got to be fast—and good. We've got four anchored ships ahead; three fathoms under the keel and God only knows what's in the air.—Lively on that TDC.

"Up periscope. Check bearing and shoot!"

Face tense with excitement, Lynch swung the periscope onto his first target. "Bearing, mark!... Three four nine."

0912: "Fire one!... Bearing, mark!... Three five 0.... Fire two!"

In seventy seconds six torpedoes left the bow tubes for a 2600-yard run to the target. All were set for a shallow six feet, but even in the choppy sea they ran well. Two minutes and twenty seconds later the first of five explosions crashed out like a great firecracker on a Chinese New Year.

Before his fish had commenced to hit, Ozzie had begun his swing to a reverse course, but with eye glued to the periscope he checked off each hit. Three landed in the second medium AK. Within five minutes the large AK was sitting on the bottom. The smaller vessel was sinking. Total score: one ship of 4000 tons and two of 1000 tons each. The aggregate, 6000 tons sunk. In addition, considerable damage was inflicted on a fourth ship, a 4000-ton AK.

"That's really knocking them down," applauded Huston when his voice could be heard above the roar that rose from bow to stern of the *Skate*. The crew went wild! This was the old *Skate* that, under McKinney and Gruner, had knocked down Japs from the equator to the Empire! With a cruiser, a destroyer, and four freighters already to her credit, she was really piling up a score!

"True, but not good enough," answered Lynch. "One of those ships hasn't been hit and one is only damaged.

"Standby for set-up for the stern tubes!"

As the *Skate* swung around to the new firing course, her fathometer showed only two fathoms of water below the keel. Pretty close quarters. At the same instant, gunfire was noted and that, too, was pretty close. The sub and the ships were now so near each other that it seemed to Lynch he was looking through his periscope down an enemy gun barrel for his next bearing and that the AK's deck gun fired smack into his face. While this was, of course, an illusion, it was not a very comforting one. Fortunately all three torpedoes fired from the stern tubes registered hits. One landed in the small tanker, one in the largest AK that was already sitting on the bottom. The third torpedo it the next larger AK, the one that had been firing at the sub with a deck gun that looked like a sixteen incher to Ozzie as he stared down its muzzle.

At 0921, the *Skate* had so little water beneath her that the fathometer would not register. Wrote Lynch in his log: "It is hereby requested that the *Skate* be considered a shallow-water helldiver as well as a submarine."

In any event it was high time the *Skate* got out of Matsugashita Byochi. Nine minutes later the opposition hove into view—a patrol boat with its deck guns slamming shells into the water all around the *Skate* as it rushed nearer. At the same time, the big AK kept firing. It had been partly sheltered by the biggest freighter and had probably received only one hit. Though the Nip's shots had only the remotest chance of hitting the sub's periscope, that did not deter the gun crews in their hymn of hate.

"Get a check on our position, Bob," sang out Ozzie. "I want to go deep and I want to get the hell out of here. All ahead, full."

To the talker he said, "Tell them to pull the five-hour rate on the batteries until we get clear. It's tough on the can but that's what we'll have to do."

At 0957 and 0958, the *Skate* was the target of a couple of depth charges, neither of which came close. At 1015, Lynch thought it safe to reduce to creeping speed.

For the remainder of that June 12 day, no shipping activity of any kind was reflected in the lens of the *Skate*'s ever-peeking periscope and all hands were rather grateful because they had had a watchful night and a busy morning.

On June 13, however, while he was on surface tracking down a freighter, Ozzie Lynch had the unpleasant feeling that someone was staring at them. At that instant a lookout

shouted, "Periscope, bearing two six O; range two thousand!"
Ozzie immediately went full right at full speed, but nobody
fired. The Japanese were cozy that way; they didn't like to
fire at long ranges—or perhaps they were not quick enough
on the trigger.

"This is a very dismal place to see one [a periscope],"
wrote Lynch in his log. However, he got ahead of his
freighter, dived, and sank her with one M O T hit. Later he
surfaced to take a look-see. Five minutes after the first
welcome breath of fresh air, he pulled the plug. Three
airplanes. Half an hour later, he surfaced and took aboard
three survivors of the sunken freighter whom Lt. West and
Ens. Earhart, the latter with a tommy gun, coaxed aboard.
Just as this rescue operation was completed, up came the
unidentified periscope again. From a range of eight thousand
yards, it stared at him for a full minute and then vanished.
Twenty minutes later, its pencil-thin outline rose once more
from the sea. Ozzie gave the survivors some emergency
rations and water, then laid a course for Honshu but in such a
way that Mr. Sneak-Peek Periscope would not be able to
guess in which direction he was really going.

The next day the *Skate* aimed her last Mark 18 torpedo
at a 2000-ton tanker, but it missed. To close the deal, he sent
a Mark 28 torpedo in its wake. This, too, missed. The latter
was a new weapon in our arsenal from which we expected
much, but it arrived too late in the war for us to get all the
"bugs" out of it.

The morning of June 17 brought periscope views of two
mine layers too far away from the *Skate* for Lynch to bother
with even if he had had any Mark 18 torpedoes left. Later he
was baited by a 4000-ton AK with a full deckload of landing
craft. Ozzie closed to one thousand yards just for fun, but it
was not fun to watch that nice fat target go bye-bye.

At noon on June 18, Ozzie was called from a much-
needed late morning siesta by his exec who wanted the
skipper to share one of the strangest sights a modern periscope ever held. The object was a destroyer—but what a
destroyer! As old as Methuselah and at least of the vintage of
the Russo-Japanese War. A slow-poking coal-burner that had
all it could do to maintain a three-knot speed as escort vessel
to a 3500-ton AK. To Lynch, the sight was interesting for
other reasons. For one, this was the first attempt at escort he
had seen in the Sea of Japan. An hour and a half later, Ozzie

beheld an ancient 800-ton steamer which, he guessed, must have been built about the time of the first big Battle of Tsushima in the earlier days of the Japanese Empire.

Next dawn, another submarine slid into scope sight of the *Skate*—a 500-tonner without a deck-gun. His zigging was so erratic that Lynch could not out-guess him and close the range. An hour later, to the second, Lynch saw another sub of the same class. His zigging was even wilder than that of the first sub. For a time Lynch hoped that he might get in a shot with his last remaining Mark 28 in the after torpedo room and swung to bring his stern to bear. Just then the enemy, as Ozzie expressed it, "uncorked a zig which the swing of the ship could not catch up with and he crossed our empty bow tubes at six hundred yards. We have had nothing remotely connected with luck this morning."

The closing days of the *Skate*'s patrol were completely without the kind of luck Ozzie Lynch was praying for. Day after day, his log would run like this:

0904: Dived.

1142: Surfaced for an hour and a half to get position by sun lines.

1200: Position: 45-32 N—138-18 E.

2001: Surfaced.

0101: SJ radar contact at 5500 yards. Avoided.

It was quite evident, toward the middle of the *Skate*'s patrol period, that as a result of the vigilance with which the *Skate* and the other Bobcats—the *Tunny* and the *Bonefish*— had operated within their assigned territories, the enemy had withdrawn into his shell in the hope he might be able to wait it out with the invaders. In other words, he kept his shipping under wraps until better protection for it could be mustered. A disappointing turn to the Hellcat skippers, but a high tribute to the efficiency of their efforts.

By the time the homeward-bound hour struck, the *Skate* had cruised 2674 miles in the Sea of Japan and rolled up a score of five vessels sunk and one damaged for a grand total of 12,650 tons put out of commission.

24

JAPS SHADOWBOX *TUNNY*

The *Tunny*, pack leader of the Polecats, still sloshing sea water off its deck and superstructure, surfaced in the Sea of Japan at 2055 on June 5, following its successful transit under the widely distributed Hellpots in Tsushima Strait. As Commander George E. Pierce lifted himself through the hatch and stepped up onto the platform under the sprayshield on the bridge, he saw a sight that truly made his eyes pop. Game—big game—was everywhere! Ships! Coming and going in all directions.

"Hank," he yelled down the hatch, "come up here quick. Bob, come see what we are up against. Holy smoking mackerel! This simply can't be true."

Laughing with belly-shaking glee, he turned to Lt. Commander H. L. (Hank) Vaughan and Lt. Commander R. D. (Bob) Quinn, respectively the exec and the prospective commanding officer, as they scrambled up the hatch.

"Take a look, boys!" he shouted. "I'll eat my hat if you've ever seen the likes of this."

He swept both arms outward so as to include all points of the compass. He wanted to draw the attention of his grinning, chuckling, spellbound audience to the fleet of freighters within easy sight.

"Better get some of this crowd off the bridge, Cap'n," warned Vaughan. "We may have to dive fast. I'll be the after lookout."

At the Captain's assent he called, "Lookouts, stand by below," and then leaning toward the hatch he spoke to the talker: "Warn all hands to be on their toes. There'll be no shooting but we may have to do some mighty quick diving. Looks like we are in the middle of a herd of AK's."

"What wouldn't you give to call the crew to battle stations and pump some torpedoes into that flock?" asked Bob Quinn.

"Man, oh man," cut in Hank Vaughan, "I didn't know there was this much torpedo bait left in the entire North Pacific."

"If this were only M-Day instead of just the end of F-Day," lamented Pierce with a real note of grief in his voice, "we could really go to work on those crates. If we've got to take this kind of punishment until sunset of June 9 we'll all crack up under the pressure."

Two smallish craft, probably patrol boats, bobbed on the *Tunny*'s starboard beam at a distance of some six thousand yards. A large ship appeared on her port bow at ten thousand yards, another on the port beam at seventy-five hundred yards. Still another was on the port quarter at eight thousand yards.

"Look sharp," warned Pierce to the OOD. "You'll have to do some broken-field running to clear these contacts."

"Radar," he called into the 1-MC, "keep ranges coming up on those tincans on the starboard beam. Bob," he said to Quinn, "hop below, please, and keep an eye on that radar scope. Let me know if anything heads our way."

At this moment, the *Tunny* slowed down to pass astern of a ship on her port bow. Suddenly the night, pleasantly starlit but without a moon, was cut by the twin slashes of two searchlight beams. To avoid them the *Tunny* swung to bring them astern at four-engine speed. But the lights did not pin the *Tunny* down or even try to follow her. The traffic was so heavy that everyone minded his own business and no one seemed to notice the obscure invader—the only ship in sight without running lights.

"Better look out," chortled Pierce to the exec. "If one of those patrol boats sees us, we'll get a ticket for running without lights."

As the *Tunny* headed northeast toward Honshu, two engines were put on battery charge in order to bring the batteries up to their peak as rapidly as possible. After running submerged since dawn, the *Tunny*'s power reserve was low, and George had a hunch that, with all this shipping in sight and being under orders to remain invisible to Japanese eyes for four whole days, he might have to spend a lot of time submerged. "Keep the can [battery] full," he warned Lieutenant Jones, the Engineer Officer. "We'll need it plenty on this cruise."

Before midnight, George had sighted four additional

ships all with lights, not one of them zigzagging. Commented the Log: "What a temptation!"

During this run, Pierce had plenty of time to wonder whether his fellow Polecats, the *Skate* and the *Bonefish*, had negotiated the mine fields of Tsushima successfully. He was sure they had because he did not have the slightest doubt that Hellsbells would see and sound them safely through.

The fine weather and the big flow of shipping ended the following day. A real storm with seas up in the scale four to five range blew up and lasted several days. Depth control of the submarine was difficult at periscope depth; so the *Tunny* contented itself with doing listening watch at 120 feet. Actually she had plenty of time to reach her initial patrol area and this inactivity gave everyone time to store up some sleep for the exciting days to come. At 2030 on June 8, Pierce reached his base station, Kyoga Misaki, a stubby point of land that sticks northward from the southern edge of Wakasa Wan, a large bay near the southern end of Honshu Island.

But the rosy dream of a spectacular torpedo bag, nourished by George Pierce since he ran into so many targets that first night in the Sea of Japan, dissolved into drab reality just before the midnight hour sent that particular June 9 into the ranks of yesterdays.

Having seen no traffic all day, George surfaced at 1958 off the entrance to Wakasa Wan. The weather was fine, visibility good, sea calm. About an hour later, after he had set course to close the coast, his radar man reported a contact at twelve thousand yards. Thereupon the skipper stationed the tracking party. At 2121, the *Tunny* had her first call to battle stations under the colors of Operation Barney. The target: a 2000-ton, engines-aft AK at three thousand yards. As Pierce waited to get his ship into a somewhat better position as well as into closer range, his radar man reported a new contact astern, also at three thousand yards. Fearful that the newcomer might ruin the setup, George unfortunately hurried his firing at the target in his sights.

2136: Fired three torpedoes. Ten-second intervals. Run: 2800 yards. Gyros: near zero. Depth setting: three feet. Track: 85-90.

As the last torpedo was on its way, Pierce, having the second radar contact in mind, went ahead full to clear the target astern. Thirty seconds later the radar man reported the contact to be a false one.

2138-45: "First torpedo hit, Captain, but it was a dud," reported the sonarman. During the long run of *Tunny's* torpedoes, sonar had been following them intently. Each seemed hot, straight, and normal. Then through the quiet ocean came a sharp thump like the blow of a heavy hammer on the hull of a ship—a heartbreaking sound to a tense submarine crew anxiously awaiting the heavy b-r-r-rom of the first hit.

"A dud, a blank-blanked dud," moaned the Gunnery Officer, a youngster on his second patrol who had dashed up to the bridge to see his torpedoes hit.

Maybe the others would hit! Maybe the dud had punched a hole in the target's side as one of *Salmon's* dud torpedoes had done. It actually sank the *Salmon's* target. Hope ran high in the little group on the bridge, but as seconds ticked by, their hearts sank—no explosions. The target was slipping away.

Suddenly they saw activity on the deck of the target. Figures with flashlights were running about. Lights were pointed over the side down onto the water. Laughter broke out as the *Tunny's* watchers pictured the consternation of their goggle-eyed enemies trying to figure out what had hit them.

"Well, we gave 'em a damn good scare," grinned Pierce. Then to the gunnery officer: "Corbeil, haul out one torpedo at a time and have a look at those exploders. Maybe some have gotten flooded."

"Aye, aye, Captain," and away went the ensign.

Two end-of-run explosions told Pierce that the exploders had been O.K. Depressed, he turned awawy from the target and headed back for the coast. Trouble with those electric exploders was something new. Were we in for another hassle with torpedoes and the Bureau of Ordnance?

Next day George dove west of Kyoga Misaki on the track used by ships running between Pusan in Korea and Wakasa Wan. Unfortunately this location did not produce the target opportunities the *Tunny* was hunting for. Time and again vessels were sighted when they were too far from the sub or too close to the coast for Pierce to head them off. All submarines had been warned not to approach this coast inside the fifty-fathom curve because it had been mined by B-29's.

On the night of June 12, he entered Etomo Ko and

closed to within eight thousand yards of the breakwater. The
eyes of the radar could pick up no ships in port. An hour or
so later, the *Tunny* crept into the harbor of Uppuri Wan right
under the flashing aircraft beacon on Hino Misaki. The sub
was standing in on the surface and the airway's beam lit up
the bridge every time it passed over the vessel at second-
short intervals. Simultaneously, two radar beams performed
their silent and invisible patrols of the harbor. The prickling
skin on George Pierce's scalp felt a little tight when the two
radar beams made shorter and shorter sweeps until they
centered upon the *Tunny*. Presently the sweeps stopped
completely—stopped smack on the *Tunny*. Somewhere ashore,
they were revealed on the screens of observers. Time for the
Tunny to hurry. The enemy radar had the stranger in their
waters pinpointed. When the *Tunny* was five thousand yards
from the harbor mouth, the Japs threw two strong searchlight
beams directly across the harbor entrance. Anyone who
ventured through that light barrier would be well illuminated.

"This is really being all lit up," Pierce said to the rangy
Hank Vaughan who was with him on the bridge.

"Yes, suh," agreed the latter, adding in his pleasant
Southern drawl as the gentlest of hints, "it's so light that I can
count every hair in your beard."

The Captain took the hint. The *Tunny* reversed course
and stood out to sea but only at one-third speed. Pierce was
fearful that a higher speed might leave a telltale trail in the
unusually phosphorescent water.

As he patrolled southward toward Shimonoseki, Pierce
ran into more and more radar interference of the mysterious
and annoying 10-CM wave length. Also airplane patrols and
most of the planes that cruised overhead were radar-equipped.

During the late evening hours of June 14, Pierce ran into
the same sort of radar temptation that his fellow Polecat
skippers had been exposed to. And at 0045 next day, he
sighted two white lights on an 060 bearing. From the same
heading he received radar interference that seemed to be
from a friendly source. Probably one of the Polecats. He was
steering toward it when one of the white lights began flashing
as the radar started to send "Vs." This had no place in the
Tunny's book; so Pierce made a quick turn to the left and
kept going that way on all four mains.

Twenty-four hours later, shortly after dawn on June 16,

Pierce made a somewhat delayed rendezvous with the *Skate* and the *Bonefish*. Larry Edge, commander of the latter, explained that he had been delayed by a successful torpedo action against a large enemy transport. Later in the day the *Tunny* came upon several rafts filled with survivors, probably from the transport sunk by the *Bonefish*. There were about fifteen rafts in all, but not a surviving soul wanted to be rescued by the American sub. In fact, most of them stretched out flat on the rafts, closed their eyes, and seemed to be prepared for swift machine-gunnings to their Oriental hereafters. Amusingly enough, the next morning, after an around-the-clock drifting on the cold sea, two men out of a group of seven soldiers on a raft were willing to be rescued. One of these was a senior petty officer whose name came to be "Who-You?"

On that first occasion—when the *Tunny* approached the rafts to invite survivors to come aboard as prisoners and failed to draw even one volunteer to go aboard the sub, get a free trip to America, and live the life of plenty in a prison camp until the end of the war—George Pierce received a lot of ribbing from his messmates.

"I don't blame them for taking their chances on the sea rather than with you," chided Quinn. "You look like the worst pirate that ever walked a ship or scuttled a plank—or whatever it is that those bold old buccaneers were supposed to do. Go take a look at yourself, George. Take a look, if you dare, at yourself just as you are. You've got a big and beautiful stand of the blackest whiskers this side of Hades—a face that only a mother tiger could love. Your black CPO shirt and your black baseball cap add the final touch. And to top it off, that black eye-patch you wear over your left eye—that's really the business. No wonder the Japs didn't want to leave their nice safe raft!"

There was more than a half-truth in Quinn's kidding. No man on the *Tunny* patrol will ever forget the appearance of their Skipper during the three- to four-day period when he had to wear an eye-patch which the ship's "Doc" fixed up for him. The *Tunny* had a hydraulic periscope and one of the oil lines developed a small leak. Pierce managed to pick up enough oil from the scope's eye-piece to get a badly inflamed eye. He modestly told me that he "must have looked a little tough" but he hesitated to take credit for keeping the Japs on their rafts. "Maybe Quinn was right when he told me that no stranger in his right mind would come aboard after looking at me," he admitted.

Oddly enough, this fear did not extend to a mouse-brown little sparrow which, coming out of nowhere, sought refuge on the *Tunny's* antenna. The poor thing, obviously exhausted after a long flight, reached the sub while it was surfacing in radar contact with the *Bonefish* preliminary to the joint attack staged by them later that day on a Japanese target.

On June 18, those aboard the *Tunny* were somewhat staggered by the sight of a mighty four-engined German bombing plane—a Heinkel He-177, no less. Shortly before that the OOD had sighted a light plane that looked like a sports craft. Those aboard the *Tunny* wondered if the smaller craft had seen the submarine on the surface and sent for its biggest brother. Taking no chances, Pierce dived to 150 feet and changed course in record time. To play absolutely safe, he decided to remain submerged until sunset.

The *Tunny* was cheated by a whimsically minded Fate out of making a score in the Sea of Japan on June 19, when, twice in a row, it was deprived of target results through no fault of its own. At noon a magnificent, brand-new 10,000-ton tanker blossomed briefly on the horizon. But the best approach the *Tunny* could make was six thousand yards with a 110-degree angle on the starboard beam at a speed of eleven knots—a shot which not even William Tell would have tried to make, no matter what the price of apples.

Hardly had this 10,000-tonner bowed off stage before a 4000 ton AK made its entrance. With a torpedo run of 3400 yards, Pierce fired four fish. The sea was calm; so he took a chance by setting them for a three-foot depth. It was risky, but he did not want to under-run the target. As bad luck would have it, one of the fish broached in mid-run and that was that. The target had seen the menace and avoided it. George could see the stern of his target in full flight for survival while his own torpedo flashed brilliantly in the sun as it skidded over the surface of the sea. A two word Log entry: "Gave up!"

And that about ends the Log of the *Tunny*—with but one exception, which happens to be a corker. On the afternoon the *Tunny* picked up her guests—two Japanese soldiers and a sparrow—it also ran into a long-range radar battle with two

Japanese destroyers. At no time were they closer than seven thousand yards. But at that range the warships opened fire with guns that were of at least four-inch calibre. Knowing that she was out-gunned, the *Tunny* reversed course at 2223 and went ahead with every horse her four diesels could muster. Shell splashes were throwing up fountains of spray at distances of two hundred to five hundred yards from the *Tunny*. At 2227, after flinging about twenty rounds, the DD's ceased fire.

Then at 2240, the started dropping depth charges at the point where—some seventeen minutes earlier—the *Tunny* had gone to flank speed to escape gunfire. By that time the sub was some 7500 yards away. "Scare charges" or "face-savers," our lads called them.

"And now," drawled Hank Vaughan as he lit a cigarette, "Tokyo Rose will report that another American submarine has bit the dust. Anyway I like depth charges at that range; it's better than having them drop in your lap."

"Right you are, Hank," replied Pierce, "but that has happened, too." Whereupon he told his young exec, who was on his second submarine combat patrol, the wonderful Christmas story about God and the *Gato*. To be sure, it was the middle of June and nowhere near the Holiday Season, but a miracle is a miracle no matter what the time of the year and it belongs in this book although the incident did not involve any of the Hellcats.

The statistical average of depth charges that drop on the decks of submerged submarines without exploding is so microscopic that not even the Univac could supply the correct answer. Here is the *Gato*'s unique story.

On December 20, 1943, the *Gato*, Lt. Cdr. R. J. Foley, commanding, on her seventh war patrol, was surfaced about two hundred miles north of the Admiralty Islands on what was believed to be the Saipan-Rabaul traffic route. Smoke was sighted early in the afternoon and the *Gato* submerged on the target's estimated track. The target group proved to be an engines-aft ship and a smaller two-masted cargo ship escorted by two new-type escorts.

Although every effort was made to maneuver for a close shot at the larger target, a zig placed the smaller target in a more favorable position and the *Gato* fired at her. The engines-aft ship was beyond and overlapping. The nearer

U.S.S. Gato

target, the naval cargo carrier *Tsuneshima Maru* of 2926 tons, was hit and sank immediately, but the *Gato* could not wait around to observe more and headed deep. The submariners heard two other explosions, which they believed to be torpedoes, and then the sound of a "gong" ringing in the distance. Shortly thereafter nineteen depth charges were dropped— the worst depth-charging the *Gato* had experienced. Said Foley: "Practically all of the charges seemed to be right on top of us and the ship was shaken violently with each."

Two hours later the *Gato* surfaced in a heavy rain squall and headed away from the pinging of the escorts. After a ten-minute survey of the situation, the *Gato* headed back for the scene of the torpedoing, which incidentally was also the bearing of the echo ranging. In poor visibility the *Gato* slowed on approaching the position of attack. Not long afterward a heavy explosion was heard and felt. Five minutes later an escort was sighted at about fifteen hundred yards and a minute later another escort on the other bow. No radar

contact had been made, but as the *Gato* swung away at flank speed, radar began giving ranges and bearings. At 3500 yards one escort fired a fused projectile which burst abeam a little high and a little to the right. Meanwhile, the *Gato* settled down on a course that would most likely overtake the big freighter.

Quoting from Commander Foley's patrol report: "2033: Situation resembled a five-ring circus. The *Gato* was simultaneously:

(a) Outrunning the two escorts.
(b) Trying to overtake the *Maru*.
(c) Reloading the forward tubes.
(d) Making some necessary minor repairs.
(e) Trying to dispose of one unexploded depth charge without blowing our rudder off."

This is the first mention of a depth charge being on board, and Commander Foley apparently considered it a small matter, being then occupied with events of more pressing urgency. It was almost an hour since the *Gato* had surfaced, and one can only conjecture the feelings of the lookout, quartermaster, or officer who first sighted the charge in the poor visibility of waning twilight. Did he sing out immediately: "Depth charge on deck," or did he gradually muster up courage as the realization dawned that here was a lethal charge which had and still held the *Gato*'s "number" on its inscrutable markings?

Commander Foley dispensed with it in few words: "2100: The prisoner and our language student, Lt. McGiven, each copied the markings on the depth charge, after which it was lashed to the rubber boat and set adrift with a slow leak. When last seen it was bobbing along in the path of our pursuers." Other submarines have thought they heard charges drop on deck and roll around, and several have recovered fragments of depth charge casings from topside, but the *Gato*, so far as we know, it the only one that ever actually found a whole one on board.

The hearty laugh which the *Tunny* had at the expense of the not-so-valiant Japanese tincan which depth-charged her at a range of seven thousand yards brings to mind an incident in which the *Harder* had a good laugh at the expense of an armed trawler which depth-charged her. While the charges were fairly close to the *Harder*, they were much too close to the trawler.

It happened after the *Harder*, skippered by Commander Samuel D. Dealey, had sunk a cargo vessel under the very nose of the man-o'-war. Diving fast, Dealey escaped several closely dropped depth charges. Then he heard a loud but distant explosion. After that, nothing.

A little while later the *Harder* nosed up for a sniff of surface news. There it saw the patrol vessel slowly sinking. Its stern had been blown off by one of its own depth charges. In her day the fame of the *Harder* was known all over the world. In all her battle-filled life she had but one Captain, Sam Dealey of Dallas, Texas. With Sam she went down in August, 1944, during her sixth war patrol, with sixteen ships aggregating 54,000 tons to her credit. In Navy annals, Dealey and the *Harder* stand as "the Submarine Force's most deadly opponents of destroyers." That was their specialty—sinking ships that bristled with guns, torpedo tubes, and depth charges. Sam Dealey sank four of these ships plus two DE's whose chief purpose was to destroy submarines like the *Harder*.

Like Mush Morton of the *Wahoo*, Dealey let his executive officer walk the periscope. To bait destroyers into attacking the *Harder*, he would run with his periscope extended well above the surface. The come-on was the scope's enticing wake. When the enemy took the bait, Dealey would blast him from either bow or stern tubes, whatever the occasion called for. Like Morton, he was a master marksman with the difficult down-the-throat shots. Dealey missed such a shot only once—and that was the end.

25

BONEFISH IN LAST TRAGIC DIVE

East and southeast of the storm-scrubbed rocks that form the high-shouldered cape of Suzu Point on Noto Peninsula two submarines lie at the bottom of Toyama Wan, the great bay of the west coast of Japan's Honshu Island.

The first of these vessels would have flown the flag of the Rising Sun; the second would have displayed the Stars and Stripes. But no flags were waving proudly in the breeze and no trumpets sounded their call when, with only a matter of days in between, the two submarines were sunk by enemy action. Submarine warfare has no background of pulse-throbbing flags or heart-stirring music.

One moment a submarine—the Japanese 1-122—is a living, pulsating entity packed with men intent on achieving victory for their Emperor. In the next moment, blasted by enemy torpedoes, she is a crumpled mass of twisted steel and broken bodies.

One moment a submarine—the United States Ship *Bonefish*—is blasting to extinction the enemies of her nation. In the next moment, crushed by enemy depth charges, she is enveloped by swift oblivion a hundred fathoms down.

Deadly enemies in life, the broken hulls of the *Bonefish* and the 1-122 lie scant miles apart in Toyama Wan, home waters for the 1-122 but thousands of miles from the quiet cottages and churches where women will mourn and memorials will honor the men of the *Bonefish*. And out there beneath the blue waters of the Sea of Japan they will sleep until Gabriel's summoning trumpet will join all of us in Doomsday's Great Review.

As related in the story of Commander Ozzie Lynch, the 1-122 fell a victim to the *Skate's* torpedoes; the time and manner of the destruction of the *Bonefish* is more obscure.

The *Bonefish*, with Commander Larry L. Edge in command, entered the Sea of Japan on the evening of June 5 from Tsushima Strait. From that day on, she was not again contacted until 2353 of June 15 when she informed the *Skate* that she had three escort vessels on her radar screen. The *Skate* also had the same targets on her screen.

The next day, at 0555, the *Tunny* sighted the *Bonefish* on the surface and pulled up to talk to her. Larry reported a successful torpedo attack to the northward. We now know from postwar reports that the *Bonefish* sank a 7000-ton freighter on June 13. The *Tunny* picked up one of the survivors from a number found on rafts.

On June 17, the *Bonefish* and the *Tunny* united in a two-pronged attack on what promised to be an important target, first sighted by the *Bonefish*. At 1856, Larry Edge flashed the *Tunny* the news that he had tops of ships in sight at a position where the contacts could be cross checked between the two Polecat submarines.

After careful submerged approaches, the two subs, at 1919, were closing on two unidentified enemy vessels. The targets, according to the *Tunny*, tracked on steady course at 330 at a range of sixty thousand yards and doing ten knots. At that time the gap between the *Bonefish* and the *Tunny* was about fifty-six thousand yards. About this time, too, both subs picked up slight indications of 10-CM radar on the bearings of the contacts and concluded that there was something phony about their targets. This could be our old radar false-face disguised as a friend.

Messages to the *Tunny* from the *Bonefish* indicated that the latter had closed the targets to ten thousand yards. However, she reported that, owing to a haze in the direction of the targets, she could not catch them in either of her periscopes. According to reports, the *Tunny* did not believe that the enemy was yet aware of the presence of either submarine.

At 2126, the *Tunny* went to battle stations on the theory that even if the enemy did know that the *Bonefish* was on hand—as indicated by their actions—there were no signs that they knew the *Tunny* was on their track. Betting his blue chips on that assumption, George Pierce closed in. He planned to go in on the starboard quarter, since the enemy now showed signs of knowing that the *Bonefish* was on their port bow. At 2222, when the *Tunny* was within seven thousand yards, the targets opened fire with a wide variety of gunpowder. In his report, Pierce said the guns "were at least" of four-inch calibre. When gun splashes fell within five hundred yards of his vessel, Pierce reversed course. When a shell exploded within two hundred yards on his port beam after the turn, George was glad that he had not continued boring in. Those seemingly innocent and invisible targets that earlier were so inviting to Larry Edge and George Pierce turned out to be destroyers. George wondered how the *Bonefish* had fared in the fray. The next morning, he sighted Larry's vessel and pulled within megaphone range. Among other things, the two Skippers talked about the incident of the previous evening.

"Those lads sure played me for a sucker," grinned Pierce. "If they hadn't been so anxious—or possibly so afraid of submarines—they might have been really annoying."

"You've got something there," agreed Larry. "Those Japs have lots of spunk, but their fighting psychology is hard to understand."

Thereupon Larry Edge asked permission to make a daylight submerged patrol in Toyama Wan, the wide, deep bay which takes shelter behind the rugged Noto Peninsula. Commander Pierce gave his sanction and shoved off for his next day's patrol area down to southward. The *Bonefish* set a course northeastward to the high cape of Suzu Misaki beyond which lie the waters of Toyama Wan.

Somewhere in those deep waters the *Bonefish* was lost. Postwar Japanese reports record an anti-submarine attack on June 18, 1945, at a point twelve miles beyond the headlands of Suzu Misaki in water shown by the chart to be one thousand feet deep. "A great many depth charges were dropped," says the report, "and wood chips and oil came to the surface." This undoubtedly was the attack which sank the *Bonefish*.

However, only eight miles from this spot, the Japanese admit the sinking of the 5500-ton *Konzan Maru* on June 19. One of these dates must be wrong, for no American submarine other than the *Bonefish* could have made that attack.

No matter which date is correct, it appears most likely that the *Bonefish* attacked and sank the *Konzan Maru* and was then counterattacked and sunk by destroyers—possibly the same ones with which she and the *Tunny* had a brush on June 17.

The *Bonefish* did not rendezvous with the other Hellcats on June 23. Messages were sent to her without reply and, since the exit could not be delayed, Hydeman took the only course open to him and ordered the departure as planned on June 24.

Once clear of La Perouse, Commander George Pierce asked permission to stay behind with the *Tunny* in the hope that he might be able to contact the *Bonefish* by radio. All hope was not abandoned, for she might have been badly damaged and forced to seek sanctuary in Vladivostok. The *Tunny* waited in the Sea of Okhotsk for two days, vainly sending out calls for her packmate, but the *Bonefish* was far beyond the call of the *Tunny*'s radio.

Of the fifty-two submarines which were lost by the United States Navy in World War II—forty-one of them as the result of enemy action—the *Bonefish* was the fifty-first. Last to be sunk was the *Bullhead*, nine days before the end of the war.

Operation Barney was the *Bonefish*'s eighth war patrol. In total, she sank twelve enemy vessels for 61,345 tons and damaged about twenty. Enemy records of sinkings are fairly accurate, but claims of damage are impossible to verify with accuracy.

The *Bonefish* began her fighting career as an active member of the Submarine Force with a patrol in the South China Sea in September of 1943. There she won her spurs by sinking two large transports and a cargo ship. From there she swept on through all the seas that wash the shores of the Philippines and the east coast of Asia, the Celebes Sea, the Sulu Sea, the East China Sea, and finally the Sea of Japan. All were her hunting grounds and all heard the thunder of her torpedoes.

Among the enemy ships that contributed to her impressive total of sinkings was one of those most deadly opponents, a 1950-ton Japanese destroyer.

The *Bonefish* was awarded the Navy Unit Commendation for the period of her first and third through sixth patrol.

It seems appropriate to highlight here—in company with the record of the only other American submarine lost in the Sea of Japan—the combat history of the *Wahoo* and what scanty intelligence exists as to her fate.

Information gleaned from Japanese sources since the cessation of hostilities indicates that an anti-submarine attack was made in La Perouse Strait on October 11, 1943. This was two days after the *Sawfish* went through the Strait. Supplementary data on the attack of October 11 state: "Our plane found a floating sub and attacked it with three depth charges." The *Sawfish* was attacked here while making her passage, and that attack is not mentioned in Jap records. However, the primary attacking agency in that case was a patrol boat, and about five depth charges were dropped.

Thus it is safe to assume that the attack of October 11 was made on the *Wahoo*, not on the *Sawfish*. Both Tsushima Strait, where the attack on the steamer was made, and La Perouse Strait, through which the *Wahoo* was to make good her exit from the Sea of Japan, are known to have been mined. This despite the fact that the *Sawfish* transited La Perouse on October 9 and reported no indication of mining. It is believed, however, that the *Wahoo* succumbed to the attack referred to above, and not to a mine

The *Wahoo* was one of the Submarine Force's most valuable units during her first six patrols and her feats have become submarine legend. She is officially credited with sinking twenty vessels for a total of 60,038 tons. As explained before, the number of ships damaged by her can only be approximated, but it must be in the neighborhood of ten. She made only seven patrols, and all except the unlucky sixth were replete with triumphs. Her fighting career began in the Caroline Islands southwest of Guam in August, 1942. That was just a warming-up round, as was her next patrol conducted in the Solomon Islands. Morton really got into his stride on Jan. 24, 1943, when he took the *Wahoo* into the shallow waters of Wewak Harbor on the north coast of New Guinea. There he gave the first classic demonstration of a down-the-throat shot by blowing the bow off a Japanese destroyer which was charging down on his deliberately exposed periscope.

As though this feat was not enough to electrify his comrades in the Submarine Force, two days later Mush wiped out an entire convoy of four ships.

Following that battle, while on his way to Pearl Harbor with no torpedoes remaining, the *Wahoo* attempted to gun a freighter but was driven off by an enemy destroyer. Morton's radio report of that battle strikes an all-time high in submarine humor: "Another running gunfight—destroyer gunning—*Wahoo* running."

For her fourth patrol, the *Wahoo* went to the Yellow Sea west of Korea. There she performed the amazing feat of sinking eight freighters and a transport with a small sized patrol boat and two luggers thrown in for protective measures.

Her next patrol in the Kurile Islands, north of Japan, netted three ships sunk and two damaged. Following these successes came the sixth and seventh patrols which were described in the opening chapters of this volume.

The *Wahoo* was awarded the Presidential Unit Citation for her third patrol. Commander Morton was considered one of the topnotch officers in the Submarine Force, and the loss of his ship was an irreparable blow to the Service.

Japanese records now reveal that the following ships were sunk in the Sea of Japan shortly before the *Wahoo*'s loss: *Taiko* (AK), 2958 tons, Sept. 25, *Konron* (AP), 793 tons, Oct. 6, an unidentified Maru (AK), 1288 tons, Oct. 6, and *Kanko* (AK), 2995 tons, Oct. 9. The *Wahoo* was the only submarine that could have sunk these ships.

And so they rest—two heroic crews—until the trumpet shall call. The *Wahoo* led the way into war's multiple dangers; the *Bonefish* followed and added its contribution toward an early and victorious ending of the war. Far they are from home. But near they shall forever be in the hearts and minds of a grateful nation.

26

TINOSA FACES HOMING TORPEDO

The dirty weather the Bobcats left behind them when they submerged for their sonar-guided transit of Tsushima Strait at dawn on June 6 was on hand to greet them in force as they surfaced after sunset on that same day. When the *Tinosa* attempted to surface about 2200, she had been submerged about sixteen hours and her battery was pretty well depleted. To his deep disappointment, Commander Latham learned that his position was not quite as far advanced as he had hoped. However, the sub was approximately on her prescribed track, which verified the reliability of the original plan to navigate by use of soundings. It was midnight-black and rough on the surface with seas of four scale. A few miles ahead were the lights of some sort of convoy proceeding from Pusan to Japan. There was plenty of radar interference and obviously the convoy was escorted by patrol boats. The *Tinosa* submerged again in order not to give away her presence. Shortly after 2100, she surfaced once more and on two mains headed for the safety of the deep water of the Japanese Sea, recharging her run-down battery with the other two engines.

Seas broke over the bridge frequently, and occasionally some of them got through the hatch and into the control room, but the crew was so jubilant over having passed the Hellpot barrier that they took little notice.

The *Tinosa* selected for her first station the most likely looking port on the east coast of Korea within her operating area, that of Bokuko Ko, and Dick became well acquainted with the soundings of that port while he waited for the "Commence fire" deadline to approach.

No traffic of any sort was sighted, however, until mid-afternoon on the final day of waiting—June 9. Deadline for "Commence attack" was set for sunset that evening. However, almost as an automatic result of her training, the *Tinosa* commenced an approach on a Japanese ship which was sighted about 1430. This vessel was well inshore and had she not slowed on approaching port, the *Tinosa* would not have been able to reach a favorable operating position. As it turned out, Dick had to get into about sixty feet of water. Even so, he was still separated from the target by a shoal of about forty-five feet depth. Finally he was able to reach a firing range of about 2600 yards with a torpedo run of about 2200 yards, but it was still only 1503, some six hours before sunset. As Dick Latham explained to me just before I started writing this book: "The sight of a legitimate target after months of waiting was too much. I simply had to let go three torpedoes aimed, one to miss slightly ahead, one to hit amidships, and one to miss slightly astern.

"Of course, I knew that all submarines would be on station by this time, and that in any event, the Japs would achieve no advantage because the firing deadline had been advanced by a matter of a few hours. As I figured it out, in violating the order, it was a situation where a Japanese ship sunk would do more toward explaining the departure from instructions than any amount of words at a subsequent investigation. Accordingly, a prayer that it would find its mark rode with each of the three torpedoes. Still the seconds seemed endless as they ticked away while I waited and watched for the explosion.

"Because the target was slowing down, it was the last torpedo, fired to miss astern, that finally hit smack M O T. Within a very few minutes the freighter buckled amidships, the bow and stern sections rose high in the air and disappeared in a commotion of bubbles and wreckage.

"Needless to say, the victory made all hands feel right on top of the wave. There is no submarine morale stimulant like a good, clean sinking."

Dick Latham's concern about declaring war in the Sea of Japan a little too early reminds me of an incident earlier in the war when another submarine skipper violated the then existing policy of not expending torpedoes on enemy destroyers.

At that time, April, 1943, we were short of torpedoes and priorities had been established as to the targets on which our small store could be expended. Destroyers, DE's, and other patrol craft were away down at the bottom of the list. They were to be evaded rather than torpedoed.

Lt. Cōmmander Roy L. Gross, Captain of the *Seawolf*, returning from patrol in the Strait of Luzon, came into my office after his arrival at Pearl Harbor with some photographs in his hand. There was an apologetic tone in his voice. The pictures, taken through the *Seawolf*'s periscope, recorded the demise of Patrol Boat #39, an old destroyer of World War I vintage. They were, in my humble opinion, among the best action shots of the war. The first of the series shows a startled looking puff of smoke from her stacks hovering over the doomed vessel after the explosion had subsided. She was hit, according to Roy Gross, right under No. 1 stack. As her forward compartments flooded, the photographs successively showed the forecastle going under, the bridge submerging, and, at last, only the stern showing at a ninety-degree down angle. Finally, the depth charges which she had been ready to dump on the *Seawolf* exploded, thus eliminating any possibility of survivors.

"I'm sorry, Admiral," apologized Gross. "I know it's against orders to waste torpedoes on tincans, but this one got in my way twice while I was trying to get shots at a big tanker and I finally just lost my temper and let him have it!"

I didn't find it too difficult to forgive Roy and today those pictures occupy a place of honor in my "Rogues' Gallery."

As the *Tinosa* reached its territory, the weather improved. A change for the better which, however, produced its own handicaps in the form of scores upon scores of Korean fishing boats—net fishermen in squat little dirty sampans—fleets of them. Their nets now and then would be great hindrances to the Bobcats, all of whom operated along the Korean coast. This was compensated for by the obviously friendly attitude of the Korean fishermen. They never lifted a finger to help or to warn Japanese targets; and, on a few occasions, they furnished fresh fish for Bobcat mess tables in exchange for a carton or two of most welcome cigarettes.

After sinking its first victim, a 2300-ton merchantman, the *Tinosa* submerged, turned, and headed east for deep water. There she dropped down to seventy and then eighty feet as the bottom fell away beneath her keel. The depth soundings had increased to about 130 feet when they suddenly indicated shoaling again. The submarine came back up to periscope depth for an observation in order to fix her position and, perhaps, account for the shoal water. It was then discovered that the fathometer ping was bounding off a layer of dense water and that the depth was actually several hundred feet. A bathythermo reading showed a fourteen-degree sharp negative gradiant at 120 feet where the water temperature was recorded as 31 degrees Fahrenheit. This unexpected discovery—a veritable fortress against enemy pingings—was as welcome as flowers in May to the *Tinosa*. In short order she went down, stopped her motors, and sat on this heavenly layer, licking her chops in satisfaction over her recent feast.

The next morning, when it came time to recharge the batteries, was brightly sunny with the deep blue of the water covered by innumerable whitecaps. As Dick Latham leaned on the bridge rail, he watched the sub's bow sliding through the ocean; the deck would sometimes come down level with the sea and sometimes be ten to twelve feet above it. Suddenly there was a peculiar rush of air through the covered-wagon section of the bridge. Dick yelled to all bridge hands to hold on tight. He knew from previous experience that this rush of air signified that a big bruiser was about to climb over the bridge. It did, but despite his preparation, Dick was knocked to the deck, and thoroughly drenched as the wave rushed over him. The water stripped the leather submarine slippers off his feet so that they hung by the ankle straps only. In the Pacific, incidents of this type were so common that at the first sound of rushing air the alert quartermaster had slammed the conning tower hatch shut to keep the deluge out of the *Tinosa*.

At 1524, on the afternoon of June 10, the *Tinosa* got herself into multiple predicaments so unusual and so dangerous that it needed all the benevolent grace of the J-Factor to pull her out.

It happened that the submarine made a radar contact on a target at the truly fantastic range of 62,000 yards. The plot showed the target to be a ship on a steady course. For the next three or four hours the *Tinosa* steamed on the surface toward a firing position. The phenomenal range which enabled the sub to make this contact was the result of atmospheric conditions that curved the radar beams along the surface of the sea.

Because the approach was conducted over such a long period, the *Tinosa* had the target, course, and speed figured exactly. Under such ideal conditions, Dick decided to fire his stern torpedoes, since none of these had as yet been used. The *Tinosa* submerged. After a short wait, the target came by in an almost ideal firing position for a stern tube shot. Firing data generated by the computers indicated a torpedo run of about twelve hundred yards, ninety-degree track, and zero gyro angles. In order to make certain of the kill, Latham decided to fire three torpedoes.

"How're they running?" asked Latham of the soundman after the three fish had been fired from Stern Tubes 7, 8, and 9.

"Hot, straight, and normal," replied the latter as he focused his electronic attention on the trio of torpedoes boring away toward the target.

Suddenly he straightened up with a startled oath, almost shouting: "Captain, Captain—one of the torps is changing bearing fast!"

With instant attention the Skipper leaned toward the sonar set.

"It's the second fish—the one from Tube 8," explained the operator. Suddenly the sonarman's voice changed pitch as a note of terror crept into the tone of his words. "It's a circular run, sir! A circular run! It's getting louder."

Latham received this truly terrifying news with his usual unshakable calm. Nothing ever stampeded Dick Latham, but he knew only too well that of all potential sources of submarine extinction there is none worse or more terrifying than that which threatens when one of your own torpedoes turns into a homing pigeon, bearing, not an olive branch, but 750 pounds of high explosive ready to blast into eternity the very vessel that sent it forth into the sea. A circular run is exactly what those words imply, namely, a torpedo that stops its advance toward the target because something goes wrong with its steering gear and goes around in a circle, the orbit of which may include the vessel that fired it.

In this case, the fish from Tube 8 had become a homing pigeon and it might well hit the *Tinosa* unless quick action was taken to escape it. At a speed of thirty-three miles per hour, it would not take the torpedo long to return to its starting point. Nor was it necessary to listen for its approach with the sonar gear. The high-pitched whistle-like whine made by its screws as the missile rushed through the water could be heard—and plainly—through the hull. First faintly, then louder and sharper as the Doppler effect of its sound built up in intensity while it approached closer and closer only to swing off again in its vicious and unpredictable circle.

Aboard the *Tinosa* all hands knew that death was approaching on screaming screws. News of the circular run had spread throughout the ship as the talker desperately called for all stations to close watertight doors and ventilation flappers to minimize the flooding in the event the torpedo hit—a hopeless precaution, as everyone realized. There are few secrets on submarines during combat. For a second, it was as if every man aboard was petrified. Men seemed to stop breathing. It was as if the low but increasingly louder whine robbed them of all life, all thought, all motion. We did not know then of the terrible boomerang run by a *Tang* torpedo which had scuttled that submarine with a loss of all but nine hands, or of the earlier loss of the *Tullibee*—the only two instances on record in World War II of American submarines being destroyed by their own torpedoes. Both of these circular runs had occurred while the subs were surfaced and therefore better targets for runaway fish than the submerged *Tinosa*. However, there are no guarantees that a boomerang torpedo will not run deep.

Before the rapidly approaching runaway torpedo could reach the *Tinosa*, Skipper Latham, who seemed proof against petrification, issued an order that brought life back into the human waxworks in the *Tinosa*'s vital compartments.

"Flood negative! All ahead, flank! Take her down fast," he ordered in his calm, steady voice. He did not want to scare anyone into inactivity by shouting above his usual voice level. "Take her to seven hundred feet," he added. Circular runs are so infrequent and so dreaded in a sub that even a skipper with boiler plating over his emotions can be pardoned for freezing momentarily. Dick's brief yielding to the pressure of events was indicated by his order to go to seven hundred feet, which is far beyond even extraordinary diving depth.

Without a second's pause between the issuance of the order and its execution, the *Tinosa* headed deeper as, with lightning speed, the Diving Officer pointed her for the bottom with a fifteen-degree down bubble.

Moments later the voice of the Diving Officer reported: "Passing 250 feet, Captain. How deep do you wish to go?"

By now, Dick had recovered completely from the instant of pressure. He replied smoothly, as if seven hundred feet had never even been mentioned, "Oh, level her off at three hundred feet."

Interwoven with this action was still another. A split-second before the circular run was reported, a fourth torpedo had been shot at the target. By this time, one torpedo had hit the enemy vessel. A dud. All that happened was a low-order explosion, probably of the airflask on the fish from Tube 7. The one from Tube 9 was a miss. So, alas, was the fourth torpedo from Tube 10. By the time the latter reached the target the ship had swung away from its original course. In fact, executing a completely unexpected high-speed turn, it had swung toward the *Tinosa* and now—with an ugly bone in its maw—it was boring right down upon the spot which the Japanese skipper believed to be the position of the submarine that had attempted to torpedo him. Obviously this fellow was bent on revenge.

2050: Those aboard the *Tinosa* rocked with their vessel as it shuddered under the concussion of the first depth charge.

2053: The ex-target delivered a second calling card.

2100: Dick Latham started the *Tinosa* back up from three hundred feet. Perhaps the circular run, by driving the *Tinosa* to such a depth, actually saved her. None of the eggs was close; all of them were set at approximately periscope depth. Dick was boiling mad. He was fed up on Japanese merchantmen that carried depth charges and put on offensive airs. He would show them. "I'm going to sink that ship!" was his determined promise to himself.

On the *Tinosa*'s way to the surface, the target dropped another egg.

"That junk was insignificant," wrote Latham in his Log, "after listening to that circular run. That awful whine still rings in our ears."

The destruction of the *Tang*, through a circular run, as previously mentioned, took place on September 24, 1944, at the very start of her fifth war patrol. Her skipper was Commander Richard H. O'Kane, who received his battle training at the hands of Mush Morton in the *Wahoo*.

At the time of the incident the *Tang* was enroute to her patrol area between Formosa and the China Coast. In the Navy's official "U S Submarine Losses in World War II," the following account is given of this unusual disaster.

The story of the *Tang*'s sinking comes from the report of her surviving Commanding Officer. A night surface attack was launched on October 24, 1944, against a transport which had previously been stopped in an earlier attack. The first torpedo was fired, and when it was observed to be running true, the second and last was loosed. It curved sharply to the left, broached, porpoised, and circled. Emergency speed was called for and the rudder was thrown over. These measures resulted only in the torpedo striking the stern of the *Tang*, rather than amidships.

The explosion was violent, and men as far forward as the control room received broken limbs. The ship went down by the stern with the after three compartments flooded. Of the nine officers and men on the bridge, three were able to swim through the night until picked up eight hours later. One officer escaped from the flooded conning tower and was rescued with the others.

The submarine came to rest on the bottom at 180 feet, and the men in her crowded forward as the after compartments flooded. Publications were burned, and all assembled to the forward room to escape. The escape was delayed by a Japanese patrol, which dropped depth charges. Short circuits caused by sea water started an electrical fire in the forward battery. Thirteen men escaped from the forward room, and by the time the last made his exit, the heat from the fire was so intense that the paint on the bulkhead was scorching, melting, and running down. Of the thirteen men who escaped, only eight reached the surface, and of these but five were able to swim until rescued.

When the nine survivors were picked up by a Japanese destroyer escort, there were victims of the *Tang*'s previous sinkings on board, and they inflicted tortures on the men from the *Tang*. With great humanity, O'Kane states, "When we realized that our clubbings and kickings were being administered by the burned, mutilated survivors of our own handiwork, we found we could take it with less prejudice."

The nine captives were retained by the Japanese in prison camps until the end of the war, and were treated by them in typical fashion. The loss of the *Tang* by her own torpedo, the last one fired on the most successful patrol ever made by a U.S. submarine, was a stroke of singular misfortune. She is credited with having sunk thirteen vessels for 107,324 tons of enemy shipping on this patrol, and her Commanding Officer has been awarded the Congressional Medal of Honor.

*   *   *

When Dick Latham surfaced, bent upon destroying the freighter that had tried to depth-charge him, the ugly customer had vanished completely. Latham simply could not understand how such a rambunctious target could be more than twelve thousand yards away. Dick instituted a through radar search, but when he did locate his late assailant at ninety-one hundred yards, he found that the *Tinosa* had already trespassed some thirty-five miles into *Bowfin* territory and decided not to continue the chase.

It would have been some consolation to Latham had he known that his target was destined to run into Alec Tyree's *Bowfin* very shortly and get herself properly sunk—but more of that elsewhere.

Understatement of the day (in the *Tinosa*'s Log): "Things seemed to be happening with great rapidity."

At noon on June 12, the *Tinosa* began a flirtation with a sea-truck, a 1500-ton motor-driven vessel of a type popular and useful as a bearer of Japanese maritime burdens. After making his approach submerged, Dick lost the target in a heavy fog. He surfaced for a look around, sighted the sea-truck at a distance of six thousand yards, and decided to sink him with his deck gun. Accordingly "Battle stations surface" was ordered. The plan was to approach through the fog to point-blank gun range before being detected.

While executing the plan, however, the fog lifted as suddenly as it had descended, and the *Tinosa* was as naked as a newborn baby as it steamed along about three miles off the coast attempting to overtake the target.

Figures could be seen running forward on the small Japanese freighter to man a deck gun on her forecastle. When the range had closed to about four thousand yards, the *Tinosa*'s five-inch deck gun barked for the first time. . . . What marksmanship! The crew was amazed to see their first shot land squarely on the bow gun of the freighter, demolishing gun and gun crew.

The *Tinosa*'s exuberant gun crew continued to put slug after slug into a spot at the waterline in the vicinity of the engine room. The photographer's mate sat on the periscope shears and proudly recorded the entire action in motion pictures for posterity. The *Tinosa* finally came within a range of about three hundred yards, and before long the freighter sank stern-first while her crew in a lifeboat pulled away from the action on the disengaged side.

The entire fracas took place in bright clear sunshine and came to an end within a mile of the Korean coast. As the *Tinosa* steamed seaward, still on the surface, she passed close aboard many Korean fishing vessels whose crews had had box seats for the engagement and waved in friendly fashion to the passing submarine. . . . Later, when the film was developed, it was found that the entire record had been overexposed and no pictures whatever resulted. Thus pride goeth before the fall.

Contrary to expectations, Bokuku Ko did not prove productive. In the *Tinosa*'s area it seemed that sailing sampans and shallow-draft small craft carried most of the cargo up and down the coast of Korea. Dick Latham concluded that the few large ships the enemy had left were used in the relatively long hauls across the Sea of Japan between Korea and the home islands. In search of better pastures, he headed south toward Tsushima but the time for the La Perouse rendezvous was getting so near that he did not have much opportunity to discover worthwhile targets.

However, there were two noteworthy exceptions. Both came within range of the *Tinosa*'s weapons on June 20 as she was returning northward. The first contact was a 4600-ton medium AK at 0305. The submarine discovered herself to be well on the starboard quarter of the target. This meant that a long end-around run was required to reach firing position. The initial range was 11,500 yards. The submarine commenced a surface run for position at high speed, keeping the mast of the target in sight through the raised periscope.

At 0539, the submarine dived ahead of the target and waited for him to come by. The target was a Japanese merchant ship making about nine knots. Three torpedoes were fired at an easy range of 750 yards. The last torpedo had a run of about 420 yards. To the crew's intense satisfaction, all three torpedoes hit and exploded properly. The target took about a ten-degree down angle and appeared to be still making nine knots when it completely disappeared from sight about thirty-seven seconds after the last explosion. To Dick, following its course through the scope, it looked as if the vessel was plowing toward the bottom under full steam. The only thing left of that ship was a crate about the size of an outhouse, with a very dejected and bewildered Japanese seaman seated atop it.

After sunset that same day, the submerged *Tinosa* sighted smoke on the horizon at an estimated distance of twenty thousand yards. Battle stations were manned and Dick took sights of the target at twenty-minute intervals with one eye. With the other, he kept an uneasy check on the steadily decreasing battery voltage. Running all day on his batteries leaves a submariner small margin to operate on when urgency for re-charging arrives long before sunset, as on this particular day.

Not until 1924, when twilight still hung over the sea scape, was the *Tinosa* in position to fire a salvo of four torpedoes for a run of twelve hundred yards. Two were hits. The first hit—aft—was followed by a spectacular broiling orange flame that rose to a height of eight hundred feet. Chances are that this maru was carrying aviation gas. Four minutes later the *Tinosa* felt the severe shock of a close and loud explosion, like that of an aircraft bomb. Latham, who had been too busy to do much looking around, did so, and swiftly. But no planes were in sight. It so happened that the Number 2 poppet had failed to work—a dead giveaway for a sub—because a large impulse bubble had risen to the surface when the Number 2 torpedo was fired. This might have drawn some bomber's fire. Taking no chances, Dick went to 250 feet, rigged for depth charges, and secured from battle stations.

This was the last shot to be fired by the *Tinosa* during Operation Barney. On its way north to the meeting place for the homeward run it met no targets of any sort. During its cruise of 3522 miles in the Sea of Japan along the coast of Korea, the *Tinosa* sank four vessels for a total loss to the enemy of 12,100 tons.

One mystery remained unexplained. One day, just as he submerged after shooting his noon position, the Skipper of the *Tinosa* heard a large and unidentified airplane fly overhead. Just as the sub went under, its radio picked up, loud and clear, a voice speaking English and saying: "Hello, fellow! This is Flight Seven. I have a message for you."

To this day, Dick has never found out what that message was.

27

FLYING FISH IN ROCK GARDEN

Despite their warm foul-weather clothing, the four lookouts on the periscope shears of the *Flying Fish* drew themselves up as small as they could in futile efforts to resist the cold, wet air that got down their necks, up their sleeves and trouser legs. The well-gloved hands of the watchful quartet were almost stiff with the tensity of their grips on the hand-rails of the periscope shears.

There would be no need of shaving the next morning, thought the port forward lookout. His station, in the full face of the breeze, gave him the worst position in the lookout arrangement. "This duster," he mumbled to himself, "could give Joe Stalin a shave as smooth as a baby's bottom."

Everyone of the four wondered when the Old Man—meaning Commander Robert D. Risser, skipper of the *Flying Fish*—would pull the plug and go down into nice and steady depths. To them, just then, the best sound in the world would be: "Lookouts below! Clear the bridge! Take her down deep!"

Down there at three hundred feet submariners would be as snug as torpedoes in their tubes. Their only contact with what was going on beyond the sub—like all personnel not in the conning tower—had been the voice of Joe, the talker, up in the conning tower, a glib operator who most of the time fancied himself a topnotch newscaster talking to a nationwide audience on a coast-to-coast network, not just to fourscore men in a submersible sardine can. But you had to hand it to Joe and his fellow talkers on other submarines. They really knew how to tell the action stories and how to make them good and hairy. When occasion called for it, as on the Tsushima Strait transit, he would now and then give the gang a bang by taking his mike over near the sonar set and picking up the sound of Hellsbells giving off like the bell of a village church whenever a string of mines came into range. Incidentally, don't let the fact that lookouts do laundry work on subs lead you to believe that they hold a menial status. On the contrary, they are a highly select breed of cats. I use that phrase deliberately because they must have sharp feline night vision. They are given laundry work below deck because it is relaxing in their two hours on and six hours off watch schedules.

From his slightly elevated platform on the bridge—a submarine captain's bridge chair—Bob Risser, Skipper of the *Fish* and boss of the Bobcats, estimated that he was heading into a scale-six sea driven by a north wind which, according to the still falling glass, would increase in velocity during the night. As of that moment, 2300 on June 6, the *Flying Fish* was making poor headway on two engines. It was on a northeast course into the Sea of Japan on the first leg of its journey to northern Korea, a matter of some 450 miles as the snowy albatross flies. The port of Seishin was her station for attack on Mike Day (just three days off) and it was not going to be easy to reach in the teeth of the storm that battered her.

A new day had been born when at 0220 strong gusts of wind and heavy blasts of water bombarded the *Fish* with new and unexpected ferocity. Bob slowed to one-engine speed to make the sub ride easier, but not soon enough. The seas that marched down from the north in serried ranks suddenly rose and stormed the *Flying Fish*. The quartermaster in the conning tower could not slam the upper hatch fast enough to keep out a heavy influx of sea water. It cascaded into the sub's conning tower and on down into other parts of the vessel, including the engine rooms. This flooding created a lot of shorts that put some highly essential electric apparatus out of business for the time being. There were, however, no shorts in the vocal circuits of engine room crews who shouted voluble and ear-burning oratory.

Not until 0447, when all batteries had been "topped off," did Bob Risser take his vessel down. In weather such as that, periscope depth is not deep enough for comfort when you pull the plug. The *Flying Fish* had to descend to 120 feet before it found itself in quiet waters. At lesser depths it bobbed like a cork in a kettle, and even the sturdiest seaman could stand in need of Mother Sill's pills. Bob spent the entire day submerged, and most of the time was devoted to clearing up the grounds caused by the cascading sea water to electrical equipment in general.

That night was a carbon copy of the one gone before. And so, to cover a lot of ground briefly, was the entire twenty-four hour stretch that followed it. In fact, wind and sea did not abate until the early morning of June 8. From then on, the *Flying Fish* made knots to the northwest to make up for lost time.

The morning of June 10—shooting season had opened at sunset the night before—found Bob at his station off the harbor of Seishin which lies quite near the boundary line that separates Korea from Russian Siberia. The visibility was only fair but good enough to give Bob and his exec—and good right arm—Lt. Commander Julian T. Burke, Jr., a chance to discuss and analyze the situation.

Prominent in the picture were many smokestacks and large buildings which bore out the conclusion that the town had considerable industrial activity. What might be a refinery could be seen to the southwest of the city. But no tankers were at anchor near the plant. In fact, no freighters were to be seen anywhere in any part of the harbor that was visible from the periscope of the *Flying Fish*. Nor were any in sight to seaward. The only water-borne craft in view were a number of small fishing boats under sail or at anchor just outside the breakwater. Up and down the seashore, from the center of Seishin, ran rows of low-roofed fisherman's shacks that were almost hidden by drying nets held aloft by stakes.

At 1145, the submerged *Flying Fish* sighted a sea-truck. It proved to be, according to the ONI (Office of Naval Intelligence) book of silhouettes, a Type E-2 of 880 tons and some 230 feet long. Two torpedoes, one of which hit, gave the target a list to port. At first it looked as if its crew was about to quit the ship. Then the men evidently changed their minds. While some of them fired at the sub's periscope from a small-calibre deck gun and machine guns. others tried to take the sea-truck into port. To put an end to this nonsense, Bob fired a third torpedo. He could, however, have saved that trouble and expense, because just as he said "Fire—" the sea-truck up-ended and sank,

About 1900, the *Flying Fish* surfaced and—following its Skipper's hunch—went a-hunting on a course that paralleled the coast and covered the approaches to the port of Rashin.

Some four hours later this paid off in the form of an SJ radar contact at 8450 yards. On tracking, the plotting team discovered that the target was zigzagging radically on a base course for Rashin. However, the legs of his zigs were rather long, which tended to make the tracking quite easy. As far as the radar pips revealed, there were no escorts. About one hour after midnight on June 11 the target was at a range of 2800 yards when it unexpectedly made a one hundred-degree zig to the left.

What could have happened?

To begin with, the night was very dark—so dark that the *Flying Fish* at no time had visual contact with its prey nor could she possibly have been sighted. In addition, a heavy fog had pulled a blanket over anything beyond a range of five hundred yards.

"Do you think he has radar?" asked the wondering Julian Burke.

"No, not likely. Probably some jittery lookout reported a torpedo which was only a porpoise," answered Bob. "Let's have all four mains on full and chase him. We'll have to try a quarter attack. Stand by with three torpedoes from the bow tubes when I give the order."

0130: Three torpedoes left the *Flying Fish* for a run of sixteen hundred yards toward a target no human eye aboard the sub had ever seen. It had never been more than a pip on a radar screen.

0131-33: One torpedo hit. Through the night came the flash and flare of heavy explosions. Then the night was still and empty as before. Also, the pips that had sailed so proudly on the radarscope had vanished.

The technique of making radar attacks against invisible targets was one that developed by leaps and bounds from about the middle of the war when we got the SJ and later the ST. The way a good operator could deduce the type and size of a target was uncanny. Sometimes disaster attended such attacks, as it did with the *Awa Maru*. On the other hand, thousands of tons of enemy shipping was sunk and hundreds of lives of our own men were saved by the aid of newly discovered electronic applications which now have useful peacetime jobs.

The parallel to the use of the atom is obvious—but back to the *Flying Fish*.

The *Flying Fish*, with only the low murmur of one-engine speed to herald its coming, headed toward the target area. Her radar eyes started to pick up debris which was translated into groups of dancing pips on the electronic screen. Soon those aboard the sub heard the shouts of men fighting for survival on the surface of the calm sea. They wanted to live—that is, up to the moment of rescue at the hands of their enemies.

So effectively had these people been indoctrinated with the belief that Americans inflicted cruelties on their prisoners that they would rather perish in the bitter cold sea than suffer capture. Besides, it was a blemish on their honor to survive defeat—or mumbo-jumbo to that effect.

At any rate, as the sound of the approaching submarine was heard, the shouting ceased. The voices went dead. Repeatedly Commander Risser called: *"Osore naide, nobettei—kinasai; osore naide, nori na sai!"* All of which is the Japanese equivalent of: "Don't be afraid! Climb aboard!"

But out of the night, from men clinging to debris on the top of the water, came not a single answering shout.

In World War II, Bob Risser had been in many combats. He had faced death at close quarters on several occasions—in battle, in storms, in wrecks. But never until that night, when the *Flying Fish* was surrounded by living human flotsam ready to die just because their masters had told them that they must die, had Risser felt a dread that made him shiver to the core of his soul. A one-line summary of the thoughts that shot through his mind on that occasion could have been: "Dear Lord—one of those, but for the grace of freedom, could have been me!"

Only one survivor came out of the debris. He was Siso Okuno, an elderly soldier who, unconscious, clung to a floating piece of timber. He wore the uniform of a superior private in the Japanese Army. At first he would not give his name. He said he lost it in dishonor when he failed to die as the vessel he was on sank. The superior private was eventually taken to Midway Island for interrogation. He had been a member of the six-man crew of a deck gun on the sunken ship, a 2000-ton freighter. For want of a better name he was called "So-So" because his initials had been S. O. The man actually considered himself dead. He was as affable as he was silent, and his English was limited to: "I thank you, sir."

To help him kill time, the POW was put at work cleaning the bright work on the torpedo tubes—a chore that hurt him deeply because he was called upon to keep weapons used against his countrymen in working order. What became of him? No submariner knows. By and large, he was a sad little man who spent nearly all of his time pining for death and making beautiful Japanese hen-tracks on sheets of paper. Some of these, it later turned out, were a letter to "The Captain, Officers, and Men of this Ship." In it he wrote:

"Even though I may have been unconscious when I was helped out of the sea by your country, as a Japanese I realized a great shame, and in order to erase this biggest of all humiliation, I made up my mind to attain death by some means. I have been suffering greatly during the last few days in an attempt to gain this end, but recently I feel a very warm feeling of friendship coming over me. At first I thought this was merely a temporary trick that my feelings were playing on me, and tried to pass it off with a strong opposing feeling. From a long time back I have been a person who was easily influenced by sentiment. Now I found that I have succumbed to this humane feeling, which is greater than any force I have heretofore encountered. Even my philosophy seems to be changing from day to day.

"*Death is easy, it can be attained at any time* seems to be my attitude at this time. The force that made me feel this strong friendship seemed to be the unlimited humanity of your crew. It is the enormous capacity for friendship that these men have. As the days passed the intensity of this feeling grew, and within less than a month I was led to the point where I cried many times from gratitude. If there had been no language barrier, I would have been eloquent in my words of gratitude. Because our countries use different languages I have failed, but here, as poor as it is, I am taking this opportunity to state my feelings and express my thoughts. To be able to do this is a great joy for me.

"What I regret most now is that, receiving such a gentlemanly compassion, I have no way of repaying you for this. You may think that I have repaid you with animosity. That my everyday routine called for the maintenance of certain of your military equipment caused me great discomfort. Even though I was the recipient of this great kindness from you people, I could not dispell from my mind the thought that what I was handling was there for the sole purpose of taking the life of my own people. This equipment was the basis of this present tragedy of the world. To one like myself, who wishes for the people of the world love and happiness above all else it was very difficult for me to even look at this equipment, let alone handle it. I felt that this must have caused a great deal of discomfort among you and your men. Because it is as I have explained previously, I beg of you to be released from these duties. At the same time, I do not wish my actions around this equipment to be judged as any criterion on how the Japanese people can work. That the Japanese people are extremely hard-working people when it comes to matters of their country I believe firmly, and I wish to have you understand this.

"My life is in the hands of your country. At a not too far off time I believe my soul will be given up to God. Actually, I died on the day on which I was captured. I do not fear death. I will receive it with no compunction. At least it is to me a far better state to be in than to have to make my hands work with the equipment that bears nothing but tragedy.

"While I am alive, I desire above all else that at least one drop less of blood is spilled, that the minimum amount of destruction of civilization takes place, and that peace and happiness will befall the people of Asia. If by fortune I should be able to die for the peace and happiness of all mankind, this would be the most fortunate thing that could befall me. My mind is clearly made up to leave this world for this one cause. By means of this I hope to repay you, the Captain, and your officers and your men, to some extent for the debt I feel toward you. Please excuse the scrawling and accept my prayers for the health and happiness of you, the Captain, and all your officers and men. As crude as the foregoing may be, I present it herewith as a token of the appreciation I feel for your acceptance of me.

"(Because I am a person who has once died, please excuse my abbreviated name)

S. O."

Bob Risser's diving team spent several hours trying to recover charts and log books from the still-floating chart house of Siso Okuno's vessel. For many additional hours, crew members worked in the engine room to dry them because Risser hoped to get some really worthwhile intelligence information.

"When we finally got them to the ward room for perusal,

imagine our feelings to find the charts to be a series of the Yangtze River with carefully plotted fixes indicating a passage up or down."

On June 12, the day after Siso Okuno, the superior private, came aboard, an incident occurred which nearly produced casualties—split sides from laughing. It was during the mid watch, about 0330, when Risser decided to run in close to the entrance of Rashin harbor for a careful inspection of its occupants. The harbor itself, inside the breakwater, was much too shallow to permit submerged entry by anything larger than a midget submarine. Those midgets could dive in a gold fish pond, but the Flying Fish—product of the hearts and hands of John P. Holland, Simon Lake, and several Navy Department Bureaus—required real water to dive in. It needed forty-eight feet to cover her periscope shears and sixty-four feet if she wanted to hide her attack periscope when fully raised.

The night was bright with frosty-looking stars and the prospects at last seemed good for a day unmarred by fog, heavy weather, or those blasted fishing smacks. Risser and his crew were in a good mood. From a slump, her sinkings had taken a decided up-trend. Behind her stretched a record of thirteen sunken enemy ships, a record built up under three iron-nerved and imperturbable skippers—Donk Donaho, Frank Watkins, and Bob Risser. Then intervened a year of frustration and bad breaks that had ended only two days before with an exciting gun action followed next day by a sinking that was a test of anyone's shooting eye. The future looked good.

In the galley, in the crew's mess, and in the wardroom quiet—coffee drinking groups joked and chatted over the recent events. The tension of running the mine fields and barging into a private ocean was broken. Where were these mighty Japanese defenses they had been warned about? This job looked like a pretty soft touch.

Suddenly, at 0610, the radarman's voice broke into their discussions: "Contact; bearing 045."

Instantly the Captain and the TDC operator gathered at the instrument, feeding ranges and bearings into its computer, studying the pip on the radar scope. Morning mists reduced visibility to five hundred yards so that the bridge watch could not pick up the newcomer.

"Not a big pip," said Risser, disappointment in his voice. "When do we get some sizable targets?"

"Not this time, Captain," replied the radarman. "This is either a trawler or a patrol boat."

"From his course, he's not heading for the fishing banks," said the TDC officer. "He's the dawn patrol going out to look for us."

"That's a laugh," chuckled Bob. "Wish him good hunting. While he's left the door open we'll have a look at the hen roost. Might be some fat ones there."

The *Flying Fish* stood on toward the harbor entrance, sweeping constantly with her radar and finding nothing. However, she could not be sure about the docks because of background interference. One lonely fisherman seemed to be the only occupant.

By this time, the visibility was improving and at 0650 two hoarse blasts of the klaxon—"Ah-oooh-wa, ah-oooh-wa"— sent the sub plunging to periscope depth as the Skipper headed out to patrol in a little deeper water. And there in the morning light they saw their friend the patrol boat, or one just like her, heading back for port. She seemed to hang her head as though she were disappointed. She was not pinging, evidently thinking that no sub commander would dare to enter such shallow waters—certainly not in daylight. And certainly not in the face of such bold opposition as one of the Mikado's own patrol boats.

There was nothing Gilbert and Sullivanish about the vessel. It bristled with lookouts, guns, and depth charges. In truth, Risser wanted no fracas with him in these confined waters, so they passed almost within baseball toss of each other on opposite courses. One exploratory ping by the PC boat and the *Flying Fish* might have been in a plenty hot frying pan.

The situation was so extraordinary that the Skipper turned the talker loose on the mike. The crew was quietly having breakfast and Joe, the talker, with the resonant voice of a well-known radio entertainer, convulsed his audience with his version of the delinquency of this guardian of the Emperor's ocean going off and leaving the hen house door open.

"Where you been, Big Boy?" he demanded. "You done been out all night like a big brave Keystone cop. And you done lef' de do' open! I'm gonna tell Miss Tokyo Rose 'bout you. But what I wants to know is—where the Hell is them chickens?"

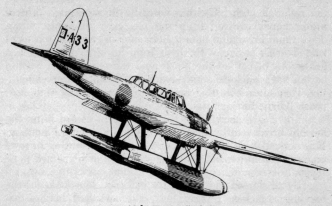

Aichi E 13A "Jake"

The roar that followed boosted the noise level of the ship far too high according to the watch officer's ideas. "Okay, okay, Joe, sign off for now—or do you want that PC fellow to hear you?"

Joe did not; he rang down the curtain.

As it did for other Hellcats, June 13 turned out to be a drab day for the old *Fish*. Two targets, six torpedoes expended, no sinkings. All misses were due, probably, to timely evasion warnings given to the targets by planes which were flying overhead at the time of attack. At the end of the day, Risser entered this in his log:

"2230: This was a very sorry day—missed two and couldn't get in on one. Six torpedoes wasted. The misses were undoubtedly caused by target maneuvers, but the spread applied might well have given us a hit or so with any luck. The 27.5-knot torpedo speed was certainly against us. We were probably sighted by the JAKE at same time and it is possible that he saw an impulse bubble when we fired. Visibility was excellent (best of any day in the Japan Sea) and the sea was flat calm. We did not use high speed at any time, however, used only 1-2 feet of attack scope and, without boasting, my periscope exposures were reasonably few and extremely short. In retrospect, I should have trailed and taken them on after dark, but the set-up was perfect for a double kill and missing was the last thing I thought of."

On the morning of June 15, the deck of the *Flying Fish*

ran red, not with blood but with the thinly diluted dust of bricks newly pressed from the red clays of Korea. From dawn, and for several hours, Bob was busy sinking ten large loaded brick barges with shells from his five-inch gun. The explosions had filled the air around the entrance to Seishin harbor with brick dust and dyed the *Flying Fish* crimson.

That afternoon the *Flying Fish* had one of the most unusual experiences that ever befell a submarine. It all began in the late afternoon when the *Flying Fish* closed in on the Seishin breakwater at periscope depth. Without enthusiasm, Bob noticed four or five AK's in the harbor, but all beyond reach of his torpedoes. Through the lens of his attack periscope, Risser watched trains pull in and out of the town on tracks that skirted the shore. He had only sour looks for the bustling launches, puffing tugs, and awkward barges that moved about inside the port area. Nothing there of interest to a wolf-pack commander in quest of sinkable bottoms.

With bored and detached interest, Risser watched a small tug with two deep-riding barges in tow head toward his position near the end of the breakwater. Without giving a second thought to the situation, he ordered the *Fish* taken to ninety feet. Not so much to avoid discovery as to prevent the tug or the barges from fouling his periscopes, antennas, and other gear. He also went ahead at ⅔ speed, thinking that would bring him well out of the way of the approaching vessels which, according to all indications, were about to pass down his port side. The tugs' propellers were plainly heard within the sub as they passed overhead. And then—all at once—there were no more propeller noises. The tug had stopped. Bob waited for it to start up again, but when after several minutes of somewhat impatient waiting the silence continued, Bob became curious to know what was going on. So with the greatest care in the world—lest he ram his scope into the bottom of a tug or a barge—he came to sixty feet and told the periscope "jockey" to run his precious mechanical eye aloft but at the slowest possible speed. When it broke through the surface in open water, the Skipper found himself looking right into a scow heaped high with boulders. At its stern stood a steersman. However, he was so busy preparing to open the bottom doors of his lighter in order to dump the boulders into the harbor that he never saw the periscope. Bob succinctly observed, "He could have spit on it!" Then he added: "The man did not see us, but a quick look showed me that the barge was full of large boulders which, at any second, would plunge down upon the *Flying Fish*."

This was no place for a submarine, what with a depth charge of boulders about to descend upon it. Either the Nips were building a new breakwater or else they were extending the old one. Whatever the answer was, Bob did not care so long as he got out of the way—but quick! Said he: "Take her back to ninety feet, fast. Right full rudder. All ahead full and don't spare those galloping horses."

Having heard their talker describe what the Captain had seen through his periscope, all hands bent to their respective tasks with enthusiasm.

"That could have been a close one," observed Risser in giving the details. "I was scared, sure; even though they could not have done fatal damage I didn't want any part of those stone age depth charges and I didn't want those boulders piling on my nice new decks. But I couldn't help laughing at the novelty of the situation. I'll bet no sub has ever been threatened with becoming a permanent part of somebody's breakwater. . . . You know something like the fairy book story of the jealous king who walled up his queen's lover in the closet of her chamber."

The *Flying Fish* had only one encounter with the real thing in depth charges. That was on June 20, the day after what one might call the Seishin incident. At 1607, the sub swung on a large AK and fired three torpedoes. It was a fast set-up that should have been sweet, but it turned out sour. What saved the AK was a quick course change to enter Seishin harbor. The end-of-run explosions of the three torpedoes that missed evidently alerted a destroyer escort in port. Soon after the torpedoes exploded, the *Flying Fish* heard echo ranging from the inner harbor. Also screws and an ST contact at sixteen hundred yards. All of this data came too late for the sub to surface and start running from the high-explosive rub-down that was evidently coming her way.

As expected, depth charges came the sub's way, but by then the *Fish* was at three hundred feet, rigged and ready. . . . Thirteen ashcans. . . . Not one was close, but each was dropped with great deliberation. All fell far astern. At 1845, when the coast was clear, the *Flying Fish* surfaced and stood seaward to patrol in deep water and charge her batteries. Ten minutes after she surfaced, Risser had his tilt with the mysterious 10-CM contact which had harrassed all the Hellcats. At the outset, this interference—so typically American that it seemed to come from a real "friend"—came from the southeast. *Bowfin* territory. And yet it seemed phony to Bob's experienced and suspicious radar man. After careful listening, he declared it to be a Jap 10-CM. The interference remained on a steady bearing of 119 degrees, true, for about twenty-five minutes. Then, suddenly, it switched to 150 degrees, true, where it remained until the *Flying Fish* lost it some twenty minutes later.

"'He was very, very cagey," explained Risser. "And he obviously had our SJ Radar nailed down cold. It was almost like two people meeting and dodging each other in the same direction the way we both turned our radars on and off."

As in all the other 10-CM contacts in the Sea of Japan during Operation Barney—and thanks, undoubtedly, to the bitter lesson learned the hard way by Commander Harry Greer aboard his valiant *Sea Horse* in the East China Sea attack—none of our submarine captains fell for the ruse that was intended to lure them into contact under the guise of friends. One cannot realize how strong is the temptation to establish a friendly contact in combat territory, to say "Hello"— only to discover a relentless enemy at the depth-charge distributing end.

On June 23, the Hellcats' last full day in the Sea of Japan, Bob Risser was working his way up along the Siberian coast without knowing his exact whereabouts. This was due to low visibility and a monotonous shore line. At long last, he and his navigation officer convinced themselves that they were opposite Egorava Point Using that as departure point, they stood eastward to the place of Bobcat rendezvous. Enroute, the *Flying Fish* sighted only two Russian freighters. Just after dark, it reached its destination and there met up with the *Bowfin*. But no *Tinosa*. A while later, Bob heard unmistakably friendly contacts to the east. They turned out to be the *Sea Dog* and her Hepcats. Risser had just reported his score to Hydeman—two AK's, one small tug, and ten brick barges, for a total of 3180 tons sunk—when his voice radio cut out. This was most annoying, for Risser had much to talk about. Still, he was able to listen in on the free and fast flow of conversation among the other Hellcats. During the night of June 23-24, Risser dashed around in search of the *Tinosa*. He was just on the verge of becoming a bit worried when he met up with Dick Latham's sub at 0103 in company with the *Bowfin*

and the *Spadefish*. At that hour, also, Bob Risser's voice radio
was back in commission. And Bob, as previously indicated,
had plenty to talk about—from heart-breaking torpedo misses, to the unusual incident near Seishin breakwater when he
barely avoided a boulder depth charge. He led of by saying,
most seriously: "The diving conditions were pretty good up
near Boulder Damn!"

"What's that," chided a listener, "Boulder Dam? You're
'way off the beam, boy. That's back in the blue-chip country,
near Las Vegas."

"If anything, you must mean Hoover Damn," injected
the voice of a Republican.

"No," answered Risser, "I mean Boulder Damn. It used
to be Seishin. But on my chart it reads: *Boulder D-a-m-n*.
And if you gents will lend me your ears, ever so briefly, I'll
gladly tell you why."

And he did.

28

BOWFIN FIGHTS FOG AND FISHING

The afternoon of June 17 was one of scattered islands of
fog as well as light, intermittent rains on that part of the Sea
of Japan where the huge bay of Tongjoson Man cuts deeply
into the Korean coast. Over these dreary waters the *Bowfin*,
skippered by Comdr. A. K. Alec Tyree, was returning to its
patrol area after having tried to attend a scheduled rendezvous with the other two Bobcats, Latham's *Tinosa* and Risser's
Flying Fish. But, for reasons unknown to Alec, the meeting
never came off and the radio inquiries he subsequently shot
forth to the other two vessels were not answered. Nearly all
of his ship contacts along this Korean coast had been little
ones. Either thirty to forty-foot sailing vessels or Korean
fishing sampans. Since taking station, almost a week earlier,
Alec had seen so many of these vessels that the rare sight of a
steamer was a distinct novelty.

In the early evening hours of June 17, the *Bowfin*

Skipper decided to swing north into *Flying Fish* territory in the hope of contacting Bob Risser. Later, during the mid watch—a couple of hours after he had sighted Kozakov Light—he picked up an ST radar bearing at 12,750 yards. It was a small in-and-out contact which, some eight minutes later, turned out to be two contacts of the same size. At that particular time, Tyree did not associate the arrival of this pair with his own almost continuous sweeps with the *Bowfin*'s SJ radar. He doubted the foe would have the ability to make SJ intercepts.

At 0330, it looked as if the two radar pips had taken station astern of the *Bowfin*. The range was now 8800 yards. Alec, cruising on the surface, was course-clocking at one-engine speed. The visibility was, at its best, 150 yards. As he maintained a vigilant radar watch, the skipper concluded that his tail-drag consisted of two nosy destroyer escorts. Apparently they were in column at five hundred yards apart. An hour later the snoopers were still there and still in column, but the range had closed to 7250 yards. At 0445, the range was down to 6800 yards; evidently the Nips were trying hard to close the gap between them and the sub. If they were looking for a gun battle, thought Tyree, it was just about time for them to start the music. Or perhaps, for a DE, a 6800-yard range on a dark and miserable night was too much. He had detected no radar interference from them but, obviously, they must be so equipped; otherwise they could not track him so accurately. Two minutes later, as though to answer his mental questioning, came the sound of gunfire astern.

"All engines," he ordered. "Ahead full."

More gunfire. Now he could also hear the dull thud of shells exploding deep in the surrounding fog. The visibility had closed to one hundred yards, the range to 6500. Rather thrilling to play blindman's bluff this way, thought Tyree. But for safety's sake he called the lookouts down and sent them below. At the same time, the *Bowfin* was ordered to set up a zigzagging course that would take it from 090 true degrees to 135 true degrees.

At 0449, the radar revealed the pip of one shell splash about five hundred yards astern. At 0450, another exploded four hundred yards abeam to starboard. At 0451, the bracketing became really effective. The enemy gunners were getting on their target. The next splash was twenty-five yards off to port and abreast the conning tower. It was so close that fragments ricocheted across the *Bowfin's* bow and slashed the sea on the other side.

This was getting a bit tiresome. Awfully good shooting and all that, but Alec decided not to be there when the next one landed; so he pulled the plug and pointed her down for three hundred feet where exploding shells could not threaten to scrape the paint off his boat. As the *Bowfin* submerged, to Tyree's surprise and pleasure, she had to flood in considerable water at 175 feet to force her way through a fourteen-degree negative gradient. All hands were pleased because the cold layer would be a wonderfully protective blanket from eager-beaver pingers.

Meanwhile, topside, the steadily approaching enemy slammed some fifteen to twenty more shells in the *Bowfin's* presumed direction. Perhaps they continued to fire in the belief that their gunnery had scored a demolishing hit on the sub and that they therefore could not see their target on the radar scope.

Enemy shells kept falling until 0458; then came the pingings. Battle stations were manned; the ship rigged for depth charges and silent running and, for safety's sake, dropped to three hundred and fifty feet. The patrol vessels were now about five hundred yards astern. But apparently the sharp jog in the temperature gradient, which acted as a protective umbrella over the *Bowfin*, was too much for the pings to penetrate. At any rate, no depth charges were dropped. Tyree felt certain that his foe was never able to make sonar contact. By 0608, the pinging was very weak and at 0708, the *Bowfin* rose to periscope depth. A peek showed nothing in sight in visibility conditions of about one thousand yards.

In his Log, following this encounter, Alec Tyree entered these highly pertinent remarks:

"1241: Sound lost all pinging astern.

"In retrospect, we should have deduced that these contacts had radar from their actions and from the fact that they were maintaining station on each other in a fog. We learned a lesson. The enemy radar must have been at a frequency higher than 1000 mcs., yet it did not appear on the SJ. It took this demonstration to fully convince the C.O. that the Japs have some radar which is really good. Furthermore, it is considered highly probable that these craft had SJ radar interception receivers."

From that time on, and in view of this conclusion regarding the exposure to which his SJ radar subjected him, Tyree used his SJ intermittently instead of continuously as he had before. He knew now that it was capable of summoning very, very unwelcome companions.

Two of the three sinkings accomplished by the *Bowfin* took place quite early in the game of hide and seek in the Emperor's Sea. Tyree's first attack, June 11—on an unescorted but zigging 4000-ton AK—could be considered routine, but there were odd circumstances about it which were far from routine.

At 0005 on midnight of June 11, the *Bowfin* picked up a radar pip as tall as a pine tree. Bearing: 135 true. Range: 65,000 yards. Strangely enough, the target seemed to have a 10-CM radar which it was using sparingly. After the contact had been traced all the way down to thirty thousand yards with a good pip, Alec stationed the tracking party. For all he knew, from the size of the pip and the terrific range on contact, he might have a battleship approaching from the south, from *Tinosa*-land. How had Latham ever missed as big and as juicy a berry as this? Tyree could not figure it out, but he did know that odd radar contacts—sort of mirages—had been made farther south—in the Yellow and East China Seas. This thing might be only a sampan.

Of course, the answer was that this was the very vessel which not so many hours previously and some seventy-five miles to the south had given the *Tinosa* so much trouble when all four of her torpedoes missed, when one of those torpedoes staged a circular run on the sub, and when the pursued became the pursuer by counterattacking and dumping a pattern of charges on the surprised submarine.

The vessel—a 4000-ton, 360-foot AK freighter—was standing up from the south at a speed of nine knots. It was unescorted but zigzagging from 240 to 300 true. Evidently the skipper of the ship had learned a lesson as the result of his encounter with Dick's submersible. Eventually Alec got a true picture of his target. It was not a battleship and it had no radar—10-CM or otherwise. What Alec saw turned out to be a reflection of his own radar from the target—an unusual circumstance, but submariners had learned to expect all kinds of antics from radar in oriental atmospheres. In Luzon Strait they even encountered ghosts at night—pips that raced across the screen at twenty-five knots and never were identified—albatross, maybe.... or could the fabled Flying Dutchman still be at sea looking for his redeeming love?

At 0210, just as he was making ready for attack, Tyree had to dodge a small fishing boat. As the *Bowfin* bore down on it, someone aboard the fisherman began to flash a white light on the sub. Tyree was about four thousand yards ahead of the target at that time. When he was clear of the fishing boat—which kept on flashing its white light, much to Tyree's annoyance, for it could be a warning signal to his quarry—he bored in to the attack. Four tubes were fired from forward at 0236. Three minutes later—after a wait that seemed much longer—he heard one torpedo hit followed by several loud internal explosions. At 0242, the target's bow pointed to the sky and thirty seconds later it had completely disappeared. A final taps over the sinking of this merchantman, which had tried so valiantly to sink the *Tinosa*, was sounded by her own depth charges that went down with the torpedoed hull. Within ten minutes the *Bowfin* secured from battle stations and resumed the task of completing her battery charge.

Two days later, on June 13 in a daylight attack, she sent a 2300-ton SCL to its wet grave without trace other than an overturned lifeboat.

During this attack, trouble developed in the after torpedo room—an apparently jammed outer torpedo tube door. This was bad news, for it meant an ice-cold bath for someone.

5″ Gun

However, two members of the *Bowfin* chapter of the Polar Bears club, Lieutenant C. J. Flessner and W. E. Cole, Torpedoman 1st Class, dived over the stern to take a look-see. All they got for their pains was a good swim, for the tube door was O.K. A jammed indicator had made it appear partly closed. They reported the water in the Emperor's private lake was very refreshing—the thermometer registered a bracing thirty-seven degrees.

The *Bowfin*, submerged ten miles south of Joshin at dawn on June 20, was not too happy. So far, only two rather small freighters were in the bag and time was beginning to run out. True the five-inch gun's crew had added a paltry twenty tons to the ship's score by blowing the daylights out of a two-masted schooner about midnight on June 14. Gun actions are always exciting, but at night, with the muzzle flash of the gun blinding the pointer and trainer, it's difficult to get your hits into the waterline and, without that, a wooden ship will float a long while. However, when the skipper called the fight off, it was evident that that shell-swept mass of wreckage would never make port.

The Captain had been called to take the dive at daylight—in fact he had been on the bridge most of the night. Dawn comes awfully early in summer at latitude 40 degrees north, and the *Bowfin* dove at 0342 when honest folk at home were still deep in their sacks—or whatever it was we called such things before World War II coined the word "sack."

A northerly course was set for the Joshin breakwater since Commander Tyree wanted to have a look into the harbor. He estimated that any shipping bound from this area to Honshu would proceed on a southeasterly course; hence the station he had selected should yield some targets.

However, the visibility did not seem inclined to play on the side of the *egin-san*—meaning Mr. Hairy Barbarian—invader, and the usually cooperative ST periscope radar had chosen this morning to "flip its lid," as the radar technician expressed it. Now and then that morning the mountains back of the coastline stood out in their clear blue beauty. But when the next wave of fog swept down, it was hard to tell whether the periscope eye was above water or below it.

After one such interval, Alec Tyree swore he saw a seagull sitting on the fog. This striking bit of news, gravely confirmed by the officer-of-the-deck and relayed by the talker, started a brisk argument in the forward room where a third-class torpedoman, earphones on his curly brown head, questioned the verity of the report.

"My dad," he argued, "was a bar pilot out of New Orleans where they got plenty fog and he never told me about no seagulls sittin' on it. But he did used to cuss that river water—said it was too thick to drink and too thin to walk on. I cain't figure why he worried about water—he drank mighty little of it anyhow."

About 0500, the visibility began to cooperate and the quartermaster, who was spelling the O.O.D. at the periscope for a few minutes, reported he could see smoke on the port bow. Thereupon the sub's course was altered toward it. By 0530, the contact was definite and the Captain was called to have a look. There it was, a canopy of black coal smoke and under it a large engines-aft freighter, bearing 330 degrees true, range fourteen thousand yards, angle on the bow forty-five-degrees, port.

"Not so good, not so good," murmured Tyree. "It will be a minor miracle if we get ahead of that baby. . . . Too much angle on the bow. . . . What's the course?"

"Two, seven, O," from the TDC operator.

"Bring her to two, seven, O, all ahead full; battle stations, torpedo."

The ship rang with sound as the sleeping hands tumbled out and manned their stations. Busy electricians checked the gravity of the batteries; torpedomen charged their torpedo impulse tanks; ship's cooks replenished the coffee makers—in the old days this was the time to spice the main brace with a tot of rum to all hands, but our modern Navy does its work on coffee.

As the superstructure hummed to the rush of water through it and the range decreased, Alec discovered by quick periscope looks that two smaller vessels were in column astern of the big AK. They were of perhaps 1000 and 1500 tons respectively, but the big boy of an estimated 7000 tons was the one which made his heart beat faster and on which all hands pinned their hopes. If they could just sink that baby, the *Bowfin* would really be back in business.

The sea was so glassy calm that periscope peeks had to be few and cautious, and Tyree resented having to slow down each time before he called "Up periscope," in order to avoid a high feather of spray around the extended scope. His targets were hugging the beach, and he cursed himself for not having selected a patrol position closer inshore.

With the conning tower tense and silent, there came the sound of someone scrambling up the ladder from the control room. A wardroom mess boy's grinning face appeared. "Cup of coffee, Cap'n?" the steward's mate asked.

"Sure could use on," replied the distraught Skipper, ". . . black. . . . Ask the Chief if he's giving us all the juice he's got."

"Maneuvering room!" called the talker. "Captain wants to know if you are giving us all you've got?"

Hoarse squawkings came from the phone receiver. "Yes, sir, he says you've got all the battery can stand; we'll have to slow down pretty quick."

For a moment the coffee broke the tension. Thank God for Central America and Brazil! How could we run a war or even a Navy without them? Of all subjects of paramount interest to submariners at sea, food is always one of the first two. Napoleon spoke a true word when he said an army moves on its belly. That goes for submarines—plenty. The greatest morale builder invented for undersea warfare in World War II was not the luscious pin-up girl but the ice cream machine. The men might grow blasé about a pin-up girl but never about that ice cream machine.

After an hour's run at full speed, the attack situation was critical. It had to be: "Shoot, Luke, or give up the fowling piece!"

The minimum range predicted by plot and the TDC would be 3500 yards. After that point the torpedo run would lengthen—the target would be going away.

But 3500 yards? . . . Oh, sure, that distance is almost point-blank range with a sixteen-inch gun, and it does not sound like much when you say it fast, but let's see how it sounds in more familiar terms. Roughly it is two miles. To New Yorkers that would be a walk from Washington Square up Fifth Avenue to the 42nd Street Library. To San Franciscans it would be the haul from the Ferry Building up Market Street to Van Ness Avenue. In any man's town it would be a long range for a turkey shoot and with a thirty-three-mile-an-hour torpedo it means a three-and-a-half minute run while your target is moving across the line of fire at ten miles per hour.

The *Bowfin* had six bow tubes ready. In three more days Operation Barney would be over. Those torpedoes would not be welcome back at Pearl Harbor. The place was stacked with them—besides there was that long chance of a hit and on such a target! Even one hit would slow her down so the *Bowfin* could go in and finish her off that night.

Like the England of Lord Nelson, so the USA of Alec Tyree *expects.*

"Well, Johnny," he said to the exec, Lt. Commander C. L. John, "we didn't bring those fish all this way just to haul 'em home again. TDC set?"

"All set, sir."

"Check bearing and fire. Stand by forward. Up periscope." 0614: "Fire one—fire two—"

Six torpedoes went on their way when suddenly the soundman shouted, "One torpedo changing course; it's coming in! Bearing 050!"

"Take her down fast!" yelled Tyree. "Flood negative."

On the way down the sonar operator reported he had lost contact with the erratic torpedo. The danger of being hit by a circular run disappeared and Alec started back for periscope depth.

On the way up, several explosions were heard. Some were probably scare charges but one sounded like a torpedo hit. This attack might pay off, after all. The race was run: would the *Bowfin* cash her tickets at the hundred-dollar window or was her entry an "also ran"?

The tension was high as the skipper, watching the depth gauge needle move upward finally gave the order, "Up scope." When he grasped the training handle he noticed how damp were his palms.

"Must be slipping," he upbraided himself. "Can't you take a little excitement without getting jittery?"

The talker—in fact everyone in the conning tower except the steersman, whose eyes were glued to the compass repeater—was intent on the Captain as he swung the scope onto the target, made a quick run around the horizon, and came back on target. Hope was still high in their hearts.

They hardly believed their ears as Tyree, with a tired motion, rose erect from his semi-crouching position before the scope. "Nothing!" he said. "Not a blankety-blank thing." Through his lens, Alec had seen the big 7000-tonner, its stern looming large against the coastline with its two smaller pals scuttling for safety. Wrote Tyree in his Log: "A sad sight!"

Three possible targets. Six torpedoes. All runs and all errors. The distance had simply been too great, he concluded, for the Mark 18 electric torpedoes. As for the impending circular run? For a moment his pulse had been jumping. But the homing threat had faded out. The erratic fish suffered a change of mind and went elsewhere.

As I back-tracked over Alec Tyree's experiences that morning, a rather poorly forged rhyme ascribed to the pen—in 1803—of Henry Kirke White, self-billed as The Wonderful Juggler, entered my mind. It goes like this:

This new Katterfelto, his show to complete,
Means his boats should all sink as they pass by our fleet;
Then as under the ocean their course they steer right on,
They can pepper their foes from the bed of old Triton.

This verse, anticipating the submarine, was written almost a century before the submarine became a really useful implement of war, but almost two centuries after a merry tub of a Dutchman, named Cornelius Van Drebbel, took King James the First of England down the Thames River in the year 1620 aboard a submersible tub of a rowboat. When one stops to think of it, submersibles have been going up and down for a lot of years—sometimes in public favor, sometimes not.

To us of the Submarine Force, submarining was a game—a grim game, to be sure, but fascinating. Sometimes our little ships had luck, sometimes they had none, but lucky or unlucky, they were always first in our hearts.

The ever-ready, completely prepared battle-feel of a submarine on war patrol or even during target practice had always been the one most fascinating thing in submarine operation. The air aboard is so electric that one can almost hear it crackle. Little chills run up and down the nape of your neck. While each man stands quiet as a statue, you know that underneath this calmness there is explosive emotion under iron control. The men who go into our submarines are well selected. Carefully picked. Born for the job.

Each of the three watch groups into which a sub's complement is divided is able to "work the ship." This means that the men of each watch—from twenty-five to thirty in each group—can take their sub through all its phases: submerge, surface, run the complex electronic equipment, set up tracking parties, and launch submerged or surface attack. There are no stand-ins on submarines. Every man is not only a specialist in his own field but a capable pinch hitter at the other fellow's job. The only exceptions are the cooks. Two on each sub. And if any cook ever knew how to make his chow appetizing, smell good, look good, taste good—it is your under-water chef.

The last vessel sighted by the *Bowfin*—on the morning before the exit-La Perouse meeting—caused a hot but brief flurry of excitement aboard the sub. On the morning of June 22 it sighted a large freighter at twenty thousand yards. After an end-around-run and the usual careful attack preparations, including the manning of battle stations, Alec discovered at noon that his intended target was not only a properly marked Russian vessel but also an American-built Liberty ship. He took several pictures at twelve-hundred-yard range and stole on his way with a face that was mildly magenta. The following night Tyree exchanged recognition signals with the *Flying Fish* and the *Tinosa*. Then, for all practical purposes, the show in the Sea of Japan was at an end.

True, the northeastern coast of Korea had provided a minimum of good targets and the *Bowfin*'s territory was fogbound at least 75 per cent of the time. On top of that, the *Bowfin*, as well as her other Bobcat companions, had been handicapped by having to play hop-scotch with Korean fishermen. There were literally hundreds of the craft, and their nets, time and again, were major hindrances to submarines slipping in and out of fishing waters adjacent to harbors that should have contained a lot of large shipping but to the sorrow of our Maru hunters failed to do so. On one occasion, just outside Joshin harbor, the *Bowfin* stopped one fishing boat to make sure that it did not carry radio-sending apparatus. For their trouble, the five grinning Koreans aboard gave the sub a nice mess of newly caught fish. But sinkings or not, the ship had done her share toward destroying the bridge of self-sufficiency Japan had built across the Sea of Japan.

The *Bowfin*'s total sinkings added up to three ships, including a 20-ton schooner. Her score, in tons, aggregated 6320. An idea of the type of antiquated vessel Tyree was up against is found in the following June 15 Log entry:

"1025: Sighted two-masted lugger of about a hundred tons proceeding down the coast. Speed six knots. JK and QB picked up lugger's screws at two thousand yards.

"It was quite a novelty to see a craft proceeding under power instead of sail. Target passed ahead. Did not attack. We had hopes of something better. But no, nothing but fog."

29

OPERATION BARNEY SECURED

Operation Barney—so far as the approach, break-through, and combat phases were concerned—was finished. Day by day, or rather night by night, I had followed its progress by trying to weave into one thread the strands of radio interceptions, top-secret intelligence, aircraft reports, and news flashes from Radio Tokyo that came to our Submarine Headquarters at Guam.

From the outset we had ruled out any thought of arranging scheduled communications on anything but the most urgent emergency messages from the Hellcats. In their position—right under the guns, as it were, of enemy radio direction-finding stations—any attempt at high-powered or lengthy transmission might easily have been suicidal. Faced with similar problems during the height of the Battle of the Atlantic, German electronics experts had developed a "Squirt" radio transmission for their U-boats whereby an entire message could be shot into the air in a few seconds—so fast that a DFing station could not center on the transmitting submarine. We, however, had no such equipment; hence our information on the progress of Operation Barney came to us by indirect means. However, we had been able to keep remarkably close track of what was happening. For instance the Army Air Corps sent me a picture taken by a photographic plane at thirty thousand feet, showing the three sunken and one damaged targets of the *Skate* at Matsugashita Byochi only a day or so after the sinkings were staged.

I felt that we had done our best with respect to providing the safest possible passage for our submarines through the mine fields of Tsushima Strait by fostering and promoting the development of FM Sonar and by planning the areas of attack for and the duration of the initial invasion of the Sea of Japan. All of the hurdles which blocked the pathway of Operation Barney would have been negotiated by the dawn of June 24—Sonar Day at La Perouse Strait, the day for setting "course zero nine zero"—east—homeward bound for the Hellcats!

The days of June 4, 5, and 6—the invasion days of Tsushima Strait—were grueling enough to those of us left behind on the *Holland* in Guam, with thoughts of the perils which the Hellcats were encountering constantly in our minds, but the days and nights of June 23, 24, and 25, the exit days through La Perouse, were infinitely worse.

They made me recall the hard and seemingly endless chain of hours back in the fall of 1943 after I allowed Mush Morton to go back into the Sea of Japan on a second patrol when his first venture sprouted a miserable crop of dud torpedoes. While it is true that no single submarine nor any single crew can be considered as more important than any other in the mind and heart of a Force Commander, it is equally true that circumstances do arise wherein a ship and its men can become more closely identified with the thinking of "The Old Man" than other men and vessels under his jurisdiction.

Such was true of the *Wahoo* and Mush Morton. First, because Mush, by virtue of his torpedo troubles, had come deeper within the orbit of my personal thinking than ordinarily happens during combat operations. Second, because Morton had the kind of personality that impresses itself upon people.

All I need do to envision the typical face of a determined seagoing fighter is to close my eyes and, to this day, there comes before me the youthful face of Dudley Morton made darker by the shadows his well-justified anger and disappointment cast upon ordinarily sunny features.

War is a game you must take in your stride. There is no time for mourning, no time for revenge. To me World War II was a bloody business of killing enemies and sinking ships. But with Mush Morton and the *Wahoo* it was as if, on the gray, cold waters of desolate La Perouse Strait, there rode a shadowy submarine, a *Wahoo* without substance. It was as if, from the broken periscope of this barnacle-covered wreck, there flew the signal: "Avenge Us!" It was as if the fighting face of Commander Dudley W. Morton, U.S.N., would never relax into a sunny smile until Japan had paid the price for destroying his ship and his crew. That was why the *Wahoo*, why Morton and his men meant something personal to me—why the successful invasion of the Sea of Japan would become the successful way of avenging the *Wahoo*.

Although the *Bonefish*—Larry Edge and his men—had failed to rendezvous with the other Hellcats, there was as yet insufficient reason to consider her lost. Many factors could have delayed the promptness of her return. It was not unusual for submarines to be overdue and eventually reach port.

As for the eight submarines that had gathered west of La Perouse Strait, one leading question was: What traps might the enemy have laid for our exiting submarines in that long and narrow alley?

La Perouse was our first and most natural choice for an exit. The swift current pouring eastward through it was an important consideration, as was also the fact that Russian ships ran through it with impunity. Perhaps they had secret information as to channels through the mine field. Perhaps, as Intelligence said, the mine fields were laid at forty to forty-five feet—a safe depth. We did not know.

Both Tsugaru and Shimonoseki were out of the question, but if Commander Earl Hydeman had found a fleet of enemy anti-submarine vessels and/or flights of planes guarding La Perouse, he would have had to contact me or make his own decision whether to force his way out of La Perouse or run out submerged; whether to make an end run to the north through the shallow tortuous Strait of Tartary, or head south and buck the current back through the mine fields of Tsushima Strait.

It is axiomatic that a good commander plans his retreat before he stages his advance. But the Hellcats' withdrawal had to be performed ad lib without a prepared operational script. The decision was entirely up to Hydeman.

As I have learned since, there was much speculation among the crews of the Hellcats over the point of exit. Most had skippers who considered it unwise to divulge too much of the operation order to their crews lest someone be captured and forced by drugs or torture to "sing" for his captors. (How industrious and adept our enemies were as "singing teachers" we learned at that end of the war when our POW's came back to us.) It was unfortunate that anyone worried about the escape route or whether or not they would be interned in Vladivostok for the duration, but scuttlebutt is scuttlebutt whether in the Navy or on the great outside, and reactions of that kind are so inborn in us that they are inescapable.

Exit speculations were comparable to those of passengers in an airplane, regarding which a non-flyer once said to me: "I never worry when I'm in a plane. I figure the pilot probably wants to live as much as I do and if he can't get us to our destination alive, there surely isn't anything I can do to help him."

I am sure Earl Hydeman worried plenty—as did I back in Guam. I find in my notes for June 22 this entry: "Nothing exciting going on except up in the Japan Sea. We are all holding our breath till those boys come out—and I pray to God they will all come out. Years will be lifted from my shoulders."

Remember this: For all practical purposes, World War II had never reached the Sea of Japan until sunset on that ninth day of June in 1945, when Mars descended upon the Sea in all his modern electronic panoply. All around the rim of Hirohito's oceanette rose the periscopes of American submarines—a whole forest of them, or so it seemed to a thoroughly bewildered Japanese public. Submarines that sent scores of torpedoes into dozens of Japanese freighters; submarines with electronic ears that heard all and saw all while they remained submerged; submarines that sent shells of destruction into cargo sampans and food-producing fishing vessels; submarines that disrupted shipping schedules and paralyzed maritime operations between Japan and Korea; submarines that put a large crimp in the shallow remnants of Japan's self-confidence.

To Nipponese observers, it appeared as if the Sea of Japan was swarming with hostile underwater craft. They were seen in the approaches to important harbors, in ship-sheltering coves and anchorages, at the breakwater entrances of vital ports, on coastal ship lanes and on the steamer tracks that link Korea with Japan. Those submarines had torpedoed twenty-eight vessels, large and small, including one submarine. The grand total loss to the Nips was 70,000 tons, not including the many small craft which were sunk by gunfire and the irreplaceable cargoes of food and raw materials sent to the bottom. But most disastrous of all was the damage to Japanese morale and the will to fight. The shock of the numerous sinkings had given additional spread to the "what's the use, we are licked" attitude which, even then, was prevalent throughout the Empire.

In the light of all this, it was safe to assume that the Japanese had not been inactive in planning to destroy the Hellcats when they attempted to exit from the well-enclosed Sea of Japan.

But what specifically had the Japanese done to that end? How would they stop the Hellcats from getting out? Had they guessed how our subs entered the Sea of Japan?

If so—and the chances were that they had—what had the Mikado's High Command done to tighten up the holes in the strait or to extend or change their mine fields so that our charts would be fatally inaccurate?

As for La Perouse, what could we look for in that sector? As a starter it would be reasonable to expect that additional mines would be planted because our enemies might conclude that we, in exiting, would try to use the same type of information we evidently had gathered in entering Tsushima Strait. They never dreamed that we had invented a device to take the sting out of their Hellpots. Our guess turned out to be sound. Because, as they stood out of La Perouse Strait, Hellcat skippers saw in the early dawn a mine layer at work planting its deadly eggs in the narrow alley south of the island of Nijo Gan.

What formula Earl Hydeman used in working out the probabilities and chances involved in ordering the exit of the Hellcats as he did, I did not know. He was the commander in the field and, as such, the decision and responsibility were his. We had informed him concerning activities of mine layers reported by Intelligence in La Perouse Strait; and we had told him that, in view of the success achieved in penetrating the mine fields of Tsushima Strait, a submerged exit through the former might be advisable—this to allow for the possibility that shallow-set mines had been added to the existing deep-set hellpots.

However, Earl had good information on which to base his decision. He knew that the anti-submarine forces of the Japanese in that theater were pitfully weak; hence an imposing show of strength at La Perouse was not at all likely. Furthermore, he had seen Russian ships still plowing through the strait and had noted the general area which they traversed. Finally, he knew that his own FM Sonar was not working and that the fairly shallow depths of La Perouse—not greater than two hundred feet—would make passage under the mines more hazardous and undesirable unless it was the one and only way out of the Sea of Japan.

Hence his decision was clear. No sonar. No electronics. No tricks. No gadgets. Just salt horse seamanship on the part of the Hellcat captains, taking their ships and crews back to their home ports by running over the mine fields of La Perouse.

30

ALL MAINS FOR GOONEYVILLE

It was a high-spirited occasion as the Hellcats gathered for the exit hour on Sonar Day—after sunset of June 24. It would have been a merry occasion, too, if it had not been that the protracted delay of Commander Larry Edge and his *Bonefish* was viewed with increasing apprehension. At that early hour no one could know, but all could dread. However, since no submarine is ever regarded as lost until it is long overdue, members of the task force radioed each other all sorts of explanations for her absence. These opinions ranged from breakdown of the *Bonefish*'s communications equipment to escape to Vladivostok because of major hull damage or engine failures. Some skippers suggested that if the Hellcats postponed the homeward journey a day or so, the *Bonefish* would show up. Others, like George Pierce, sought permission to remain in the Sea of Japan. This was refused by Hydeman who, however, gave Pierce permission to wait for the *Bonefish* for two days at the eastern end of La Perouse Strait in the Sea of Okhotsk after completing his transit. But, as revealed previously, the *Bonefish* had made its last dive in the bay of Toyama Wan.

Two points of land and an island form a triangle at the spot where La Perouse Strait runs between Karafuto and Hokkaido. The longest of the three legs of this triangle runs from Nishi Notoro Misaki on the north to Soya Misaki on the south, a gap of some twenty-five miles that reaches practically due north and south. The gap from Nishi Notoro Misaki to the rock-like island of Nijo Gan, to the southeast, is some ten miles long; while that from Nijo Gan to Soya Misaki measures about twenty miles on its south by west line.

The southern part of Karafuto ends in two sharp points like the great claw of a tremendous crab. One of these is Nishi Notoro Misaki, the other—and it lies some fifty miles to the east—is Naka Shiretoko Misaki. About halfway between these two points run two important south-north telegraph and telephone cables. About fifteen miles east of Naka Shiretoko Misaki runs the Hundred Fathom Line.

The distance from the center of the strait, where depths of around thirty fathoms obtain, to the safety of the Hundred Fathom Curve to eastward is about seventy miles—a four-to five-hour run at four-engine speed.

In making our analysis at Guam and Hawaii of the probable mine situation at La Perouse, we had only scant information on which to work. A strip approximately fifty miles wide was suitable for mining across the entire north and south extent of the strait. A swift current, sometimes as much as three and a half miles per hour, presented problems both as to laying and maintaining a mine field. Hence we judged that it might have quite a few unintended gaps in it. However, such gaps would not be useful to us except by accident.

Also we believed the mines would not be laid too close to the telegraph and telephone cables between Karafuto and Hokkaido. This narrowed the dangerous area considerably. But our main dependence was upon bits of intelligence which indicated that the mines were set at a depth of forty to forty-five feet, which meant that they would not endanger surface ships—such as the neutral Russians—while submarines, forced to dive by air or surface patrols, would be fairly sure of destruction. The enemy's strategy would be to patrol the strait heavily and thus drive submarines down to their destruction. This may well have been what happened to Mush Morton and the *Wahoo*.

The operation order called for a rendezvous of the

hellcats south-southwest of the high, mountainous island of Kaiba To. From there, the course would be 120 degrees, true, until south of the mid-channel island of Nijo Gan where the traditional and well-remembered "Course Zero Nine Zero" would ring throughout the compartments of every ship.

For making the sortie, Hydeman decided to form his ships in two columns of four each (the *Bonefish* still being absent); interval between columns, two thousand yards; distance between ships, twelve hundred yards. One line-up would be headed by the *Sea Dog* followed by the *Crevalle*, *Spadefish*, and *Skate*. The other lineup, with the *Flying Fish* leading, inclouded the *Bowfin*, the *Tinosa*, and the *Tunny*.

It was long after sunset when the eight little vessels began their exit. The night was made for their trip. Even the flying fish were swimming. Thick clouds shrouded the moon and a friendly fog had rolled its white blanket over the surface of the sea. Earl Hydeman called it the most wonderful fog he had ever seen.

Before they stood out, the captains agreed that there would be no submerging, at any cost for any reason, once the Hellcat go-ahead signal was given. With their compact formation and with the heavy fire-power of eight five-inch guns, plus twenty or more rapid firing forty- and twenty-millimeter guns, Hydeman's flotilla could really give very good account of itself in a surface engagement with anything up to and including a brace of destroyers. Of course, there was no way of knowing what the Japs had waiting for them in La Perouse in the line of anti-submarine vessels. But they were determined that any anti-submarine vessel, so ill advised as to try to stop their surface exit, would know she had been in a fight.

31

"WE'LL SHOOT IT OUT..."

The threat of Japanese men-of-war—with blazing guns and depth charges, safety pins removed, ready in their racks—storming upon the Hellcats out of the black and misty night kept the Hellcat skippers and their crews, especially gun and torpedo crews, quiveringly alert.

Rounds of ammunition for all deck guns were stowed in their respective pressure-proof deck lockers. Some Hellcats had small gun-access trunks built near the forward gun position adjacent to the bridge. Into those, the gun captain, pointer, and trainer were ready at the first sound of "Battle stations, gun action" to squeeze, sardine-tight. From the gun trunk they would swarm out to man the gun the instant the order for gun action was given. Other gun crew members would follow them, including the hot shell man, whose elbow-length asbestos gloves enabled him to handle the empty shells, hot enough to fry catfish on, as they popped out of the breech off the five-inch piece. In subs without the access trunk, gun crews gathered in already overcrowded conning towers leaving elbowroom for nobody. Lined up from conning tower to the ship's magazine below the control room were the four ammo passers who handed along each sixty-odd-pound projectile from storage to gun.

Lookouts—as well as observers who patrolled the electronic beats—were keyed to the highest pitch. They were good to begin with, but on that night they were better than they had ever been before—or, perhaps, since. There were no tricks in the peeping trade these boys were not familiar with as they scanned their respective fragments of the fog-cluttered horizon or shot their invisible probing beams through the air and beneath the sea to await their return with news of invisible lurkers in the night or navigational hazards which according to their charts should not be there.

Because of the weather, airplanes did not constitute a very formidable danger that night. But Japanese Hellpots were a very real and—well, why not admit the fact—terrifying menace. The subs might swerve away from the crown of what these skippers believed to be "the safe Red Russian Road" and slip into a ditch lined by shallow planted Japanese 93's.

Some of the Hellcat men remembered the loss of the *Flier*, which struck a mine in Balabac Strait where her eight survivors swam for seventeen or eighteen hours to reach an island. There would be no swimming in La Perouse. Death would come swiftly in those freezing waters. Each skipper had his own way of reducing tension among his men on that score. For instance, Commander George Pierce of the *Tunny* had his talker describe the *Tunny's* progress through the strait. Earlier, he had described his mine charts to the crews and, as they passed over each of the three or four lines, he would announce the passing.

Aboard the *Skate*, Skipper Ozzie Lynch had put ten pounds of air pressure into the forward torpedo room. "I'm not so sure," he explained later, "that it would have helped to keep us afloat if we had hit a mine, but, anyway, it was a good idea for morale purposes."

The bad radar luck that pursued the *Sea Dog* intermittently during the entire operation again asserted itself on the way out of the Sea of Japan.

"We had hardly gotten under way on the night of our departure," explained Earl, "before the *Sea Dog's* pet radar quit once more. Steiny with the faithful *Crevalle* was next astern of me in our northern exiting column; I gave him the bad news, told him to guide us out, and fell in astern of the last ship, the *Skate*, where Ozzie Lynch coached us along—through the only beautiful fog I've ever seen, a really thick one. About dawn, when we were pretty well clear of any area in which mines would probably be, our radar was again brought to life."

Keyed up as they were for resistance to their exit by A/S Japanese destroyers, the Hellcats arched their backs and extended their claws when talkers on all ships—except the *Sea Dog*—repeated this flash from the radar watchers: "Contact! Bearing 330, range 8600."

Aboard the *Crevalle*, the Exec left Steiny on his bridge platform. In a flash, he was down the hatch, scanning the radar scope. Seconds later he appeared under the hatch and called to the Skipper: "That's right, Captain, it's a ship and a good-sized one. It could be a destroyer or bigger."

For a split second Steinmetz, who was now the column leader, weighed the situation. "It could be a Japanese destroyer, if they've got any big ones up here. It could also be a Russky," he thought. Should he order battle stations, gun action? If he did that, should he inform the ships astern? If it were a Russky and someone got trigger happy, there would be a heck of a mess. He decided against battle stations and called down the hatch: "Track her closely. Get her course and speed as soon as possible and let me know instantly if she seems to be heading our way."

"Aye, aye, sir."

"We'll sweat it out for a while," decided Steiny to himself.

Meanwhile, throughout the little fleet the beams of radar and eyes of lookouts probed through the murk of the night toward the oncoming vessel. Was it a Jap or a Russky?

Seconds ticked into minutes. On some vessels gun captains, pointers, and trainers slipped up into their gun-access trunks. . . . "Just in case," they said.

The chatter of voice radio that had linked sub to sub had come to a dead stop. Aboard the *Sea Dog*, trailing at the end of the column, the radar was not working and she had to be told what was going on. What with the stoppage of phone conversation, the tenseness increased. The *Sea Dog* felt herself alone in a most uncomfortable darkness.

One might have thought that under the pressure somebody would yield and the cry of "Battle stations, gun action" would go up. But no one did. These were battle-hardened, seasoned sea fighters who mentally, physically, and emotionally could hold their ground with steady eyes and nerves. Any gun action at this time, even though successful and without casualty to the submarines, could bring most undesirable responses in the form of patrol craft and bombers.

Lt. Lynch's voice came up the hatch: "She's on an opposite course, Captain, making twelve knots and she'll pass us about eight hundred yards to port. No sign of any move toward us. She's not zigzagging."

Suddenly a lookout sang out and the lilt of intense relief was in his voice: "There he is, Captain. Almost on the port beam and he's all lit up like a new saloon! He's a Russky all right."

Not a very professional report from a lookout and no standard nautical phraseology, but all hands understood it and heaved a sigh.

Now the vessel was close enough for all bridge eyes to see her lights. Skippers among the Hellcats who had seen Russian vessels—and especially those who had fired at or even sunk them because they failed to show required identification lights and markings—grinned with relief. Maybe the so-and-so's at last were going to play ball with us.

Never had a Russky been such a welcome sight. Never had a Russky profited so completely from its compliance with the international requirements of wartime regulations. I hate to think what might have happened to that freighter had she been running darkened or had she made any false move toward those embattled Hellcats. Their five-inch guns and forty-millimeters would have torn her to ribbons before anyone could have said "Jackimir Robinsonowitz."

The relaxed Hellcats might even have given the blighter a cheer had she not at that moment turned on a twenty-four-inch searchlight which played up and down the columns, accurately and slowly, until its long white finger came to rest on the *Spadefish*—an intrusion into her privacy which she greatly resented.

"I thought that Russky was never going to turn that searchlight off," said Bill Germershausen of the *Spadefish*. "He doused that glim just as I was seriously considering dousing it for him!"

Suspect as the *Spadefish* was of having sunk a Russky off the Rebun Shima group three nights before, this might not have been the wisest action to take, but under the circumstances it would have been difficult for anyone to blame Bill Germershausen.

"That trip out was a real thriller," grinned Commander Steinmetz, Skipper of the *Crevalle*. "We were in the northern group as we stood out through the strait and were second ship in column, next behind the *Sea Dog*. We hadn't gone too far when we saw the *Sea Dog* swing sharply to starboard and proceed down the line. Shortly thereafter we got a message from Earl Hydeman, its Skipper, telling me to take charge, that his radar had gone out just as it did on the way to Tsushima Strait before the shooting started.

"Naturally everyone was following in the exact water of the ship ahead, and we did not particularly relish being in the van position. When we had completed our battery charge we speeded up to eighteen knots. It was just about this time that we picked up a ship contact, the already mentioned Russian freighter. I directed a change in course so we would all put a little more distance between ourselves and the stranger. Actually, sighting this contact gave those who thought we should have made the run submerged a bit more confidence in our tactic of going out on the surface.

"Later, when the formation had cleared the contact, we resumed base course. The visibility during the entire passage was not much more than six hundred yards. Yet our PPI showed one of the most perfect examples of station-keeping that I have ever seen, and that included top-level fleet maneuvers.

"One point that I remember vividly was that never was I treated so solicitiously. It seemed every time I put my hand out, a fresh and hot cup of coffee was placed in it."

32

MISSION ACCOMPLISHED—*WAHOO*

Shortly after daybreak, Earl ordered the Hellcat formation slowed and resumed his spot at the head of the column. Once in position, he announced that his radar had been repaired and that he would again take charge. As the subs were now well clear of the mine fields, Steiny could not resist the temptation to go out over the air with a wisecrack to the effect that "my eyebrows are lifted!"

This gentle insinuation by Steiny as to the fortitude of the flagship had a hilarious effect on the rest of the column, and the laughter broke the tension that had gripped the nerves and hearts of all hands from top to bottom. Even the snorting of seas spouting up through the bullnose and through the deck gratings seemed to soften into a long sigh of relief.

About ten that morning the *Crevalle* had to pull clear of the formation because one of her cable guards had come loose and become caught in its starboard screw. Bill reported his troubles to the *Sea Dog*, and Earl sent the remainder of the group on their way while the *Sea Dog* stood by the *Crevalle* the entire time it took to clear her prop. Bill tried to clear by sending Lt. Walter Mazzone over the side with the shallow-water diving rig. However, the combination of cold water and strong current made him give up this method. He finally succeeded by alternately backing down and going ahead until the cable cleared itself. Incidentally, Walt Mazzone was a Reserve who later took a course in Pharmacy and went on active duty in the Medical Service Corps. He was probably

Submarine Combat Pin

the only one of his kind to be entitled to wear Dolphins and the Submarine Combat Pin.

The *Spadefish* was first into Midway. She arrived there without slowing down a single turn after leaving La Perouse, a whole day ahead of the nearest Hellcat. Commander Johnny Waterman, first captain of the fabulous submarine *Barb*, who had begun his career with her by acting as a lightship and radio beacon for the North African landings in November, 1942, met Germershausen as the *Spadefish* docked. "How come you got here so fast, Bill?" he asked in his smooth Louisiana drawl. "You must really run scared, eh, boy?"

An interesting and comprehensive summary of the La Perouse transit was given me by Bob Risser of the *Flying Fish*.

"By far the most exciting and remembered moments of the entire patrol were those taken up in our exit through La Perouse (Soya Strait). We had experienced some communication difficulties the preceding night and thus were somewhat left out of the proceedings. Trying to find out who was who and where was no easy task. By departure time, however, we were straightened out and radio was working perfectly. The *Flying Fish* was guide of the southernmost column—a distinguished but none too enviable position.

"It is impossible to describe that evening in logical narrative form. I remember it as a series of rather disconnected events and odd occurrences: the perfect station-keeping behind us—no ships ever followed so precisely in our wake; our gun crew standing by in the crew's mess; the *Bonefish* not present; a sudden radar contact on the starboard bow—darkened and to this day unexplained; our engineers squeezing considerably more than rated power out of our four trustworthy Fairbanks-Morse engines; the lighted ship standing westward on an opposite course, suddenly lighting off her searchlight and slowly sweeping southward from dead ahead to just abaft the last ship in our column and extinguishing just as suddenly; the innumerable cups of steaming hot coffee. . . .

"The tenseness and excitement of that night might be illustrated by my own actions in using the voice radio. I remember suddenly realizing that I was talking in almost a whisper! No matter when we may have passed out of the suspected mined area, our feelings persisted throughout the night and it was not until dawn—a cold foggy one—that our minds and bodies returned to a normal existence. After passing through the Kuriles I think that I must have slept through to Midway."

But the payoff for that transit and perhaps for all of Operation Barney took place aboard the *Crevalle* when its Skipper, Commander Steinmetz, went below for the first time during the run, but that was not until the *Sea Dog* had resumed its place at the head of its column and the mine fields were far behind. It so happened that the day coincided with the second anniversary of the commissioning of the *Crevalle*. Steiny was asked to go to the after battery. There he found practically everyone who was not on watch gathered around the largest birthday cake he had ever seen. Prominent among the birthday greetings on the snow-white icing was an inscription in big red letters: "Was This Trip Necessary?"

Answering the query, as one who spent almost two years preparing for it and who now looks back on it from a range of almost ten years, I feel even more strongly than in those breathless days of 1945 that it was necessary—vitally necessary. Not only did it deliver a terrific defeat to the enemy, destroy the last remnants of his shipping, cut him off from the support of the mainland and his armies therein; but it also did tremendous damage to the morale of his fighting forces and the people of Japan whose will to win or to die in the last ditches fell lower and lower even as their Rising Sun flag sank in the Sea of Japan. Remember, too, the first atom bomb was yet to be dropped.

To the officers and men, living and dead, who manned and fought the Hellcats, go my most sincere thanks, admiration, and respect for their courage, determination, and ability. They were a splendid cross-section of the lads who composed our Submarine Force, Pacific, and were without exception a tremendous credit to the Force and to the Navy of the United States.

I felt that the dauntless spirit of the Hellcats and of

Dudley Morton's *Wahoo* was with me when I reported their success to Fleet Admiral Nimitz. Together we drafted this dispatch:

"Commander in Chief Pacific Fleet is extremely gratified by the success of this operation which has not only sunk an important number of the enemy's few remaining ships but has also demonstrated your faith in your new equipment and your daring and skill in its operation. You made a shambles out of Hirohito's private ocean. Fleet Admiral Nimitz and I join in sending you a hearty well-done."

It was late evening when I left Admiral Nimitz's Guam Headquarters on Cinepac Hill, after drafting the final message to the Hellcats, and returned to my flagship *Holland* in Apra Harbor.

The night was beautiful with stars, a moon submerging and surfacing through fluffy clouds, and only the whisper of a breeze. I stood for a moment at the rail on the quiet boat deck enjoying its coolness and indulging in pleasant recollections of this fine old ship, cradle of the modern submarine service. When I first saw her, an old submarine hand named Chester W. Nimitz, as Commander Submarine Division Twenty, was beginning his swift climb to the five stars of a Fleet Admiral. Later I served on her when the inimitable, irrepressible, and well-beloved Admiral Dicky Edwards began his rise. A generation of submariners had trod her decks. Some of them would come back wearing the star-studded ribbon of the Medal of Honor, or the coveted blue and white of the Navy Cross; some of them—legendary heroes even before the war had ended—would not come back: Gilmore, Cromwell, Dealey, and Morton.

As I stood there, alone, gazing westward over the sea, it was as if, when the moon was beclouded, I saw once more the wraith of the *Wahoo*. She was heading out—fading into the moon streak on the water. Then I noticed that there had been a change in the signal flags that fluttered from her broken periscope above the rusty and barnacle-covered hull.

The signal no longer read: "Avenge Us!" Instead, distinct in the waning light, I read: "Mission Accomplished!" . . . And the broom—the broom which had not been lashed to the periscope on the *Wahoo*'s return from the Sea of Japan—swept proudly again above her shattered bridge.

Now I could say in sadness and in pride: "Go with God, *Wahoo*!"

EPILOGUE

Thus Operation Barney passed into history. Whether it was the one-two punch that floored Japan for the count may never have been firmly decided in high councils at Navy Department or even Fleet levels.

But over foaming beakers, where hard-handed torpedomen argue with bearded black-gang or "underground savages" as to the merits of their respective departments, the subject is frequently under discussion. Not by torpedomen or motor machinists' mates is the subject of Operation Barney broached, but by quiet sonar men, weary of the endless claims to preeminence voiced by the rival gangs.

"Yes, yes," they say with soul-weary patience, "we know that you torpedo guys won the war. But who was it took you through the mine fields of Tsushima so that your fish could give Hirohito boys the old one-two?"

And in wardroom bull fests, during long submerged runs with the surge of the seas overhead, where bright-eyed young submarine geo-strategists settle the problems of the universe, the pronouncements of the men who rode with the Hellcats through the Hellpots into the Japan Sea to deliver what the Big Boss pridefully called the "knockout punch," carry weight. They have passed the acid test for courage; theirs was the honor of first pitting the magic of revealing sonar beams against hideous death from exploding mines that pressed in from every side.

No one makes the threadbare claim that so-and-so or such-and-such "won the war." However, there is no doubt in the minds of the men who fought in the Sea of Japan as to the supreme importance to final victory of the terrific damage they wrought and the morale-shaking fear they created.

They know that the heavy bombardments laid down on strategic areas of the Empire's eastern shores by Admiral Bill Halsey's battleships and cruisers; the air strikes by Vice Admiral Marc Mitcher's carriers; the bombing raids by General Le May's B-29's; and, last but not least, the liquidation, one by one, of the Japanese Pacific outposts by the hard-fighting soldiers and marines of Generals MacArthur and Holland Smith—all made their contribution to the final victory. Each added its crushing weight to the overwhelming burden which ultimately destroyed that vital factor, that indispensible element without which no armed forces, no civil population can carry on—the will to win.

They also know—as who does not—the punishment the British took from the air and the disasters they suffered in the field without cracking. But what was the haunting dread that dominated their thinking in World War II as in World War I? The fear that they might be isolated—have their vital supplies, their bread and beef, their beans and bullets, cut off by enemy submarines. We can all remember those frantic days of 1942 when German submarines were sinking tankers, freighters, even lightships, right in our own front yard, fouling the Gulf Coast and Atlantic or Venezuelan wells, silting the bottom of the ocean with priceless nitrate and manganese from South American.

That was the threat which drew banner headlines, that tensed the faces of planning boards in Navy and War Departments—the threat of being cut off from indispensable strategic supplies, of having munitions plants idled and fleets immobilized.

Part of that threat our Nation neutralized by building pipe lines—the Big Inch, for one. The other parts we neutralized by building up air and sea anti-submarine forces which conquered the German U-Boat in the Battle of the Atlantic.

Japan could build no "Big Inch." She could build up no air and sea anti-submarine forces. Her industrial potential had been destroyed long before by the sinking of tankers and freighters by U. S. and Allied submarines. . . . When Operation Barney ended, Japan was on the ropes, and the Hellcats of the Sea played a proud part in putting her there.

CHARLES A. LOCKWOOD
Vice Admiral, U.S.N.-Ret.
Commander, Submarines, Pacific, W W II

Los Gatos, California,
July 1st, 1955

SAILING LISTS OF THE *WAHOO* AND THE HELLCATS

Following are the officers and men who, according to the Navy's official "U.S. Submarine Losses in World War II," went down with the *Wahoo:*

OFFICERS

Morton, D.W., Cdr.
Skjonsby, V.L., Lt. Cdr.
Burgan, W.W., Lt.
Greene, H.M., Lt.
Henderson, R.N., Lt.

Fiedler, E.F., Lt.(jg)
Misch, G.A., Lt.(jg)
Brown, D.R., Ens.
Campbell, J.S., Ens.

ENLISTED MEN

Anders. F., F1c
Andrews, J.S., EM1c
Bailey, R.E., SC3c
Bair, A.I., TM3c
Berg, J.C., F1c
Browning, C.R., MoMM2c
Bruce, C.L., MoMM1c
Buckley, J.P., RM1c
Carr, W.J., CGM
Carter, J.E., RM2c
Davidson, W.E., MoMM1c
Deaton, L.N., TM1c
Erdley, J.S., EM3c
Finkelstein, O., TM3c
Galli, W.O., TM3c
Garmon, C.E., MoMM2c

Garrett, G.C., MoMM2c
Gerlacher, W.L., S2c
Goss, R.P., MoMM2c
Hand, W.R., EM2c
Hartman, L.M., F1c
Hayes, D.M., EM2c
Holmes, W.H., EM1c
House, V.A., S1c
Howe, H.J., EM3c
Jacobs, O., MoMM1c
Jasa, R.L., F1c
Jayson, J.O., CK3c
Johnson, K.B., TM1c
Keeter, D.C., CMM
Kemp, W.W., QM1c
Kessock, P., F2c

Kirk, E.T., S1c
Krebs, P.H., SM3c
Lape, A.D., F2c
Lindemann, C.A., S1c
Logue, R.B., FC1c
Lynch, W.L., F2c
MacAlman, S.E., PhM1c
MacGowen, T.K.J., MoMM1c
McGill, T.J., CMoMM
McGilton, H.E., TM3c
McSpadden, D.J., TM1c
Magyar, A.J., F1c
Manalisay, J.C., St3c
Mandijiak, P.A., F1c
Massa, E.E., S1c
Maulding, E.C., SM3c
Maulding, G.E., TM3c
Mills, M.L., RT1c
Neel, P., TM2c
Oneal, R.L., EM3c

O'Brien, F.L., EM1c
Ostrander, E.E., F1c
Phillips, P.F., SC1c
Rennels, J.L., SC2c
Renno, H., S1c
Seal, E.H., Jr., RM2c
Simonetti, A.R., SM2c
Smith, D.O., EM1c
Stevens, G.V., MoMM2c
Terrell, W.C., QM3c
Thomas, W., S1c
Tyler, R.O., TM3c
Wach, L.J., Cox
Vidick, J., EM2c
Ware, N.C., CEM
Waldron, W.E., RM3c
Whipp, K.L., F1c
White, W.T., Y2c
Witting, R.L., F1c

The complete and official list of the officers and men who vanished with the *Bonefish* follows:

OFFICERS

Edge, L.L., Cdr.
Knight, F.S., Lt. Cdr.
Amburgey, L.M., Lt.(jg)
Johnston, R.M., Lt.(jg)
Slater, R.E., Lt.(jg)

Smith, L.C., Jr., Lt.(jg)
Abel, D.A., Ens.
Dunn, D.H., Ens.
Kern, F.B., Ens.
Rose, R.A.II, Ens.

ENLISTED MEN

Adams, T.B., Y3c
Adams, W.S., Bkr3c
Anderson, G.I., Jr., MoMM3c
Aureli, S.J., S1c
Beck, M.L., GM2c
Brown, R.W., F1c
Browning, J.A., EM1c
Burdick, G.A., MoMM2c

Canfield, K.T., MoMM2c
Coleman, J.A., RM3c
Cooley, Q.L., StM2c
Danielson, O.C., SC2c
Enos, E.R., F1c
Epps, W.H., Jr., StM2c
Feld, P.E., F1c
Fox, D.C., RM2c

Frank, R.E., CMoMM
Fugett, M.A., QM2c
Fuller, G.M., CMoMM
Hackstaff, H.J., RM2c
Harman, G.P., TM1c
Hasiak, J.J., TM3c
Hess, R.D., S1c
Houghton, W.S., TM1c
Jenkins, R.W., EM1c
Johnson, J.C., RT1c
Johnson, S.E., Jr. CQM
Kalinoff, M.W., F1c
Karr, W.G., RM2c
Keefer, R.T., S1c
King, E.W., EM2c
Kissane, J.E., S2c
Lamothe, J.L., Cox
Laracy, J.J., Jr., EM3c
Lewis, J.A., CGM
Lockwood, T.G., PhoM3c
Lynch, J.F., TM2c
Maghan, A.G., F1c
Markle, J.E., EM2c
McBride, R.J., MoMM2c
Miles, H.V., Jr., MoMM1c
Nester, S.A., EM3c
Newberry, J.R., F1c
Olson, D.H., MoMM2c
O'Toole, W.P., EM3c
Parton, J.F., EM3c

Pauley, G.W., RM3c
Paskin, T., RT2c
Phenicie, J.E., MoMM3c
Primavera, L.J., MoMM1c
Prunier, G.A., EM3c
Quenett, C.F, RM2c
Raley, C.H., F1c
Ray, R.C., Jr., SM1c
Raynes, J.A., EM1c
Rhanor, C.J., S1c
Reid, J.A., F1c
Rice, R.P., S1c
Schiller, R.G., F1c
Schmidling, C.J., FC1c
Schweyer, R.H., RT2c
Snodgrass, R.L., Y1c
Stamm, R.S., SC1c
Surber, R.M., EM2c
Tierney, D.R., MoMM1c
Velie, R.C., TME2c
Vincent, T.F, Jr., S1c
Whitright, W., RM2c
Wilson, J.R., F1c
Williams, J.J., MoMM2c
Williams, J.R., Jr., FC3c
Williams, T.F, F1c
Winegar, C.D., TM3c
Wolfe, L.E., TM3c
Wright, G.W., PhM1c

USS Spadefish (SS 411)

OFFICERS

Germershausen, William J.,
   Jr., Cdr.
Wright, Richard M., Lt.
Decker, Daniel D., Jr., Lt.
Fellows, Richard D., Lt.
Lacroix, Edward J., Lt.(jg)

Wood, Perry S., Lt.(jg)
Ware, Willian J., Ens.
Buncke, Harry J., Jr., Ens.
Dix, Ramond E., Ens.
Falconer, LeRoy D., Warrant
   Mach.

ENLISTED MEN

Armstrong, Edward Richard, PhoM2c
Asher, Warren Jay, EM3c
Babb, Maurice Lee, Jr., F1c
Barton, Thad Ralph, TM3c
Bassett, Richard Harold, EM3c
Brenneis, Harry Jerome, MoMM3c
Brewer, John Belton, Jr., MoMM3c
Brooks, Sie (n), Jr., StM1c
Bynum, William Thomas, StM1c
Carney, Hugh Patrick, S1c
Case, Joseph Bennion, RT1c
Casey, James David, EM3c
Charles, Walter Joseph, Jr., FC3c
Cole, James Douglas, F1c
Cruze, Herman Franklin, Jr., EM2c
Cunningham, Edwin William, MoMM2c
Cuthbertson, John Marshall, TM2c
Dependahl, Leonard Edward, EM1c
Dunleavy, Anthony (n), Jr., MoMM3c
Eimermann, Willard Christ, CBM
Fletcher, James Wallace, QM2
Gamby, Orville Richard, MoMM2c
Gouker, Zelbert (n), SM2c
Graf, Edward Frank, SC2c
Graff, Charles Alfred, S1c
Griffith, Charles Clain, CMoMM(AA)

Harbison, Joseph Albert, MoMM2c
Holeman, Victor Rolla, MoMM1c
Hord, Cleveland Maybee, F1c
Ingberg, Norval Owen, S1c
Ives, Victor Leon, CphM(AA)
Keeney, William Jackson, Jr., RT2c
Kelley, William Patrick, MoMM2c
Kite, Vernon Joseph, TM1c
Kreher, Emery Andrew, TM1c
Kreinbring, Irwin Henry, Y1c
LaFose, Murphy (n), F2c
LaRocca, Albert George, EM3c
Lester, Clifford Robert, MoMM3c
Lewis, Edgar Lycurgous, CGM
Lundquist, Hugo Carl, TM2c
Majoue, Paul Henry, Jr., CRM
Massar, Bernard Adam, GM2c
Melstrand, Howard Walfred, S1c
Mikesell, Robert Edward, S2c
Miller, Thomas Harry, MoMM2c
Moody, Roy Hubert, EM1c
Morrison, James Walter, S1c
Mullen, Melvin "C," MoMM3c
McMahon, Wallace Francis, TM3c
Nesnee, John (n), TM2c
Noonan, Maurice Anthony, GM3c
Olah, Andrew (n), FCS1c
O'Neil, Thomas Patrick, RM3c

Ordway, Emerson Locke, CEM
Paulson, Roger Francis, S2c
Peel, John Richard, CMoMM
Pelliciari, Nicholas John, MoMM2c
Pierce, Sam Henry, MoMM1c
Pigman, Billy Bob, EM2c
Pike, Neal (n), CRT
Potting, Roy Christian, Y3c
Powers, Kenneth Clyde, RM3c
Rewold, Radford Crowell, CMoMM2c
Riley, Thomas Gordon, SC1c
Ring, Joseph John, MoMM2c

Sandleben, Olaf Bernard, S1c
Scherman, Francis Julian, CCS
Schmelzer, Carl Thomas, CEM
Scholle, Donald Joseph, QM3c
Schuett, James Shirley, SM1c
Sergio, Michael (n), RM1c
Shaw, Thomas Eugene, EM3c
Sigworth, Kenneth Leroy, EM2c
Taylor, John Wright, MoMM1c
Terboss, William Frederick, S1c
Wells, Francis Arthur, CTM

USS Sea Dog (SS 401)

OFFICERS

Hydemann, Earl Twining, Cdr.
Lynch, James Paul, Lt.
Brown, William Stewart, Lt.
Hindert, Edward Michael, Lt.
Reed, Kelly Bruce, Lt.
Hinchey, John Francis. Lt.(jg)
Argo, Wesley Breeden, Lt.(jg)
Duckworth, Edward Weldon, Lt.(jg)
Schwind, William Francis, Ens.
Kornichuk, Arthur, Warrant Elect.

ENLISTED MEN

Bass, Joe Willie, StM1c
Bishop, Richard Ottis, SC1c
Bryant, Douglas Almon, MoMM3c

Buesing, Von Clarence, MoMM3c
Carter, Robert Lee, Jr., F1c
Codgen, Anthony Eugene, F1c
Crowley, Harold Francis, PhoM2c
Dell, Andrew Francis, CTM
Dunham, Paul Peter, S1c
Eilert, Morgan Bell, TME2c
Fails, Earl Franklin, F1c
Fickett, Albert Warren, Jr., RT2c
Fitzpatrtick, Thomas Francis. GM2c
Fisher, Ronald Gordon, TM3c
Fontnote, Sidney Thomas, MoMM1c
Gibson, Kenneth Love, TM2c
Glass, Orval Alva, S1c
Gressman, George Arthur, MoMM1c

Griffith, Eddie Everett, RM2c

Hammel, Paul Alvin, S1c

Harrell, Max Alan, FCS2c

Harry, Frank John, EM2c

Heebner, Newell Graves, CQM

Heiden, Walter Geo Erwin, CEM

Heller, David Alexander, S1c

Hessman, Robert Dale, MoMM1c

Hinkel, Russell Dale, EM3c

Hoyt, William Dennis, RM2c

Ignasiak, Bernard Albin, TM3c

Jacek, Martin Paul, MoMM3c

Johnson, Richard Eugene, F1c

Jones, Oliver Hillory, PmM1c

Juniper, Albert John, Y1c

Karn, Fred William III, CMoMM

Kiesel, Earl John, MoMM3c

Kral, Elmer Steve, MoMM1c

La Bore, Louis James, F1c

Lanczky, William Andrew, SC3c

Lennox, William, MoMM2c

Lewis, Lester Beale, CTM

Lupe, Theodore, Jr., S1c

McAuliffe, William Jeremiah, F1c

McCormick, Paul Lee, F1c

McKenzie, Thomas Scott, Jr., Y3c

McLarty, Pat, TM2c

Meacham, Arthur Jackson, MoMM1c

Misch, Frank Edward, RT3

Moser, Ben, SM2c

Mracek, Edward, MoMM1c

Murzie, William Richard, RM3c

Nicholson, William Henry, RM2c

Nicodemus, Ivan, Jr., TM3c

Noble, Willie Zemry, F1c

Pagnam, James Robert, F1c

Parker, Earl Wayne, MoMM1c

Peterson, Leonard "J," QM3c

Powell, Cecil Oliver, TM1c

Prince, James Bryan, EM2c

Ptaszynski, Arthur Clarence, S1c

Ripple, Robert Elmer, F1c

Roberts, William Monroe, EM3c

Rue, Dwayne Taylor, EM1c

Rutledge, Charles William, S1c

Saunders, Charles Mahlon, Jr., S1c

Sawyer, Albert Joseph, RT2c

Schleuter, Vernon Eugene, F1c

Shelby, Claude La Verne, SC3c

Sims, James Albert, RM1c

Steppe, Raymond, MoMM2c

Swain, Robert Raymond, EM3c

Thomas, Louis Edward, EM1c

Tompkins, Edward Ellis, GM3c

Truscelli, Anthony Frank, Jr., TME3c

Voss, William Alfred, S1c

Williams, Walter Wayne, GM3c

Wilson, Harold Lloyd, QM2c

Wilson, Richard Dorothy, StM1c

Zimmerman, Florin Wayne, EM2c

USS Crevalle (SS 291)

OFFICERS

Steinmetz, E.H., Cdr.
Seymour, Jack M., Cdr.
Westbrook, E.M., Lt. Cdr.
Morin, G.F., Lt.
Raider, A.J., Lt.

Mazzone, W.F., Lt.(jg)
Loveland, R.A., Lt.(jg)
Bowe, R.E., Lt.(jg)
Lord, E.R., Lt.(jg)
Seel, J., Lt.(jg)

ENLISTED MEN

Adams, William LaVerna, S1c
Barnes, Frank, MoMM1c
Bessette, Roland, P.P., TM3c
Biehl, Henry Tudor, CRT
Brown, Robert Joseph, S1c
Bolin, Willis Guy, TM3c
Brooks, Marvin M., GM1c
Brophy, John Paul, F1c
Coyer, James W., S1c
Flaherty, Joseph E., QMoMM
Fletcher, Chester J., S1c
Folse, John Stephen, RM3c
Freeman, Edgar Allen, TM2c
Fritchen, William L., GM2c
Gaines, Robert E., MoMM2c
Gogul, Frank Stephen, MoMM1c
Goodman, Francis W., S1c
Graham, Ivan Hugh, MoMM3c
Helix, Max Rudolph, MoMM1c
Hildebrand, Charles Frederick, EM2c
Howard, Stephen Aubry, FC(S) 3c
Howie, Robert Charles, MoMM2c
Jaycox, John A., StM2c
Jenigen, Albert, F1c
Jones, Jermone L., S1c

Katchis, Jim "A," QM3c
Keane, Edward F., S1c
Kneisly, Geroge Eliott, SM1c
Langfieldt, Maurice Edward, TM3c
Larsen, James Louis, MoMM2c
Lenatz, John Joseph, TM2c
Lubinsky, Walter, EM3c
Mallin, Ralph, F1c
McGowan, Thomas Francis, Jr., TM1c
McHugh, John Joseph, F1c
McNorgan, Joseph Whitmore, EM3c
Minaker, Russell Samuel, RT1c
Minor, Bert E., StM2c
Mushett, Robert William, Y1c
Newell, Richard Paul, S2c
O'Brien, Joseph F., CSM
Osborne, Cedric Henry, CPhM
Pablo, Marcelo Andriano, SC1c
Plachowicz, Frank A., GM2c
Polk, Lloyd Eugene, RM3c
Rennecke, Wyman John, EM1c
Reynolds, Rodney Ralph, SM3c

Roraback, Gilbert Little, TM2c

Schaeffer, John William III, MoMM1c

Schwarz, Robert Franklin, EM3c

Scisco, Clayton Sterlin, MoMM3c

Sherick, Albert Marlin, EM3c

Silvia, Richard G., TM2c

Sinclair, Joe Milton, Jr., EM3c

Singer, Jack William, EM3c

Slyter, Gilbert Gordon, EM3c

Smith, John V., S1c (FC)

Stagman, Paul Louis, EM2c

Starnes, Kenneth Jackson, MoMM3c

Stemler, Milton David, RT3c

Stokes, Frank H. SC2c

Stutzman, Gerald Wilber, RM1c

Thomas, Everett A., QM1c

Thompson, Robert, Jr., F2c

Thompson, William H. Bkr3c

Tomlin, George Lawrence, EM2c

Truman, Horace Lynn, MM1c

Wagenbrenner, Fred, EM2c

Weber, Russell Frederick, F1c

Westerlund, Alfred, MoMM3c

Wheelus, Roy Calvin, QM2c

Wiesniewski, Francis Walter, MoMM2c

Williams, George Findlay, CEM

Wilmot, George Edward, MoMM2c

Woodhouse, Robert R., Y3c

Zessman, Sam TM3c

USS Skate (SS305)

OFFICERS

Lynch, Richard B., Cdr.

Huston, Robert C., Lt.Cdr.

Edgerton, Stuart T., Lt.

West, Franklin G., Lt.

Carlin, Thomas L., Lt.(jg)

Burlin, Charles W., Jr., Lt.(jg)

Crooks, Sheridan Russell, Lt.(jg)

Debuhr, Calvin H., Lt. (jg)

Earhart, Herman M., Ens.

Doyle, Reginald E., Warrant Elect.

ENLISTED MEN

Bauer, Frederick William, TM3c

Bebeau, Walter Harold, S1c

Beste, John David, EM2c

Bird, John Joseph, EM1c

Brennan, Philip Franklyn, MoMM3c

Brown, George Edwin, SC3c

Bryson, Howard Wesley, GM3c

Champion, Ralph Arthur, Jr., S1c

Collier, John Leroy, Bkr2c

Covell, Wallace Meurling, MoMM1c

Coyne, Edward Joseph, TM3c

Davis, William Middleton, S1c

Dearing, Harry James, MoMM1c

Donovan, John Leonard, EM2c

Dzuik, Emil Frank, EM2c

Eastwood, Freddie Ray, TM1c

English, Cannon Miller, CMoMM

Ewald, Marcus Henry, SM1c

Faurotte, Harvy Richard, TM1c

Farnof, Arthur (n), Jr., S1c

Foster, Theodore Arthur, MoMM3c

Galles, Lester Daniel, MoMM1c

Gann, Earnest Elwood, F1c

Glaab, Richard George, RM3c

Goss, Herbert Wallace, TM2c

Heissenbuttel, Samuel, EM3c

Hermance, Frank Jay, Jr., MoMM1c

Hill, Joseph Thomas, TM2c

Hinton, Floyd James, MoMM2c

Jordan, James Ivan, F1c

Kenyon, Frank Crosby III, S1c

Kice, Everett Faye, EM1c

Kichline, Reginald Grant, CMoMM

Knold, Vernon Ottmar, GM2c

Lee, Arnold (n), S1c

Ledbetter, Frank Thomas, CRM

Lemier, Billy Bullock, SM2c

Levy, Stanley Stephen, S1c

Marshall, Douglas Seymour, Jr., S1c

Mileskie, Stanley Joseph, EM2c

Moser, Adam Dean, EM3c

McCracken, Chadwick Neyman, SC2c

McFadyen, Peter James, QM2c

Miller, Robert Enoch, MoMM3c

Millspaugh, Stanley Clements, MoMM3c

Moller, Edwin Raymond, RT2c

Mudore, Thomas Anthony, MoMM1c

Murphy, Robert Langdon, Jr., EM3c

Naylor, William Rockafellow, Jr., S1c

O'Donohue, Robert Joseph, S1c

Olufsen, Albert Emil, RM2c

Ostrom, Norman Henry, MoMM3c

Parker, Edgar, Jr., RM2c

Paul, Clinton Jerome, F1c

Perigo, Robert Louis, S1c

Potter, John Romans, FCS2c

Praskievicz, Wallace Michael, CEM

Rayner, William Andrew, MoMM2c

Roberts, Grady Everett, S1c

Ruediger, Manfred Warner, TM1c

USS *Tinosa* (SS 283)

OFFICERS

Latham, R.C., Cdr.
Smith, H.J., Jr., Lt. Cdr.
Sanders, C.R., Lt.
Brooks, F.C., Lt.
Weaver, B.S., Lt.(jg)

Salisbury, G.F.,Lt.(jg)
Siegfried, C.W., Lt.(jg)
Grose, H.G., Lt.(jg)
Olsen, J., Ens.
Clutterham, D.R., Ens.

ENLISTED MEN

Anderson, Jack Homer, EM3c
Atnip, Tolbert Boyd, S1c
Ault, Earl Edward, F1c
Baird, Floyd Calvin,
    MoMM1c
Barr, George, MoMM3c
Bennett, Millard M., TM3c
Bentham, Robert E., TM3c
Bolinder, Ralph H., F1c
Boyd, Edgar, SM1c
Brady, Ferris Gehr, RT3c
Brumfield, Floyd E., S1c
Burke, Charles M., MoMM3c
Burlew, Harry Alfred,
    MoMM3c
Carlen, Robert C., S1c
Carpenter, Rex N., S1c
Carpenter, Clarence A., S1c
Clement, William R., TM2c
Costabile, Joe Frank, S1c
Daranowich, Walter H.,
    PhoM3c
Daughtry, Herbert, MoMM2c
Dismukes, Alvin Cleo, FCS2c
Dixon, Richard Leroy, TM1c
Dowler, Melvin Leon, QM2c
Eterovich, Matthew, F1c
Freeburn, Harry D., EM2c
Garner, Frank Eugene,
    PhM1c

Gibson, Jack Richard, EM3c
Giltner, Thomas W.,
    MoMM1c
Goen, Louis Erwin, TM3c
Gould, Harold Ray, S1c
Grigg, John Robert, MoMM3c
Groves, Russell C., RM1c
Hall, William "F," MoMM3c
Harris, Frederick B., Y1c
Hinds, Lawrence, P., RM2c
Huson, Loyal Arthur, TM3c
Irvin, Frederick L., SC3c
Jackson, Nathaniel, StM2c
Keepers, Harold J., S1c
Klag, Donald James, EM3c
Larson, Allen Gene, F1c
Leonard, Carthel F., EM3c
MacPherson, Malcolm, RM2c
McDaniel, Jessie J., EM3c
Minor, James Paul, EM2c
Nylander, Raymond E., S1c
Otis, Donald Joseph, TM2c
Owens, Robert Lowell, EM3c
Paquette, Clifford N., F1c
Polis, Jack Salem, EM3c
Reif, Harry William,
    MoMM2c
Richeson, Edward M., GM1c
Robbins, Kermit E.,
    MoMM1c

Robertson, James C., MoMM3c
Rodman, George W., QM3c
Sanders, Aubrey Ray, S1c
Scott, Dale Verne, S1c
Scruggs, Robert C., SC1c
Searles, Dayton, Jr., GM3c
Settle, Spaulding B., ST3c
Shelden, James F., S1c
Smith, Richard Paul, MoMM3c
Soutiere, Clement, EM3c
Stamant, Wilfred J., Jr., S1c
Stanford, Samuel E., MoMM3c
Stevens, Charles R., MoMM3c

Stokes, Victor L., CEM
Stripling, Ernest R., MoMM2c
Thompson, Robert M., MoMM2c
Tyler, John Phillip, RT1c
Vannatter, Charles H., RM3c
Voegtlin, E.P., EM1c
Wagner, Charles H., Jr., TM3c
Welch, Freeman, CTM
Whipps, Jack Carl, RT3c
Wicker, William A., QM3c
Wilson, Eldon Rogers, TM3c
Wilson, Norval D., CMoMM
Young, Buck Rodney, FC2c

USS Flying Fish (SS2 229)

OFFICERS

Risser, Robert Dunlap, Cdr.
Burke, Julian Thompson, Jr., Lt.Cdr.
Kilgore, William Huey, Lt.
Hopley, Eric Earle, Lt.
Doheny, Edward Laurence III, Lt.

Ostergren, John Frederick, Lt.
Korn, Carl Andreas, Jr., Lt.
Jerbert, Arthur Henry, Lt.(jg)
Sly, Richard Harmon, Ens.
Emmons, Robert C., Warrant Elect.

ENLISTED MEN

Anderson, Lloyd Craig, CMoMM
Anthony, Melvin Lawrence, RT2c
Apostolopoulos, Vasilios, QM3c
Bartocci, Lawrence Edwin, F1c
Beardslee, Ralph Currier, Jr., SM1c

Bennett, Wilfred Arthur, TM2c
Birkner, Francis Richard, PhoM1c
Canaday, Gerald Benart, TM1c
Caramenico, Lewis Joseph, F1c
Cates, Don Brady, FC1c
Chereek, Benjamin, EM1c

Christensen, Charles Raymond, CMoMM

Collins, Joel Walter, III, RM2c

Cooper, Earl Boyd, MoMM2c

Cronin, Joseph John, MoMM1c

Drozdowicz, Edward John, MM1c

Dougherty, John James, RT2c

Dunn, Matthew Daniel, EM2c

Earley, John Anderson, Jr., F1c

Evans, Cassel Joel, TM2c

Fiedler, John Emanuel, F2c

Field, Sidney Frank, F1c

Funkhouser, Edward Morris, RM3c

Geiswer, Robert Frederick, RM3c

Giannelli, Frank Anthony, MoMM3c

Griffin, Charles William, SC3c

Hall, Lloyd Alfred, RT1c

Haney, Arthur Alvin, RT2c

Hayes, William, EM3c

Herbert, Edward Robert, F1c

Holland, Noble Vernon, Bkr1c

Holloway, Harold Edmond, S2c

Holzwarth, Jacob Taber, MoMM2c

Jasinski, Leon Frank, EM3c

Johnson, Kenneth Wallace, EM3c

Kenworthy, Harvey William, F1c

Kocon, Joseph Stanslaw, TM2c

Laster, Robert, StM1c (SS)

Logan, John Edward, GM1c

Lort, Joseph McCrea, Jr., QM2c

Lusse, Melvin Reel, EM2c

Lynsky, Mark Vincent, Jr., MoMM2c

Mahoney, Robert Cornelius, TM1c

Mattingly, John William, CTM

McGee, John Singleton, Y1c

Miller, Kay Dean, F1c

Moody, Dick, MoMM2c

Nelson, Chester Raymond, F1c

Nelson, William Carl, S1c

Nickerson, Bryan Webster, S1c

O'Brien, William James, FCS2c

Peterman, John James, Jr., TM2c

Ragsdale, Glenn Earl, S1c

Rainer, William Horace, Jr., RM3c

Rankin, Walter Hodge, MoMM2c

Rodgers, James Louis, S1c

Rusin, Nicholas, TM3c

Schmersahl, Jacob Benjamin, Jr., MoMM3c

Schoonmaker, Edward Philip, S1c

Schulke, Oscar Joseph, EM2c

Shaw, Harold Milton, RM2c

Smith, Billy Roy, SC1c (SS)

Smith, Carl, MoMM3c

Smith, Paul Thomas, S1c

Sproull, Raymond DeLost, Jr., S1c

Sunbury, George Glenn, RT3c

Thacker, William Odell, StM1c

Thompson, Earnest Lester, MoMM1c

Wakshinsky, Albert Stanley, EM2c

Ward, James McVey,
    MoMM2c
Weeks, Richard Lance, S1c
Whitefield, William Burgess,
    CPhM

Wildes, Warren Freeman,
    EM3c
Wilson, Robert Grant, F1c
Witt, Ishmael Clinton,
    MoMM2c

USS *Bowfin* (SS 287)

OFFICERS

Tyree, Alexander K., Cdr.
John, Clary L., Lt. Cdr.
Flessner, Conrad J., Lt.
Anderson, Hubert C., Lt.
Van Kuran, Peter, Lt.(jg)
Elliott, Michael M., Lt.(jg)
Cummins, William E., Lt.(jg)
Ayres, James M., Ens.
Wise, John Philip, Ens.

ENLISTED MEN

Alexander, James Reid, Bkr3c
Alexander, Robert Emmet,
    CPhM
Aplin, Cater Freeman, Jr.,
    EM3c
Beales, Austin William,
    MoMM1c
Benson, Gordon Howard,
    RM2c
Beyer, Walter Louis, QM1c
Beynon, Robert Paul, EM3c
Bruderly, Robert Earl, EM2c
Buckman, Horace Tomlinson,
    F1c
Burkeen, Keys Yandle, TM1c
Carberry, Jack Stanley, F1c
    (MoMM)
Carden, Olie Lee, MoMM1c
Carter, Arthur Lee, FC(S)1c
Chisum, Albert, TM2c

Choquette, Hugh Eugene,
    TM3c
Cole, William Edward, TM1c
Curran, John Edward,
    MoMM2c
Ely, John Andreas, S1c
Erickson, John Howard,
    EM1c
Ervin, Norval Leo, Jr., S1c
Fletcher, Earl Thomas, EM3c
Gilkes, Thomas Horace,
    MoMM1c
Gillespie, Clark Hurt, RM3c
Gilmore, Paul David,
    MoMM3c
Gosnell, Marshall Smith,
    MoMM1c
Hadland, Fred, F1c(MoMM)
Harrington, John Leo,
    MoMM2c
Heinz, Robert LeRoy, Y1c
Holder, John "A," F1c
Howard, Homer Lamar, F2c
Jackson, Ted Douglas, F1c
Jackson, Wilbur Lee,
    MoMM1c
Johnson, Gerald Burton,
    EM3c
Johnson, Henry Neal, S1c(SM)
Gaito, Eugene, CMoMM
Jordan, William Michael,
    F1c(MoMM)

Kear, Charles Burns,
  F1c(MoMM)
Kenney, Albert Patrick, Bkr3c
Knox, Joseph Michael, Jr.,
  CMoMM
Knoche, Eugene Alfred,
  MoMM2c
LaCour, Marshall, W.,
  PhoM2c
Lancaster, Wallace Eugene,
  S2c
Launius, John Jeptha, RT1c
King, Henry, Jr., TM1c
Lundgren, Walter Edward,
  MoMM3c
McMillion, George James,
  F1c(MoMM)
McNeven, Vern, MoMM2c
Molloy, Leslie Robert, RT2c
Nash, Paul Gilford, GM2c
Odoms, Edward Arnold,
  StM1c
Ohlund, Arley "V.," S1c
Olsen, Rolf Sander, EM2c
Patterson, Robert George,
  CEM
Perske, Earl William, CCS
Poppleton, Sidney Robert, S1c

Price, Lloyd Raymond, S1c
Rasp, Vincent Robert, F1c
Reiner, Morton Maurice, S1c
Rodskiaer, Aage Edward,
  RM1c
Rohrbacher, Virgel Harold,
  GM1c
Ryan, Ronald Redge, S1c
Scaglione, Peter, T., RM3c
Stack, Thomas Patrick, TM3c
Sweat, James Grantham,
  SM1c
Taylor, Richard Southard,
  EM2c
Turner, Charles Robert, StM2c
Updegraff, Jack Lockwood,
  QM3c
Verkinder, Victor, MoMM1c
Videkovich, William Paul,
  MoMM2c
Waddell, Kenneth Albert,
  EM2c
Waugh, William Lee, TM2c
Weidner, Alpheus S., Jr.,
  MoMM3c
Weller, Homer Glen, QM2c
Winning, Edward Gary, CEM

JAPANESE-ENGLISH GLOSSARY

BANA, point
DANI, valley, stream
DAKE, mountain
GATA, lake, inlet, bay
GAWA, river
HAMA, beach
HANA, point
HANG, harbor
HANTO, peninsula
IWA, bluff, cliff, rock
JIMA, island
KAIKYO, strait
KO, anchorage, harbor, river
KAI, bay, gulf
KAWA, river
MACHI, city, town

MAN, bay
MAL, point
MISAKI, point, cape
MINE, mountain
NADA, gulf, sea
SAKI, cape, point
SE, reef, shoal
SAN, hill
SHIMA, island
TAKE, mountain
TO-DAI, lighthouse
URA, bay, inlet, lake
WAN, bay
YAMA, mountain
ZAKI, point, cape
ZAWA, river

NOTE:

1. Digit and small letter "c" appearing after the rate indicates class.
Example: MoMM2c—Motor machinist mate second class.
2. Capital letter "C" before rate indicates chief.
Example: CMoMM—Chief Motor machinist mate.

Bkr	Baker	GM	Gunner's Mate
CBM	Chief Boatswain's Mate	Lt	Lieutenant
CCS	Chief Commissary Steward	Lt (jg)	Lieutenant, Junior Grade
Cdr	Commander	Lt Cdr	Lieutenant Commander
CEM	Chief Electrician's Mate	MoMM	Motor Machinist's Mate
CGM	Chief Gunner's Mate	PhM	Pharmacist's Mate
CK	Cook	PhoM	Photographer's Mate
CMM	Chief Machinist's Mate	QM	Quartermaster
		RM	Radioman
CMoMM	Chief Motor Machinist's Mate	RT	Radio Technician
		S2/c	Seaman, 2nd class
COX	Coxswain	SC	Ship's Cook
EM	Electrician's Mate	SM	Signalman
Ens	Ensign	ST	Steward
F	Fireman	STM	Steward's Mate
FC	Fire Controlman	TM	Torpedo Man's Mate
FCS	Fire Controlman (Surface Weapons)	TME	Torpedo Man's Mate (electrical)
		Y	Yeoman

BANTAM IS PROUD TO PRESENT A MAJOR PUBLISHING EVENT
THE ILLUSTRATED HISTORY OF THE VIETNAM WAR

Never before has the Vietnam War been so vividly presented. Never before has a full account of the controversial war been available in inexpensive paperback editions.

Each Volume in the series is an original work by an outstanding and recognized military author. Each volume is lavishly illustrated with up to 32 pages of full color photographs, maps, and black and white photos drawn from military archives and features see-through, cutaway, four-color paintings of major weapons.

Don't miss these other exciting volumes:

William L. Shirer

A Memoir of a Life and the Times Vol. 1 & 2

- ☐ 34204   TWENTIETH CENTURY $12.95
  JOURNEY, The Start 1904-1930
- ☐ 34179   THE NIGHTMARE YEARS, $12.95
  1930-1940
- ☐ 32335   WM. SHIRER BOXED SET $25.90

In Volume 1, Shirer recounts American/European history as seen through his eyes. In Volume 2, he provides an intensely personal vision of the crucible out of which the Nazi monster appeared.

Anthony Cave Brown

- ☐ 34016   BODYGUARD OF LIES $12.95

The extraordinary, true story of the clandestine war of deception that hid the secrets of D-Day from Hitler and sealed the Allied victory.

Charles B. MacDonald

- ☐ 34226   A TIME FOR TRUMPETS $11.95

The untold story of the Battle of the Bulge.

John Toland

- ☐ 34518   THE LAST 100 DAYS $12.95

The searing true drama of men and women caught in the final struggles of the epic conflict. World War II.

Prices and availability subject to change without notice.

Special Offer
Buy a Bantam Book
for only 50¢.

Now you can have Bantam's catalog filled with hundreds of titles plus take advantage of our unique and exciting bonus book offer. A special offer which gives you the opportunity to purchase a Bantam book for only 50¢. Here's how!

By ordering any five books at the regular price per order, you can also choose any other single book listed (up to a $5.95 value) for just 50¢. Some restrictions do apply, but for further details why not send for Bantam's catalog of titles today!

Just send us your name and address and we will send you a catalog!